HELLO AUSTRALIA

a memoir

Sam Moshinsky

❖

To Ada
with love and gratitude

First published in 2023 by Real Publishing
www.realpublishing.com.au

Hello Australia
ISBN: 9780645681116

A catalogue record for this
book is available from the
National Library of Australia

Edited by Romy Moshinsky
Editorial assistance by Georgie Raik-Allen
Cover design and book design by Jacki Starr

The author and the publisher respectfully acknowledge the traditional
custodians of the land this book is published on, the Bunurong, Boon
Warrung and Wurundjeri Woi Warrung Peoples of the Kulin nation.
We pay our respects to First Nations Elders past, present and emerging.

REAL
PUBLISHING

Prologue

My last few days in Shanghai were fraught with anxiety. I had enjoyed a comfortable and sheltered childhood, and was now, at the age of 17, preparing to depart, on my own, for a long journey by rail and ship to start a new life in Australia. I would be staying with strangers in Melbourne and had been tasked with finding accommodation for the rest of my family, who would follow at an unknown time in the future.

While Father and Eva were preoccupied with the difficult job of winding up our complex affairs in Shanghai, Grandmother, sensing my increasing disquiet, drew me aside for a chat. After expressing her confidence in me, she shared some valuable insights. According to her, there were only three important decisions in life: who to marry, who to work with, and who to befriend. The rest, she assured me, was merely detail.

This book was written with those dictums in mind. I am so grateful that Grandmother met Ada and that she was able to attend our wedding. Unfortunately, she did not live long enough to witness how conscientiously I have adhered to all her guiding principles.

Throughout my life, people have struggled to place my accent. This has inevitably led to numerous questions and long conversations about my childhood in Shanghai. Ada encouraged me to write my first memoir, *Goodbye Shanghai*, in the hope that it would stop these seemingly endless Shanghai-based discussions. Instead, to her frustration, the success of the book resulted in even more interest in my childhood, including invitations to speak at events and to share my knowledge about the history of Shanghai during those tumultuous years.

Since I have now spent much more of my life in Australia than in Shanghai, and have enjoyed interesting experiences, both as an accountant and in senior roles in a variety of community organisations, Ada encouraged me to write a second memoir. The idea was compelling, particularly as, with the passage of time, my sharp memory would surely start to fade.

I soon realised, however, that the process would be challenging. Daunted by the task of writing about my life, whilst preserving privacy and professional confidentiality, I let the project lapse.

Finally, on my 85th birthday, 10 years after the launch of *Goodbye Shanghai*, I embarked upon another, more serious, attempt to write *Hello Australia*. The project provided particular focus, purpose and satisfaction during Melbourne's extended COVID-19 lockdowns in 2020 and 2021.

I have attempted to reveal my struggle to adapt to life in a strange and bewildering new country. I'm certain that my grandchildren will enjoy the stories about my floundering attempts to work in a garage, hitchhike, ski and study engineering!

I hope that I have adequately communicated my consistent effort to conduct myself with diligence and integrity; allowing me to earn the trust and respect of mentors, colleagues and peers. Here again, I have responded to one of Grandmother's wise sayings: "Even the *joulikies* (crooks in Russian) need someone to trust!"

I also hope I have done justice to the satisfaction I have experienced from giving back to the community, and conveyed the critical importance of meaningful connections and close friendships in my life.

PART ONE

1951 - 1960

Culture Shock

In the epilogue of *Goodbye Shanghai*, I alluded to the twin sensations of wonder and bewilderment that I felt upon arriving in Sydney in 1951. Apart from the few months I spent with my grandparents in Japan in 1940, my early years had been confined to Shanghai, where I lived in considerable comfort. My sheltered upbringing left me ill-equipped to easily adjust to the Australian way of life.

My first experience of culture shock took place at Central Railway Station in Sydney. My close friend, Alex (Sasha) Vinogradov, who had moved to Sydney from Shanghai with his family several months earlier, came to the station to help me buy my train ticket. I was preparing to travel to Melbourne, where I would live with our distant relative, Grisha Sklovsky, his wife and children until the rest of my family arrived from Shanghai. With all my identity and travel documents in hand, standing ready to provide my reason for travel, I found it hard to believe that all I had to do was hand over the requisite fare.

I was equally unprepared to change trains in Albury, on the border between New South Wales and Victoria, which was necessary because the rail gauges were different in each of those states. Australia was only perfunctorily covered in the British textbooks we studied at school. I was more familiar with the individual counties of England than its far-flung, much larger, colonies. And so, I was quite surprised during the overnight journey when I was woken and told to walk across the platform to the designated carriage of the Melbourne-bound train, ironically named *The Spirit of Progress*.

Culture Shock

My arrival in Melbourne, on Tuesday 6 November 1951, coincided with the running of the Melbourne Cup, a horse racing event so rich in prize money and tradition that the day had been declared a public holiday. Grisha picked me up from Spencer Street Station[1], and, as we drove in his Fiat through the empty streets of Australia's second largest city, he explained nonchalantly, "They've all gone to the races." I was stunned. That was my introduction to the city I would soon call home.

My family's migration to Australia had been forced upon us by circumstances beyond our control. During the Japanese occupation of Shanghai, from December 1941 (after the bombing of Pearl Harbor) to August 1945 (when Japan unconditionally surrendered), our status as 'stateless' was a great convenience because we could not be classified as enemy aliens. Even after the war, when the Chinese nationalist government assumed legal sovereignty over Shanghai, there were still no residency issues for the stateless. However, the situation gradually changed[2] when it became apparent that the Chinese communists would emerge as the victors in the Chinese Civil War.[3] Well before Mao Tse Tung's Red Army took control of Shanghai in May 1949, European residents and wealthy Chinese people had been leaving Shanghai, perceiving correctly that there would be no future for them under the new communist regime.

My father's preference had been to emigrate to the United States of America, the 'Mecca' for most stateless Jewish residents of Shanghai. But initial enquiries revealed that immigration to the US was not an option because, even though we did not hold Soviet citizenship, the American government considered us to be Russians and the Russian immigration quota was already filled.

As Jews, we could settle in the newly created State of Israel, with its promulgation of the Law of Return. In fact, the Israeli vice consul in New York, Moshe Yuval[4], came to Shanghai to issue entry permits to

---

[1] Now Southern Cross Station.

[2] Initially, being stateless was advantageous because we were not identified with any country. Subsequently, it became a disadvantage, because no country was obliged to take us.

[3] The Civil War between the communists and nationalists started before the breakout of WWII. However, when Japan entered the war, they came together to fight a common enemy. After Japan was defeated, the Civil War restarted. The communists won in 1949 and the defeated nationalists fled to Taiwan.

[4] Moshe Yuval would later become Israel's ambassador to Australia from 1958-1963.

Israel for the stranded Jews. But those early years in the new Jewish state were fraught with problems. Israel was at war with its neighbouring Arab countries, whilst attempting to absorb Jewish refugees forced to flee their homes in Arab countries, as well as Holocaust survivors living in displaced persons camps throughout Europe. Many Jewish residents of Shanghai immigrated to Israel, but their letters to friends and relatives still in China painted a dismal picture.

As a result, my father decided we should immigrate to Canada, reasoning that its proximity to the United States would eventually facilitate our entry into that country. At first, all seemed to go well, and we were granted entry permits to Canada. Through connections of Brother Julius, the principal of my school, St Francis Xavier College, I had also been accepted to study chemistry at the Catholic Laval University in Quebec. Then disaster struck. We were suddenly informed, without explanation, that our entry permits had been revoked. Apparently, the large influx of immigrants from China, in the wake of the communist victory, had prompted the Canadian government to rethink its liberal entry policies. I can still recall the anguish that accompanied the realisation that our family was stranded.

We desperately needed a new plan. Fortunately, my stepmother, Eva, had the address of a distant relative living in Melbourne, Australia. Eva had never met Grisha Sklovsky, whose genealogical connection to her family dated back to nineteenth century Siberia, but she wrote to him and asked him to sponsor us to settle in Australia. When he agreed, the relief was immeasurable.

Leaving Shanghai involved securing exit visas from the new authorities. This was a complicated process for those, like my father, who owned a business in Shanghai. When his exit visa negotiations struck yet another delay, it was decided that I should be sent to Australia on my own as I had completed school and there was little for me to do in Shanghai. As I would arrive in Melbourne in time for the commencement of the academic year, I wrote to the University of Melbourne to see if my admission to Laval University would qualify me to enrol there. I was pleasantly surprised by the prompt and favourable response.

Sponsoring our migration to Australia, which included providing financial guarantees, was an act of incredible generosity. Grisha and his Australian-born wife, Celia, also kindly agreed to accommodate me in their home, pending the arrival of the rest of the family. They lived in a comfortable house set in a spacious garden in Camberwell, regarded as one the best residential suburbs in Melbourne. The car ride from the train station through the deserted streets took about half an hour. On arrival, Celia, nursing a teary little Anna, who was suffering from measles, cordially welcomed me. I was assigned the spare room, whose dimensions were similar to my bedroom in the Doumer Apartments in Shanghai. So far, so good.

Until then, there had been few demands on my reserves of self-sufficiency. From the moment I was escorted onto the departing train in Shanghai, to my arrival in Melbourne, others took care of any difficulties I encountered. My first challenge occurred that afternoon, when a carrier delivered my well-crated belongings, deposited them in the garage, and drove off. Grisha handed me a hammer and other tools that I had never seen before and suggested that I get on with the job of unpacking before it started to rain. I had no idea how to go about it. Sensing my panic, Grisha eventually began to help me. He already had my measure!

My next challenge was the food. For dinner that night, Celia had prepared a welcome dish of rabbit stew, which sent me into another panic as I had a strong aversion towards certain foods. Somehow, my ingrained Eastern politeness helped me survive the crisis. Doing the 'washing up' was a welcome relief even though I had never, until that night, touched a dish after eating from it.

That evening, Celia helped settle me into my room before Grisha outlined some of the duties expected of me as part of the Sklovsky household. Apart from helping with the washing up after meals, every Sunday morning I would mow the lawns with a hand mower and, on Sunday evenings, I had to take out the rubbish bins, which, back then, were metal containers without wheels. Grisha explained that everybody in Australia did these chores as, unlike in Shanghai, there were no servants.

The next morning, by the time I awoke, Grisha had already gone to work. Celia left me to continue with my unpacking and to write some letters. In 1951, letting my parents in Shanghai know that I had safely arrived in Melbourne and settled into the Sklovsky household, involved writing a letter on wafer-thin paper and sending it by airmail. A telephone call or even a telegram seemed unnecessarily extravagant. I also wrote to Sasha in Sydney and to other friends in Australia and overseas.

In the afternoon, while Anna was having a nap, I had a cup of tea with Celia, who was interested in my life in Shanghai. No doubt, she had some thoughts about my future in Australia, but she left that discussion to Grisha. That evening, after I washed the dishes, Grisha and I talked about my next steps.

Most urgent was the need to open a bank account and deposit the money draft my father had given me. This I duly did, at the head office of the then Bank of New South Wales at 360 Collins Street, the most prestigious business address in Melbourne at the time. Once again, I was surprised by how quick and easy the process was, and how little was needed in the way of paperwork.

The next imperative was to sort out my enrolment at the University of Melbourne.[5] Grisha facilitated the process by contacting his friend, Sid Rubbo, a professor of microbiology at the university. Through his intercession I was able to secure an appointment with a Mr Johnston, the registrar with whom I had already corresponded from Shanghai. My admission was, in theory, assured by virtue of my admission to Laval University in Quebec but the registrar had to ensure my English was up to standard. I spent more than an hour chatting with Mr Johnston over a cup of tea in his office. He was extremely interested in Shanghai, particularly its recent takeover by the communists. Our

---

[5] The only university in Melbourne at the time.

discussion was in English, which I spoke fluently. At the end of our meeting, he thanked me for my time (a level of courtesy from such a senior official that, coming from China, surprised me) and signed an authority permitting me to enrol into the faculty of engineering to study chemical engineering. Grisha had persuaded me that chemical engineering would offer better employment and remuneration prospects than just studying chemistry, which had been my original intention.

I had no problem settling into the pleasant routines of the Sklovsky family and the chores really posed no difficulties. Most evenings after dinner, Celia, Grisha and I would retire to his library to listen to the radio. Then, after Celia went to bed, Grisha and I would sit up and discuss how I could successfully integrate into Australian society.

Back then, modern notions of multiculturalism were not yet understood or accepted. Migrants who had recently arrived in the country were labelled 'new Australians' and were expected to fit into the mainstream as quickly as possible. This often involved anglicising the family surname to make it easier for the general population to pronounce. Integration involved avoiding being conspicuous, in terms of dress and behaviour.

Grisha subscribed to this assimilationist approach and was critical of recent migrants who insisted on retaining their European mannerisms and preserving their narrow social cliques. With every good intention, he encouraged me to adopt his attitude and our discussions revolved around how I could most quickly integrate. Firstly, he felt that I should get a job that involved physical labour. He saw this as an important way for me to shed the indolent culture associated with my youth in Shanghai. To this end, he arranged for me to be interviewed for a job as a garage hand. I was initially aghast—and even more so when I actually got the job. He also felt that I should go on a hitchhiking trip to acquaint myself with 'the bush', a concept I found mystifying.

Above: *The Anking*. The cargo ship that took me from Hong Kong to Sydney
Below: Washing the dishes

Working at H.E. Gilbert & Son in Tooronga Road, East Malvern

Grisha & Celia Sklovsky with their children Anna, Janie & Michael

Hitchhiking

My parents, grandmother and two brothers were due to arrive in Sydney in March and, as vanguard of the family, it was up to me to find somewhere for us all to live. That was no easy matter in Melbourne where there was a severe postwar shortage of accommodation. The obvious place to start looking was the large classifieds section of *The Age* (dubbed 'the river of gold' by the newspaper mogul Sir Frank Packer). Initially, I was too slow in responding to the advertisements in the 'houses to rent' section and every call I made was rudely rebuffed by the agent or owner. I resorted to turning up at the offices of *The Age* in Collins Street as early as seven in the morning so that I could scour the advertisements and be among the first to call. To no avail! I was starting to get desperate as my hitchhiking trip to Sydney, where I would greet my family, was fast approaching.

Celia was quietly observing my efforts and suggested that I also look in the classifieds section of the *Camberwell Free Press*, a local paper that was delivered to every home in the suburb. I had never heard of a free local newspaper. Nothing like that existed in Shanghai. Sure enough, I found an advertisement for a house to rent in nearby Allambee Avenue, Camberwell. I called the number and spoke to a Mrs Broadbent, the owner, and arranged to meet her the following day. Mrs Broadbent turned out to be a pleasant, recently widowed woman who wanted to rent out her family home for a fixed term of six months, before deciding whether to sell it. The house was in a side street that was only a short walk from the Riversdale Road tramline. The position seemed ideal, and the house had enough bedrooms, a generous kitchen, a separate dining room, a lounge room, and a bathroom. My only concern was how my family would react to the septic tank toilet in the back garden. Despite my youth, I must have made a reasonable impression on Mrs Broadbent who agreed, in principle, to rent us her house. Once she had spoken to Celia, my referee, she confirmed the arrangement. I was extremely relieved and could not thank Celia enough.

With the house arrangements sorted, I could focus on my upcoming hitchhiking trip with Sasha Vinogradov, whom I hadn't seen for several months. Our communication had been limited to letter writing and I was keen to compare notes on our relative experiences in Australia.

After studying the route, we decided to meet in Goulburn, then detour to Canberra, after which we would head to the Pacific Highway all the way along the coast to Sydney. Sasha would look after the sleeping arrangements by bringing along a tent.

And so, early one February morning, Grisha dropped me off at the Sydney Road entrance to the Hume Highway. Whatever qualms he may have had about leaving me there to fend for myself, he didn't share with me. In those days, hitchhiking was an acceptable mode of transport and it certainly was not considered dangerous.

It did not take long for me to realise what a novice I was. A few yards ahead was a young man, in military uniform, who was also attempting to hitch a ride. I approached him, introduced myself, and asked if I could join him. He was quite affable and suggested that I go on ahead and wait. He told me that as a recently discharged soldier, it would be easier for him to score a ride, and that he would ask the driver to stop and pick me up. I felt embarrassed and naïve when, a short while later, he waved at me from a passing car.

Eventually, I was picked up, dropped off and then picked up again. Sometimes the lifts came quickly, but often the wait was agonisingly slow and a bit scary. I recall being amazed by the lack of cars on the most travelled highway in Australia. If a passing car was full, or declined to pick me up, it could be hours before I caught the next ride. At those moments I sincerely regretted agreeing to undertake the journey.

However, I did also have some good luck. One afternoon, a car pulled up and the driver offered me a lift. He introduced himself as Jeff Bate, a member of parliament headed for Canberra. I told him I was a newly arrived immigrant from Shanghai, and he expressed interest in the events taking place in China. As dusk approached, he said he would be camping overnight and that he could drive me to Goulburn in the morning. Without any other options, I gratefully accepted his offer. Jeff Bate turned out to be a gregarious and entertaining individual and the evening was a highlight of the trip. The following day, he dropped me off at Goulburn Railway Station and urged me to visit Canberra.[6]

Finally, I met up with Sasha who had been patiently waiting for me. It was a wonderful reunion and all night we swapped stories about our lives in Australia. Sasha was more settled than me, as he was living with his family, who were socialising with the expatriate (non-Jewish) Russian community, and he had already started studying at a Sydney technical institute. His father, who had previously held a position with the Shanghai Power Company, had experienced no difficulty obtaining employment with the Sydney Power Company in a similar capacity.

The next morning we hitchhiked to Canberra, where we easily found a camping ground to pitch our tent. Canberra, in early 1952, was a far cry from the city it is today. Walter Burley Griffin's vision for a modern national capital[7] had been deferred due to the Great Depression and World War II. Lake Burley Griffin was not yet built, nor were the iconic buildings now gracing its shores. The city's layout was extremely confusing, and the traffic was light, making hitchhiking very difficult.

We took up Jeff Bate's suggestion to visit Parliament House, now known as the Old Parliament House, and had no trouble gaining admittance to the visitors' gallery at the House of Representatives. To us, coming from China, it was particularly special to see Robert Menzies,

---

[6] Jeff Bate would later marry Zara Holt, the widow of former prime minister Harold Holt. My naturalisation certificate was signed by Harold Holt in 1954.

[7] In 1912, American architect Walter Griffin won an international competition to design a federal capital city for Australia. He declared, "I have planned a city that meets my ideal of the city of the future."

the prime minister, and various other dignitaries, including Jeff Bate, on the floor of parliament. After a while, we noticed a change in tempo. Ministers started to whisper to each other, and normal business seemed to come to an end. I recall saying to Sasha, "Something is going on!" Then, Robert Menzies stood up to make a special announcement to the hushed chamber. He announced that King George VI had died and followed up with, "Long live the Queen." That proclamation, on 6 February 1952, became another memorable highlight of our adventure.

After another day of sightseeing, we decided to hit the road. Thanks to Sasha's calm demeanour, I became accustomed to the rhythm of hitchhiking, the search for a suitable campsite, pitching the tent, organising meals, and then heading off in the morning. I stopped being anxious about being picked up. Although some days we would spend more time on the side of the road than riding in cars or trucks, somehow things always worked out. We were struck by the friendliness of the drivers who expressed genuine interest in our backgrounds.

Eventually we arrived at a small seaside town called Pambula. At the post office, I made a long-distance call to Grisha to see if there was any news from my parents regarding their arrival in Sydney. Grisha was relieved that I had rung as he had just received a telegram from my father, advising that the ship transporting them to Australia would, in fact, be arriving in Melbourne, in about 10 days' time. I would have to cut short my trip and head back to Melbourne. I was disappointed about this abrupt change of plans, and particularly upset to be leaving Sasha.

I was emboldened to hitchhike my way back to Melbourne. However, without Sasha to reassure me, some of my anxieties returned. Eventually, after about four days, I finally arrived back at the Sklovsky residence. It was a relief to be home and to know where I would sleep that night but, to my great shock, I was informed that a second telegram had arrived to say that my family's ship, *Changsha*, would be disembarking in Sydney after all!

Our tent

Travelling light

Settling In

The *Changsha* was due to dock on the evening of 8 March so, to save time, I decided to fly to Sydney instead of hitchhiking again. There were three airlines to choose from: TAA, the government-owned airline; ANA, which was privately owned; and the new airline founded by businessman Reg Ansett.[8] I booked the Ansett Airways flight because it was the cheapest; the plane was a DC3, probably purchased as postwar surplus. I also booked several rooms at the Astor Hotel on Campbell Parade, overlooking the famous Bondi Beach, for the family to stay for a few nights.

The flight departed, like all Melbourne flights at the time, from Essendon Airport[9] and the travellers waved farewell from the top of the plane's boarding stairs. I was excited for my first ever flight and I was, once again, amazed that all I needed was a ticket, and no other official documentation. I was also excited that I would soon be reunited with my family, after nearly six months.

Standing on the pier in Sydney, I thought about how much I had missed my family during our separation. I reflected on all that I had experienced since leaving Shanghai, and I felt proud that I had facilitated the start of our new life in Australia.

The wait for them to disembark seemed endless, and I started to fear that my grandmother had become sick during the long and arduous journey. Finally, I saw my father, Eva, Grandmother, Nathan (now nine years old) and Elijah (aged six) walk down the gangplank and off the boat. Later, my father proudly explained that they had been delayed because Australian officials (he called them 'intelligence officers') had questioned him about Shanghai and the new communist regime. He seemed quite chuffed that they had asked him about the political situation in China.

---

[8] Ansett was a bus service before becoming a successful airline business. In 2001, Ansett Airlines went into administration following financial collapse. We were lucky that international flights we had booked were honoured by the airline before its liquidation. [9] Tullamarine Airport opened in 1970.

Settling In

I was very close to my grandmother, and I was relieved to see how well she had weathered the trip. When I had left Shanghai, we had both feared we might never see each other again. I had missed her very much, particularly her wise sayings, which I continue to quote to this day.

Our few days in Sydney were a whirlwind of activity as Eva was keen to catch up with her Shanghai friends. She particularly wanted to thank her friend, Mrs Prosterman, for accommodating me in her new home in Dover Heights when I had first arrived, and we all visited the Vinogradovs, who had settled in Chatswood. I also accompanied Father to meetings with businesspeople from Shanghai to learn about their experiences in Sydney. Most were still struggling to adapt, including our jeweller in Shanghai who, unable to find work in his trade, had reluctantly retrained as a baker.

I took Nathan and Elijah for a ride on the open Bondi tram, as well as to the pictures to see their favourite cartoons. It was difficult for Grandmother to move around, so I spent time with her in her hotel room, telling her, in great detail, about my life in Melbourne.

Once again, Sasha accompanied me to Central Railway Station so I could pre-purchase tickets and I warned my family about the early morning changeover in Albury. We finally arrived in Melbourne and travelled in the several taxis I had arranged to transport us to our new home in Allambee Avenue, Camberwell.

A freight company delivered all the personal possessions that my parents had been allowed to take out of China. The truck arrived with furniture, trunks filled with handwoven tablecloths and other reminders of our former life. Sadly, most of our family wealth—the Shanghai Card Box Company, two properties in the former French Concession and two properties in Hongkew—had been surrendered to the communist authorities without any compensation.

I was, of course, anxious about how the family would react to the house I had rented as, in several respects, it did not measure up to the two flats we had occupied in our Doumer Apartments. Whatever they really thought, they expressed their satisfaction and gratitude.

We spent the rest of the day unpacking and, later that afternoon, we visited the Sklovskys' house.

Father and Eva brought lavish presents for Grisha and Celia to thank them for sponsoring our migration to Australia and for letting me stay with them. After the welcome dinner, I took my very tired family back to our new home for their first night in Melbourne.

The school year had already started in February, so enrolling Nathan and Elijah was the priority. On Grisha's advice, they started going to the local state school, where they both settled in quickly and did well academically.[10] Another priority was to set up Father's bank accounts, so I took him to the Collins Street banking chamber where I was already a customer so he could meet with the manager.

Celia advised Eva about where to purchase groceries, a chore that had been handled by our cook in Shanghai. Large supermarkets did not yet exist, but Celia had an account with a store called Crittendens that delivered her orders each week. You had to be a 'person of good standing' to get onto Crittenden's exclusive delivery list, so we were grateful when Celia put in a good word for Eva and they agreed to take her on as a new customer. Celia also arranged for her cleaner to come to our house for a few hours once a week. This was a coup because, we were surprised to learn, home help was very difficult to come by. We were even more shocked when the cleaner nonchalantly sat down to eat lunch with us.

Grandmother could not speak English and was not particularly mobile. She helped Eva as much as she could with running the household, but we worried that she would become lonely. Fortunately, we discovered that Mrs Segal was living in the nearby suburb of Kew. My parents' friendship with the Segal family dated back to their early days in Shanghai. In fact, when that family's apartment building in Shanghai was commandeered by the Japanese authorities in 1944 (so the Japanese could place their anti-aircraft guns on the roof to shoot down the American bombers flying overhead), they moved into the residential apartment above my father's factory.

---

[10] From the beginning, both Elijah and Nathan did very well in their studies and were eventually accepted into Camberwell High School. Elijah quickly distinguished himself by attaining one of the highest marks in Victoria in the matriculation exams.

Settling In

The next issue for my parents was how to connect with the Jewish community in Melbourne. In Shanghai, we were well known in the Russian Jewish community and had enjoyed a vibrant social life, as well as a moderately religious life. Grisha had not joined any of the Melbourne Jewish community's religious or social organisations, so he could not guide us in these matters. Furthermore, because we were not part of an official influx of Jewish refugees, we were not known to the Jewish organisations facilitating the integration of many new arrivals.

From our enquiries, we discovered that the two main synagogues, the Melbourne Hebrew Congregation in Toorak Road, and the St Kilda Hebrew Congregation, were dominated by established Australian Jews and that, in any event, all the 'seats were sold'. However, we were also told about a small congregation which had recently been established in a large house in Camberwell, that conducted Friday evening services fortnightly. Membership of this congregation, an offshoot of Temple Beth Israel[11], was largely composed of Central European Jews as well as Australian Jews and called itself 'Liberal', rather than 'Orthodox'. Men and women sat together and many of the prayers were in English, as well as Hebrew. This new form of Judaism was bitterly resented by many Orthodox adherents.

While most of the new Jewish arrivals settled in the traditional Jewish areas of Carlton and St Kilda, it was sensible for this new movement to establish a congregation for the sprinkling of Jews who settled in the eastern suburbs of Melbourne, including Camberwell, Hawthorn and Kew. We decided to attend a service one Friday evening and found the format totally different to what we were used to, and the atmosphere rather forlorn, but it was good to meet other recently arrived Jews. Most were from Germany and Austria, some of whom had fled to Shanghai and spent several of the war years in the Hongkew ghetto that was established in 1943. From these new friends, Eva obtained the names of kosher shops where she could purchase matzos, gefilte fish and other specialty foods for the approaching Pesach holiday.

I don't know whether we would have persevered as members of this congregation, were it not for Rabbi Herman Sanger who was visiting

---

[11] The emancipation of Central European Jewry in the eighteenth century produced this new offshoot of traditional Judaism to signify its integration in general society.

from Temple Beth Israel. Rabbi Sanger had a wonderfully warm and charismatic personality, and he made newcomers feel welcome and reassured. He was also an outstanding orator who understood how to reach into the souls of his audience. Rabbi Sanger came from an illustrious family of rabbis in Germany. He was enticed to escape rising antisemitism by coming to Melbourne, in August 1936, to take ecclesiastical leadership of the newly established, and struggling, Liberal congregation. He was an immediate success in Melbourne and was embraced by the community.[12]

Father had some capital, but he was at a loss as to how to make a start in business. Everything in Australia was completely different to what he was used to, and he must have missed his late father's confident guiding hand. Regrettably, his pride and his perception of what our family expected of him prevented him from seeking employment, which, looking back, would have probably been the sensible thing to do. It also prevented him from confiding in us, although I am not sure how we could have helped. Grandmother was quite bitter about the situation we found ourselves in. Unfortunately, she had no faith in my father and blamed him for not selling up and getting out of Shanghai sooner. Her frustration spilled over into whatever conversations they did have.

Eva was also grappling with the challenges of setting up a home without the many servants she was used to. In Shanghai, she would issue orders and requests to the cook or the *amah* who looked after Nathan and Elijah, and then go to the Shanghai Jewish Club to socialise. In Melbourne, she had to cook all the meals for the family and do most of the cleaning. It was also difficult for her without the support of friends and community.

It was little wonder that tension pervaded the atmosphere at home, no matter how hard everybody tried to adjust. I was old enough to sense these undercurrents and was also missing the active social life and close friendships I had enjoyed in Shanghai.

---

[12] Rabbi Dr Herman Sanger, a seventh-generation rabbi, was born in 1909 in Breslau, Germany where he received his rabbinical training. He was ordained at age 24 and was engaged by a Berlin Jewish congregation. His induction on 1 April 1933, two months after Adolf Hitler became chancellor, was a fateful day as it was the same day the newly-empowered Nazis unleashed their first official attack on German Jews. In 1936, Rabbi Sanger received an anonymous telephone call warning that the Nazis were on the verge of arresting him. He immediately left for London. Although only 27, he was already well known and several well-established pulpits in Britain and the US were readily available to him. But Lily Montagu, one of the founders of Liberal Judaism in Australia, was somehow able to persuade him to come to Melbourne, where he arrived August 1936. The leaders of the nascent Liberal congregation took to him immediately. But he must have wondered about his decision as he started his ministry in the parish hall of Christ Church in Acland Street, St Kilda, preaching from a rickety pulpit on an unstable podium. Sanger was tall and charismatic, which he put to good use energising and expanding his fledgling congregation. He was an excellent orator and his spiritual sermons were mesmerising.

Above: Outside our house in Lansell Crescent, Camberwell
Centre: With our Humber Hawk
Below: With Grandmother

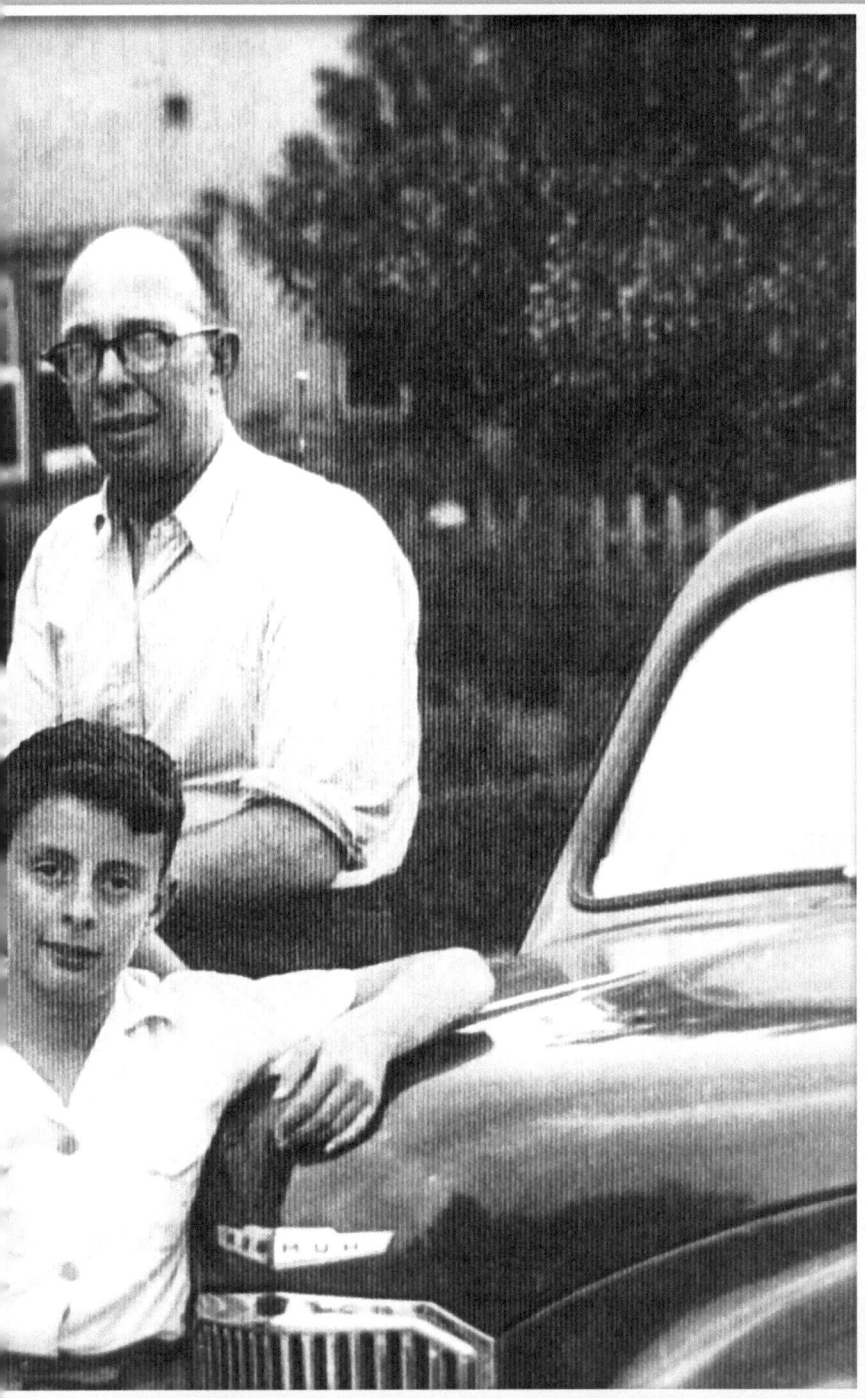

With Eva, Elijah, Nathan & Father

University Life

I commenced my tertiary education in chemical engineering at the University of Melbourne in March 1952. The first-year subjects for all engineering students were mathematics, physics, chemistry, and engineering drafting and drawing.

Keen to participate in university life, I was excited by the variety of extracurricular activities on offer and the opportunity to meet people. I eagerly joined the Union Theatre Repertory Company, an acting group founded by the celebrated director John Sumner.[13] With limited experience from my sole acting role in a Betar play in Shanghai, I brashly auditioned for a forthcoming production and was quickly rejected.

Undaunted, at Grisha's urging, I also joined the University Ski Club (USC), even though I had never skied and knew nothing about the sport. Over the Queen's Birthday long weekend, I joined the club's annual trip to Mount Buller. I travelled in a fellow member's car, and we parked at the carpark part-way up the mountain. We then set off by foot with our heavy backpacks to Mount Buller Village. My travel companion was a Canadian Jewish student on exchange from McGill University in Montreal. He was swearing in Yiddish about the mountain's primitive facilities as we trudged upwards. Finally, after several hours of excruciating hiking, we arrived at USC Lodge, which, back then, was a basic hut. The only heating was a log fire in the common room where we drank copious amounts of claret, before retiring to the unheated bedrooms where we slept, fully clothed, in sleeping bags on bunk beds. The worst part was that the toilets were in outhouses.

The skiing itself proved to be an insurmountable challenge, particularly as there were no professional instructors. I rented skis and steeled myself to face the slopes. Back then, getting to the top of the

---

[13] The Union Theatre Repertory Company would later become the Melbourne Theatre Company (MTC), an important organisation in Melbourne's vibrant cultural scene. Many years later, when I was invited to join the board of the MTC, I recounted the story of my short-lived attempt to become an actor.

run involved grasping a rough rope attached to an electric motor. I am not sure which was harder, hanging on to the rope tow for dear life, or attempting to ski back down. Both involved multiple tumbles in the heavy snow and humiliating attempts to get back up again. I was extremely relieved to arrive home late on Monday night and resolved never to ski again.

I would have liked to get involved in more clubs and societies, but I started to find my studies hard going. This came as a surprise as I had been a good student in the same subjects at school. I was used to a more didactic and disciplined approach to teaching, whereas at university I was expected to be a more independent learner. In the tutorials it was evident that I was falling behind and, after failing several exams, it was suggested that I should repeat the year.

The following year, depressingly, I once again failed every subject. Of course, this led to a crisis in my education, as I could not repeat the subjects a third time. I was devastated and confused about how I had gone from being such a good student in Shanghai to someone who received such poor results. Looking back, I suspect I was struggling to adjust, and that I was unsettled by the fact that Father was finding it difficult to establish himself. He attempted to shield us from the reality, but we knew he was finding the new business environment extremely challenging.

When Grisha Sklovsky heard that I had failed my course for a second time, he suggested that I take an aptitude test to ascertain whether I was suited to engineering. The results revealed that my true abilities did not lie in the complexities of engineering, which provided an explanation for my poor grades, but left me feeling even more confused about my future.

At a meeting in our new home in Lansell Crescent, Camberwell[14], Grisha recommended that I join an organisation that would expose me to a wide variety of businesses to determine what area of work most appealed to me. He suggested that a large accounting firm might be prepared to hire me, whereas law firms only hired graduates.

---

[14] My parents liked Camberwell, so when the six-month lease at Allambee Avenue expired, they purchased a house in nearby Lansell Crescent, where we lived for many years.

Consequently, in mid-December 1953, with Grisha's help, I compiled a list of chartered accounting firms, to whom I wrote, in my neat longhand, requesting an interview.

I successfully secured interviews with two firms: Flack & Flack (which was associated with Price Waterhouse, a firm that Father had dealt with in Shanghai) and Fuller, King & Co. Both had offices in William Street in the city.

The Flack & Flack interview did not go well, and I was not offered a position. The Fuller, King & Co. interview got off to a good start when Mr Reg Waddell, a senior partner, complimented me on my handwriting. At that moment I felt grateful to my teachers for inculcating in me the discipline of good handwriting.[15] He also appreciated my candour when explaining my struggles with engineering. Contrary to my fears, my university results did not compromise my application. When Mr Waddell asked if I'd commit to at least two years with the firm, I readily agreed. He then offered me a position as a junior at a weekly salary of four pounds, seven shillings and six pence, which, he admitted, was substantially less than the normal salary of a junior clerk. However, he added, the position should be viewed as a steppingstone to a worthwhile career.

As I was about to leave, Mr Waddell asked what I proposed to do about future studies. He suggested that I consider undertaking a part-time Bachelor of Commerce degree and added that the firm would be prepared to give me time off to attend the early evening lectures. I thanked Mr Waddell for the offer of employment and his wise counsel regarding my future studies. We fixed upon my start date, in early February 1954, and I left his office feeling elated.

Looking back, that interview was undoubtedly a seminal event in my life.

---

[15] In those days, good handwriting was considered an important attribute.

University life, 1952

Young Leadership

A significant meeting during my time as an engineering student greatly influenced the future direction of my life. One afternoon, after our names were called out to retrieve our submissions, a fellow student approached me and introduced himself as Nathan Fink. He asked if Moshinsky was a Jewish name and was interested to hear that I had recently arrived from Shanghai. Coincidentally, his father, Leo Fink, was heavily involved in the Australian Jewish Welfare Society, which was helping Jewish refugees, including Jews from China, resettle in Australia. The Fink family owned a successful manufacturing business called United Carpet Mills and were prominent members of the Jewish community. But, of course, I had never heard of them.

Nathan took me under his wing, invited me to parties and introduced me to many other young Jewish people. With more friends and a newly active social life, I started to feel more like my old self. Significantly, Nathan also invited me to join him on the Leadership Development Committee of the Melbourne Jewish Youth Council (MJYC), which he chaired.

MJYC was the roof body for all Jewish youth groups. I still find it curious that, in the early 1950s, the much smaller Melbourne Jewish community had a roof organisation for its youth groups, whereas none exists today. These youth groups represented the full spectrum of Zionist ideologies, as well as several non-Zionist cultural groups. Similarly, in the Jewish sports arena, all the different sports clubs were given the prefix AJAX and were united by their own roof body, the Judean League.

The MJYC's Leadership Development Committee was one of several initiatives pioneered by the executive committee. Our mission was to develop the leadership expertise of the head of each youth group.

The program we devised consisted of lectures on Jewish historical and contemporary topics, as well as courses on public speaking and how to conduct meetings.

Our regular committee meetings were held at night in a room in the basement of the Toorak synagogue. There was a lot of work involved and I could see why Nathan welcomed my assistance. I embraced the opportunity to engage in a communal activity and to get to know many youth leaders who would later become influential adult leaders in the community, including Isi Leibler, Philip Symons, and a young solicitor named Arnold Bloch who had recently arrived from England and established a law firm.[16]

I vividly recall one event we hosted, that required each participant to speak for a few minutes about their aspirations. One young man, the only participant whose family had lived in Australia for generations, got up and said, in a clear voice, that his aim was to be a rabbi and serve the religious needs of his community. His name was John Levi, and he would later become the celebrated senior rabbi of Temple Beth Israel, where I would one day serve as a board member and then as president.

About a year after I joined the committee, Nathan surprised me by announcing that he was heading overseas[17] and that the MJYC outgoing president, Phil Symons, had agreed that I should replace him as chair. I was nervous to take on the additional responsibility but could not summon the courage to decline. So, with trepidation, I accepted the challenge. The new role came with an invitation to join the executive of the MJYC, and the new president, Sonny Traeger, began mentoring me in the complexities of community politics.

That marked the beginning of my long involvement in the leadership of Australian Jewish communal organisations that, throughout the course of my life, would provide me with incredible opportunities, fascinating challenges, and enormous satisfaction.

---

[16] The now well-known and highly regarded law firm Arnold Bloch Leibler.

[17] I assumed Nathan was travelling to Israel for work but later discovered he went to attend his sister Freda's wedding to Martin Freiberg. Their son, Mark Regev, was raised in Australia but later immigrated to Israel where he held senior positions in the Ministry for Foreign Affairs before becoming a diplomat. He was appointed Israel's ambassador to the United Kingdom from 2016 to 2020.

E (1)   N° 12290

COMMONWEALTH OF AUSTRALIA.

Nationality and Citizenship Act 1948–1953.

CERTIFICATE OF NATURALIZATION AS AN AUSTRALIAN CITIZEN.

WHEREAS   Samson MOSHINSKY

has applied for a Certificate of Naturalization as an Australian Citizen, alleging with respect to **him**self the particulars set out on the reverse side hereof, and has satisfied me that   he has fulfilled the conditions laid down in the *Nationality and Citizenship Act 1948–1953* for the grant of such a Certificate :

NOW THEREFORE I, the Minister of State for Immigration, hereby grant, in pursuance of the *Nationality and Citizenship Act 1948–1953* this Certificate of Naturalization, whereby, subject to the provisions of the said Act and of any other law

affecting the rights of naturalized persons, the said

                Samson MOSHINSKY

shall, as from the date upon which   he swears or affirms allegiance to Her Majesty Queen Elizabeth the Second, her heirs and successors, and swears to, or affirms that   he will, observe faithfully the laws of Australia and fulfil **his** duties as an Australian citizen, become entitled to all political and other rights, powers and privileges, and become subject to all obligations, duties and liabilities to which an Australian citizen or a British subject is entitled or subject, and have to all intents and purposes the status of an Australian citizen and British subject.

Dated this   **Nineteenth**   day

of   **July,**   One thousand

nine hundred and   **fifty-four.**

(Signed) H. HOLT

Minister of State for Immigration.

CERTIFICATE BY JUDGE, MAGISTRATE OR PERSON APPROVED BY THE MINISTER.

I,   Henry Charles Stanford   do hereby certify

that on the 4th   day of   November,   195

the grantee of this Certificate

                Samson MOSHINSKY

appeared before me at   Camberwell
swore allegiance to Her Majesty Queen Elizabeth the Second, her heirs and successors, and swore to observe faithfully the laws of Australia and fulfil   **his** duties as an Australian citizen.

Signature   H.C. Stanford

Title   Mayor

[OVER.

Above: Receiving my naturalisation certificate from the mayor at Camberwell Town Hall
Below: The B'nai Brith Youth Leadership Committee

Strong Foundations

On a hot Monday morning in early February 1954, I presented myself for work at the offices of Fuller King & Co, Chartered Accountants (Australia) to begin what was to become a rewarding 30-year career as a professional accountant.

The job was intended to be an opportunity for me to work with clients across a range of businesses to help me identify my areas of interest. The plan was that I would eventually establish a new business with my father's financial assistance and possible involvement. As it turned out, it was the field of accounting and, more specifically, management consulting that claimed my interest.

The firm's offices occupied the whole fifth floor of Western House, a modern building on the northwest corner of Collins and William Streets.[18] A major branch of National Australia Bank was on the ground floor and the rest of the building was tenanted by prestigious businesses, including another leading accounting firm, Smith Johnson & Co.

At the reception area I asked for Mr Waddell, who welcomed me and introduced me to Alec Barr, the office manager. Mr Barr, a middle-aged, short man with a gruff manner, told me I would work as a junior in the audit section. There was no formal training program and, he said, I would easily pick up what was required. He then took me on a quick tour of the offices. The partners' area, known as the 'inner sanctum', which featured a bathroom for their exclusive use, was at one end of the building. In the centre of the office space was a large room for 'the typing pool', which was comprised of six typists presided over by Miss Betty Cunning. All handwritten documents were given to her and then allocated to an available typist. I was quietly advised

---

[18] The building still exists but is no longer considered modern.

to stay on her good side. Fortunately, I did get on well with Betty over the years and never experienced any problems getting my typing done.

On that first afternoon, one of the more experienced juniors took me down Collins Street to the ANZ Bank and showed me where to pick up the cheques of specific audit clients, which had been paid and bunched for collection. One of my allocated tasks was to sort the cheques into number order so they could more easily be checked against the names of the payees in the cash payments book. This tedious and intensely disliked sorting procedure was done on the large table in the boardroom where I was first interviewed. Presumably it would be my job until the next junior was hired.

Another one of my jobs at the firm was at the layby department at Myer Emporium, then Melbourne's most prominent department store and one of the firm's largest and most respected clients. Back then, Myer customers had the choice to put an item on layby and pay it off in instalments, only receiving the purchased item once the final payment was processed. Because every layby purchase generated several duplicate receipts, to prevent theft by the store's cashiers, regular audits of these receipts were required. It was my role to check whether all the numbered layby receipts were properly listed in the layby books. A few months later, I was given the added responsibility of also ensuring that there were no printer errors in the numbering sequence of the original receipt book.

The work was mind-numbingly boring, but Father urged me to persevere. Fortunately, a month later, my part-time commerce course began at the University of Melbourne, and I was given permission to leave work early twice a week to get to the 5.15pm lectures. I really enjoyed the intellectual challenge of the course and I always looked forward to the days I went to the university.

After a few months, Mable Cooper, another office manager, gave me an important new task, which had been performed by one of the juniors who had just left. Each week a new set of laundered hand towels was delivered, and it would be my job to hang the coloured striped towels on the correct hooks outside the partner's washroom. Each partner had his own hook and his colour preference and Miss Cooper was anxious that I get it right. In fact, I performed the job so well that, even as I gained seniority, I was asked to continue doing it. As menial as it was, that task gained the partners' attention and was, I am sure, the reason for my generous Christmas bonuses. Unbelievably, the partners requested that I continue hanging up the hand towels for the next five years.

Over the next few months, my life took on a pleasant rhythm. I spent several days a week at the layby department of the Myer Emporium. On other days, I would pick up the bundles of paid cheques from the various banks, for sorting. And every Thursday, I would be in the office so that I could deal with the partners' towels following the laundry delivery.

For lunch, I would buy sandwiches at a small milk bar in the laneway next to the office. The milk bar was run by a Polish Jewish lady who must have sensed that I was Jewish because she always served me first. Years later, after giving a speech at a Warsaw Ghetto Uprising Commemoration evening at the Melbourne Town Hall, the woman approached and proudly reminded me that she used to sell me sandwiches.

One morning, while waiting patiently in the lobby of the Bank of New South Wales in Collins Street for yet another bundle of cancelled cheques, I was approached by a young man who was also waiting for a delivery of documents. He introduced himself as Ian Permezel and said that he recognised me from evening lectures at the university. It transpired that Ian was also studying commerce part-time, whilst working for a stockbroking firm called Tolhurst, Henley, Munckton & Co.

Over the next few weeks, Ian and I met regularly for coffee at Union House on campus. I learned that Permezel was a French name and that one of his ancestors had rebelled against his Lyons-based French Catholic background, travelled to Australia and become a Presbyterian. Ian was also a devout Presbyterian, and he and his brother, Rod, had both attended the elite private school, Scotch College. Ian expressed interest in my Shanghai background as well as my Jewish religion, for which he professed an affinity. The two of us bonded over our shared studies, common interests, and commitment to work and community life. It was the beginning of a friendship that was as close as it was long.

Ian soon convinced me to join the Melbourne Junior Chamber of Commerce, or 'Jaycees' as it was known, which was devoted to improving the managerial skills of the young men who were gravitating to the executive ranks of Australia's fast-growing business community. Thus began a long and satisfying involvement with the Jaycees, through which I met many businesspeople, some of whom became great friends. Before long I was elected chairman of one of the sections and Ian was elected president of the entire organisation, a most prestigious appointment.

By then, my family was well settled in our new home in Lansell Crescent, Camberwell. At the bottom of the street was Willison Railway Station, on the Alamein Line, and I would catch the train at 8am each morning. Before long, I became friends with several young professionals on the train, including Ken Hyden, who worked for a stockbroking firm called A.C. Goode & Co. One day, Ken gave me a tip to buy shares in a finance company called Industrial Acceptance Corporation. I rashly decided to follow his advice and invested 500 pounds—the equivalent of two years of my starting salary—which was all that I had left from the original 1000 pounds my father had given me when I left Shanghai. Luckily, Ken Hyden's tip was good and, several months later, the shares had doubled in price! That was my introduction to share trading, which I continued to pursue with enthusiasm.

In my first year at the firm, although the work was repetitious, I enjoyed the environment, and everybody seemed to go out of their way to make me feel welcome. Most of my co-workers came from an upper-middle class Anglo-Saxon background, and many had attended private schools such as Melbourne Grammar and Scotch College. As a new Australian of Russian Jewish descent, born and raised in Shanghai, I must have been considered a real oddity. No doubt they were surprised by how well I spoke English, although my accent and formal manner of speech would have seemed strange.

Betty Cunning was the one who told me that I was the first Jew employed by the firm, although she added that a former partner had "some Jewish blood". Betty was particularly nice to me and regularly told me she would be pleased to ensure my typing was done quickly if I ever had any. Some years later, I finally started to generate some typing and Betty came good on her promise, always giving me priority. Back then, producing typed documents was a laborious exercise, often involving correcting errors with a white liquid called Tipex. This caused problems when carbon paper was used to simultaneously produce multiple copies. Tipex could be applied to mistakes on the top copy and then typed over, but the carbon copies would often be unusable.

One day, when I was in the boardroom sorting cheques, a middle-aged gentleman came in and introduced himself as Rex Prime, the manager of the firm's accounting and secretarial department. He explained that his department kept the books of businesses that were not large enough to employ their own full-time accountants. He said the job involved working closely with the owners of the businesses, explaining the financial accounts and the business implications. This sounded interesting to me and relevant to the original reason I had joined the firm. Then, startlingly, Rex explained that he had heard I was one of "the people of the book" and so he had wanted to meet me and shake my hand! Before I could register my amazement, he went on to explain that his Christian faith was focused on the Old Testament, and he believed that Jews were the descendants of the ancient Hebrew people who gave God to the world. By the time he left, I felt like I was part of an aristocratic race and not a member of a persecuted religion. When I described that encounter to my family that night, they were equally astounded.

At work, I never encountered any antisemitic comments or behaviour. In fact, leave from work for the Jewish High Holidays was readily granted without any deductions from my salary. I remained the only Jewish person at the firm until 1956 when Geoffrey Cohen, a chartered accountant from a long-established Australian Jewish family, joined the partnership. Geoffrey went on to enjoy a distinguished career at the firm and we remained friends until his recent passing.[19]

As the year drew to a close, I sat exams in my two subjects and was pleased that I did very well in both, including receiving honours in accounting 1. Just before Christmas, I was presented with a bonus cheque of 50 pounds by one of the senior partners, Les Sharp, who expressed satisfaction with my first year at the firm. Finally, for the first time since my arrival in Australia, I started to feel at ease about my life and my future. However, Father was still struggling to establish himself financially, which was concerning.

My second year at the firm started well. After the mandated two-week holiday, I was assigned to assist some of the managers in more senior audit procedures. Some of the changes to my role were incremental, and most of the work still involved routine checking, but at least I was no longer working on my own the whole time.

I now had to undertake important audit steps known as 'calling back', 'vouching' and 'ticking off', all of which involved checking for discrepancies—which were possible indicators of fraud—between cheques, payment entries and invoices. The processes involved the use of pens and different coloured ticks to indicate that the audit steps had been carried out. As the junior on the job, it was my task to obtain the requisite cash payments book, vouchers, bank statements and sorted cancelled cheques. Then I would contact the relevant partner and we would take over an available office at the client's premises.

One client I enjoyed working with was David Syme & Co, publisher of the daily newspaper *The Age*, which was listed on the Melbourne Stock Exchange. We were always assigned the 'lead writers' room', used by the journalists who wrote the editorials. The room was crammed with the latest editions of leading political and business magazines. I had already developed an avid interest in current affairs, so spending days in that room leafing through the magazines was a bonus. Fortunately, the urbane manager of the assignment, John Claridge, also enjoyed reading the publications, so he would allocate extra time during the morning and

---

[19] After our Australian practice became fully integrated into the worldwide Arthur Andersen network, Geoffrey became a partner in 1961 and then managing partner. He retired from the firm in 1994. In 1967, after a visit from Geoffrey, his wife, Ola, and their son, Randall, we chose the name Randall for our second son.

afternoon tea breaks for us to peruse them. John took great interest in my background and opinions, and we developed a lasting friendship.[20]

Bill Charlton, the manager of the firm's tax department, was another partner who showed an interest in me. Whenever I passed his office, he would invariably ask me in for a chat. Later, when I transferred to the secretarial and accounting section, and I had to clear clients' tax returns through him, our association deepened.[21]

I was increasingly selected to work with managers in the two-person audit procedures, and I received positive feedback about my reliability and ability to focus throughout the long hours of repetitive work. There was considerable turnover of staff, and gradually I was earning the trust of my superiors to take over the responsibilities of those who were leaving. However, I was still not excused from the weekly task of hanging up the partners' coloured towels.

I was soon given sole responsibility in the payroll audit area. My role was to confirm that the workers listed on the payroll of some of our larger clients, were physically on the job. Prior to the introduction of computerised bank account systems, the weekly or fortnightly pay was distributed in cash in small distinctive envelopes, marked with the name of the employee and the amount payable, and physically given to the employee. If they were not around on payday, the pay packet was held in the cashier or accountant's office for personal collection on another day.

For the audit, the procedure was to turn up with virtually no notice, and to accompany the person distributing the pay, ensuring that each packet was given to the person named on the envelope. During the audit, if an employee was not on site, I would have to keep their pay packet until they could personally retrieve it from me after begrudgingly showing identification. This audit procedure gave me the opportunity to see the scope of the client's physical operations. One memorable windy day, an employee from *The Age's* maintenance department was painting a flagpole in Collins Street and I had to clamber up the pole to ask him to identify himself before handing over his pay. On that occasion, I learned some new Australian swear words!

---

[20] Years later, when John Claridge was a partner at Mann Judd & Co, I was pleased that he agreed to be the auditor of Ada's law practice's trust accounts. Since she conducted her law practice from our home in Doncaster, his audit visits were preceded by convivial dinners. [21] Ada and I remained friends with Bill and his wife for many years.

In those days, in Australia, we were not yet required to provide detailed audit working papers. Green ticks in the various books of accounts were the main evidentiary marks left by the auditors. Another way to establish that a procedural step had been completed was to initial one of the ruled vertical columns in an account book. Before final sign off on the client's accounts, a partner would have to ensure that all the initials were in place. I remember feeling very proud the first time I was asked to enter my initials next to a payroll step.

As my second year with the firm ended, I felt satisfied with my progress, evidenced by a rise in my salary and an increased bonus. My university exam results were very good and I was also enjoying my increased involvement with the MJYC, and a social, intellectual organisation called the Jewish Study Group.

One of the Jewish students I met was Morris Mrocki. Morris had a Polish background, and his father owned a well-known menswear shop called Six Little Tailors on the corner of Elizabeth and Little Bourke Streets. Morris was a passionate member of a Jewish organisation called The Bund, which championed Yiddish language and culture. Another feature that distinguished the group from other Jewish organisations in Melbourne was that it didn't support Zionism and the State of Israel. The group, founded as a socialist network in Poland, also had strong links to the Australian Labor Party and its working-class supporters. Despite my reservations about The Bund, Morris and I became good friends. Later, I was honoured to be a groomsman at his wedding to Hannah. I was also fortunate to befriend his cousin, Maurice Burstin, and his wife Tonia.

Early in my third year at the firm, Mr Waddell asked me into his office for a chat. He told me that everyone I had worked for was happy with my performance and he was pleased that I had taken up his suggestion to commence a commerce degree. He also asked for my feedback and, recalling my initial interview, asked if I had come across a type of business that was of particular interest. I responded that I was very happy at the firm and that I had not developed an interest in any one type of business but hoped to pursue a career in professional accounting. He seemed pleased and offered me a permanent position at the firm. He also encouraged me to consider rotating between different sections of the firm, so I took the opportunity to request a transfer to Mr Prime's secretarial and accounting section.

Working directly for Mr Prime was a real delight; it would have been difficult to find a more considerate man. He, like the other partners, often singled me out for chats during the morning and afternoon tea breaks and, over the next few years, we would often walk together to Flinders Street Station to take our respective trains home. Occasionally, I would invite him over for Friday night dinner, which he appreciated as he was a bachelor who lived with, and cared for, his elderly mother.

I had been right to follow my intuition and transfer to Mr Prime's section. Working with smaller companies with more limited accounting resources, even as a junior, provided me with a comprehensive picture of each company's finances. My role was to prepare profit and loss statements, balance sheets and tax returns. Fortunately, by then I had completed several accounting subjects at university. I also had to communicate the relevant accounting information to the business owners who were often financially unsophisticated. I found the work satisfying, and my knowledge grew considerably.

Particularly gratifying were the opportunities to set up the records for newly established businesses and to become involved with the accounting and financial issues that evolved as these businesses grew to become more successful and increasingly complex. This was the case with J.H.Minet & Co, a subsidiary of a large and successful London-based insurance broker that was entering the Australian market. Mr Prime thought it would be a great experience for me to look after this account and I was pleased to be selected, particularly as I got on well with the senior team from London, including the manager, Roland de Valence. When the company decided to expand into the Sydney market, I was asked to set up the relevant accounting records. I still recall my great excitement when I flew to Sydney and was put up in the New

South Wales Automobile Club. One highlight was to reunite with my friend Sasha over dinner.

After some time, Mr de Valence and his team returned to London[22] and Joel Crow was selected to be the Australian manager. I worked closely with Joel, and we became good friends. As the Australian Minet business expanded and took on in-house accountants, it started to outgrow our section's services. Having worked on the file since the business launched in Sydney, I was proud to supervise the transfer of the account to the firm's larger audit division.

Most of my time was now spent in the office and I became increasingly familiar with the firm's various operations and more senior staff. One interesting development I noticed was its growing management consulting practice. A business under financial pressure will often be liquidated so as not to compound its debt. Common practice was to appoint a partner at an accounting firm to act as a receiver or liquidator. The senior partner usually appointed was Ken Little, who had good contacts with the banks and the business community. Entertaining clients seemed to be a big part of his role and I was often sent down the street to buy bags of ice for their drinks. Fortunately, I outgrew this role faster than the job of changing the washroom towels. One of the younger partners, Alan Dick (who happened to be a champion cricketer), persuaded Ken to have businesses evaluated for viability before liquidating them as a matter of course. So, Alan began to recruit professionals with expertise in this area, mostly men with business degrees who considered themselves to be elite and behaved accordingly. Little did I appreciate that one day I too would have a career in this emerging field of professional accounting.

The entry of Minet into the Australian commercial scene was part of a larger influx of foreign businesses, mostly American, that wanted to take advantage of Australia's expanding economy under the Menzies government. All these businesses required accounting and taxation guidance and, increasingly, I could hear American accents around the office. The American businesses were referred to Fuller King through a formal arrangement called 'corresponding relationships' set up by their

---

[22] When I travelled to London in 1960, the senior management team at Minet's head office took me out to dinner and the theatre.

affiliated US accounting firm, Arthur Andersen & Co. The English accounting firm Turquant Youngs was also part of the arrangement. The names of these firms appeared on our firm's letterhead, along with the names of our partners.

One day, I noticed an appealing publication called *The Arthur Andersen Chronicle*, left behind by an Arthur Andersen representative, which contained articles written by personnel within the firm. After reading the magazine, I experienced a 'light bulb' moment! Why not produce a similar publication for Fuller King, which was expanding throughout Australia? Looking back, I am still amazed that, as a low-to-middle ranking employee, I had the confidence to take the concept directly to Mr Waddell.

The Arthur Andersen publication prominently displayed the names of the editorial committee, and so, in my presentation, I suggested to Mr Waddell that he might like to be the chairman of the editorial committee of *The Fuller King Review*, which was the name I had devised. I indicated that I was prepared to do all the work necessary to establish and run the publication in my own time. Mr Waddell responded positively and, after consulting with the other partners, he gave me the go-ahead. Fortunately, Rex Prime was also in favour and so he allowed me to work on *The Review* during work hours as long as my client responsibilities did not suffer.

The project was an instant success as it filled a gap in the cohesiveness of the increasingly diversified operations of the firm, which now also included several interstate offices. Particularly popular was the 'News and Notes' section, which detailed the changes to personnel and other developments. There was no shortage of people willing to contribute technical or general interest articles, as staff quickly realised it was a great way to secure recognition. It was also obvious that Mr Waddell was pleased with his position as chairman of this new initiative.

For me, the firm magazine was a real boon. To secure contributions and to write the 'News and Notes' section, I was dealing with people right across the firm. Suddenly, everyone knew who I was, including

Alan Dick, who was busily establishing the nascent management consulting division. That connection was critical to my career because, in 1958, when our firm was set to be absorbed by Arthur Andersen, Alan selected me to be one of several Australian personnel to work in its Chicago head office.

This opportunity could not have come at a more opportune time. By then, everything seemed to be going right for me. I had almost completed my part-time course in five years, and I was looking forward to graduating and sitting for the additional exams that would enable me to be admitted as a chartered accountant. The family was delighted with my progress, and they encouraged me to pursue my future as I saw fit.

It had become clear that the original idea of going into business with Father would not eventuate. Father had purchased a small finance company to run until he came across something more substantial. At that stage he still had enough capital to feel some optimism about his prospects, but these issues were never openly discussed. Grandmother voiced her concerns only to me. She seemed resigned to the fact that he would never establish himself successfully. Looking back, I do feel a twinge of regret that I didn't take the initiative and ask whether he needed my help. Most probably, pride prevented him from discussing his problems and fears openly.

Uncannily, a few days after Alan Dick invited me to go and work in the Chicago office, Ian Permezel suggested we that we travel overseas together and get some international work experience.

In December 1958, the university published my results, and I was thrilled to have successfully completed my Bachelor of Commerce degree. Not only were my family and Grisha Sklovsky overjoyed, but I also had the pleasure of conveying the news to Mr Waddell and thanking him for suggesting that I enrol in the course. Normally the degree took six years to complete part-time. However, because I had received several honours in the first few years, I had been permitted to 'overload' by taking on an extra subject and reducing the overall study period by a year. This involved attending lectures and tutorials four nights a week.

From Monday to Thursday, I would rush to university from work, and often not get home on the tram until after 10pm, by which time I was too tired to do any further study. This schedule was particularly difficult on cold winter nights, and the demanding regime left only the weekends for study. Luckily, Ian, who was in a similar situation, had friends who regularly allowed us to stay at their holiday homes on the Mornington Peninsula. On Friday nights, Ian would pick me up from home in his Morris Minor (which he named 'Bernadine') and we would drive to the accommodation and spend the weekend studying intensively. On Sunday afternoons, Ian insisted we clean the house fastidiously so that we would be allowed to stay again. I often felt that we left the place in a better state than we found it.

Our approach to disciplined study worked. I graduated at a dignified ceremony held at the imposing Wilson Hall on the university campus. It was indeed a very proud moment, during which I reflected on how much I had achieved since arriving in Australia.

The next step was to be admitted as an associate of the Institute of Chartered Accountants of Australia, a condition for advancement in the profession. Traditionally, candidates attended privately run courses and sat for exams in subjects set by the institute. However, it had recently started to recognise the commerce degree as a prerequisite for admission, subject to a major in accounting, plus completion of several subjects such as taxation and professional ethics. I decided to defer tackling these additional subjects until after my stint at Arthur Andersen in America.

Life was extremely busy. At the start of 1959, I had been elected president of MJYC and I held that position until my departure from Melbourne at the end of the year. I had also joined B'nai B'rith Youth (BBY), an up-and-coming affiliate of the worldwide Jewish organisation. By then, I was also the honorary treasurer of the Jaycees.[23]

With an eye to the future, and with my bank account growing from an increasing salary and profits from several stock exchange transactions, I also made a foray into the Melbourne property market, which was a popular topic of discussion among my peers. After doing some research,

[23] Later, in 1961, I became chair of the prestigious Jaycee management training course.

I purchased a 'controlled tenancy' terrace house in Gourlay Street, St Kilda. Controlled properties were relatively cheap as the tenant's rent was fixed at an artificially low level throughout their tenancy. When the tenant left—either passing away or taking a sum of money to relinquish this right—the property would rise in value to reflect the current residential rental rates. The tenant in my newly acquired property was an elderly war widow and I was content to allow her to remain there for the rest of her life.

When Ian suggested the overseas trip, as it coincided with Alan Dick's offer of work experience in Chicago, I grabbed the opportunity. The journey became even more enticing when our Jaycee friend, Keith Lewis, who was working for the shipping company Orient Lines, organised our return tickets (colloquially known as 'boomerang' tickets) at a dramatically reduced price. The tickets were so cheap that we could afford a first-class cabin on a liner called the *Orcades* sailing in late December from Princes Pier in Port Melbourne to London.

In September 1959, a particular incident underscored how favourable my reputation had become within the Melbourne Jewish community. I was invited to a party hosted by Nathan Jacobson, president of the Victorian Jewish Board of Deputies—the community's roof body—and his first wife Martha, also a highly regarded member of the community, in their gracious home and garden. The occasion marked the beginning of the Jewish New Year and it was always followed by the annual general meeting. The function was a highlight of the community calendar, and I was pleased to be invited because of my roles at the youth council and BBY. At the event, I was taken aside by several senior members of the community to discuss a proposition. I was stunned to hear that they wanted me to apply to become a member of the Melbourne Stock Exchange, a prestigious and powerful body.[24] Apparently, sections of the community were unhappy that, despite several attempts, no Jewish applicant had successfully been elected. It was feared that antisemitism was at play within the major commercial institution. The excuses given for previous knockbacks were questionable dealings of the Jewish

---

[24] This was before the formation of the Australian Stock Exchange.

candidates. However, community leaders believed the real reason was concern that Jewish clients would shift their custom to a Jewish stockbroker if one was elected to the exchange. The group facing me felt certain my background was beyond reproach and they urged me to stand for membership to break this suspected ban on Jews. I felt flattered and momentarily interested because of my share trading activities. However, I advised them that, regretfully, I could not accept their proposal as I was committed to travelling to the US. I later learned that a Jewish man named Herbert Baer succeeded in attaining membership and went on to enjoy a successful tenure on the stock exchange.

In my final weeks in Melbourne, I had another interesting conversation that would have a beneficial outcome some years later. I had a call from a solicitor, Maurice Cohen, who was the head of the Hillel Commission, an initiative of B'nai B'rith, America, which established meeting places called Hillel House at university campuses. Usually headed by rabbis, the houses provided a Jewish social and educational experience for Jewish students. Maurice was working towards a Hillel House at the University of Melbourne and he asked me to visit the Hillel House at the University of London to form an opinion of its director, Rabbi Henry Shaw, who, rumour had it, was considering moving to Australia. I readily agreed to his request.

By then, I was 26 years of age. Looking back, I am amazed at how much I managed to cram into my first nine years in Australia. Hard work, intensive study, astute investments, extensive involvement in Jewish and non-Jewish communal activities, and the formation of lasting friendships, certainly created a strong foundation for my future.

My graduation, 1959

With Morris Mrocki, the groom, & Maurice Burstin, the other groomsman

Holidaying (with Sasha) on a Halvorsen boat on the Hawksbury River

Our Continental Tour

Our four-week journey to London on *SS Orcades*[25] was scheduled for late December 1959, and there was great excitement at home as the departure date drew close. The family was supportive of my planned holiday in Europe with Ian, which they felt I had earned through my personal and professional achievements over the previous few years. They were also excited about my future opportunities at Arthur Andersen in Chicago.

Despite their support, I started to feel anxious about leaving Grandmother, just as I had worried 10 years earlier when saying goodbye to her in Shanghai. Now she was a decade older and leading a more isolated existence. I had become her central focus and I would spend many hours talking to her about my daily life. I was concerned about how lonely she would be without me and, of course, whether she would still be alive when I returned. Undoubtedly, she was also worried about life without me but, not wanting to diminish my excitement, she never conveyed her concerns.

And so, on a sunny afternoon on 27 December 1959, the family piled into our Humber Hawk and drove to Princes Pier, where the *SS Orcades* was docked. Back then, there was minimal security and my family, as well as a few friends who had turned up to say goodbye, all boarded the ocean liner to see our cabin and to roam through the public facilities.

A blast of the *Orcades'* horn was followed by an announcement requesting that visitors leave the ship. After emotional goodbyes, our family and friends disembarked. As the ship pulled away from the pier, I threw the streamers my parents had given me. Ian and I spent

---

[25] The *SS Orcades* was an ocean liner serving primarily the UK-Australia-New Zealand route. The owner was The Orient Steam Navigation Company (Orient Line), which, in 1966, became the Peninsular and Oriental Steam Navigation Company (P&0), based in London. The ship was launched in October 1947, and mainly operated as a liner, carrying first and tourist class passengers until it was broken up for scrap metal in 1973. In her initial years she was also used for transporting migrants from the UK to Australia. She displaced 28,000 tons and was some 700 feet in length.

a few minutes gazing back at Melbourne's modest skyline, before wandering down to our cabin to unpack. Our cabin was small, but it had a porthole, bunk beds, a compact bathroom and washing facilities.

Ian surprised me by calling over the cabin steward assigned to look after us. He produced a 10 pound note, quite a sum in those days, tore it in half and gave one half to the steward. He said that if, at the end of the trip, we were satisfied with his service, he would give him the other half. Seeing the look of surprise on my face, Ian told me that he had been advised to do this by friends who were seasoned travellers.

For dinner on our first night on board we were permitted to wear casual clothes but for the rest of the trip we were expected to dress up. On some nights tuxedos were mandatory, at least in first class. After dinner, we toured the public rooms, which had the atmosphere of a British club.

Our first port of call was Fremantle in Western Australia, which involved traversing the Great Australian Bight, notorious for its stormy seas. I did not expect to succumb to seasickness but on the third night I had to skip dinner and was confined to our cabin, retching into a bucket, which our steward helpfully provided.

Ian felt fine and decided to shave and change for dinner. When he returned a few hours later, he was in an excited state. As I lay on the bunk, he shook me hard to ensure that I could hear him repeatedly saying, "I have met her! I have met her!" I was too seasick to ask him what he meant.

The next morning, over breakfast, Ian told me about his evening. Most of the other passengers, like me, were seasick so the dining room had been virtually empty. He was seated next to a young lady, and they had struck up a conversation. She came from a farming family in New South Wales, had finished school and was travelling with several girlfriends before touring 'the Continent', as Europe was often called. By the time dinner was over, Ian was totally smitten and convinced she was the love of his life. He had learnt that her name was Judith (Jane) Carroll, however he had not been able to determine whether she was Catholic or Protestant, like him. Ian's efforts to ascertain Jane's denomination and then wooing her all the way to marriage, became a defining aspect of our trip.

We arrived in Fremantle a few days later, on a beautiful sunny day, and we went on a walking tour of the small port. After leaving Fremantle, the atmosphere on board became increasingly festive and relaxed as we entered the calm and beautiful blue waters of the Indian Ocean, heading towards Colombo, the capital of Ceylon.[26]

The lighter mood of the passengers was, no doubt, the result of the ship being declared duty free for a variety of goods, including tobacco, alcohol and perfume. The price drop on items in these categories was substantial. My preferred cigarettes, an English brand called Senior Service, normally cost four shillings a packet. Once duty free, the price dropped to just one shilling! Smoking was permitted everywhere on board except for outside on the main decks for fear of fire.

In this relaxed atmosphere, we became friendly with other passengers including Geoff Smith, his wife Sue and their three children. Ian had met Geoff in Melbourne and told me he was a rising young executive at National Australia Bank who was being transferred to the UK to take charge of one of its London branches. We got on well with the family and would share a table with them at dinner. There was only one large first class restaurant on the ship, as well as a salon where alcohol or tea was served, depending on the time of day.

Ian continued to torture himself about whether Jane was Protestant or Catholic and devised ways to find out, short of asking her outright. Jane seemed oblivious to this critical issue. She seemed totally comfortable with her friends and was enjoying the social life on board.

As we docked in the port of Colombo, the distinctive smells of Asia immediately reminded me of Hong Kong. We were taken on a tour of the peaceful city and spotted a performance featuring elephants performing tricks. For lunch we were taken to an upmarket hotel where we were served a spicy curry. However, the weather was stiflingly hot, and we were pleased to be ushered back to the port. That evening, we pulled up anchor and headed back into the Indian Ocean, bound for Aden.

---

[26] Now Sri Lanka.

Our Continental Tour

Aden was also part of the British Empire and was then the main port of the Arab state of Yemen. In early 1960 it had yet to be embroiled in the internecine Arab wars of later years. It was a duty-free port and resembled a vast Arab market where virtually anything could be bought and sold. The Australian dollar, then at a fixed discount to the British pound, was a strong currency and generally accepted by the traders. Everything seemed very cheap compared with similar goods in Australia. I bought a powerful set of binoculars and some trinkets. I was careful not to eat any street food, unlike other passengers who suffered in the following days. I also bought some postcards, which I briefly inscribed and sent home to family and friends. Once back on board, we all had a great time comparing our respective purchases.

A few days later, we reached the town of Suez, the southern point of entry to the Suez Canal, the famed artificial sea-level waterway in Egypt that connects the Mediterranean Sea to the Red Sea.[27] The 193-kilometre waterway had been nationalised in July 1956 when Gamal Abdel Nasser, the charismatic president of Egypt, had wrested the canal from its joint owners, the United Kingdom and France. The event had led to the Suez Crisis of October and November 1956. As I had been a youth leader in the Jewish community at the time, I recalled the conflict well. It had involved an ill-fated alliance between Britain, France and Israel culminating in the 1956 war between Israel and Egypt.

The *Orcades* offered passengers a day tour in Egypt, including a visit to the pyramids. I was reluctant to view the aftermath of the war, so I decided to forgo the pyramids and stayed on board. I was surprised by the number of passengers who also opted to stay behind and was taken aback by the disdainful anti-Egyptian sentiment being expressed, particularly by Australians who had served in the Commonwealth forces stationed in Egypt during World War II.

As we glided north, closer to the Sinai desert, we could plainly see wrecked tanks and military vehicles, vestiges of the war. Otherwise, it was a hot and leisurely passage through the Suez Canal. In the evening, the day trippers rejoined the ship at the northern exit at Port

---

[27] The Suez Canal was the inspiration of Frenchman Ferdinand de Lesseps. Construction by the Suez Canal Company commenced in 1859 and it was officially opened in November 1869.

Said, and by nightfall we headed out in the Mediterranean, bound for Naples.

Contrary to our expectations of the Mediterranean, we encountered a storm, and the seas were choppy almost all the way to Naples. Nevertheless, the morning we sailed into the Bay of Naples was truly magnificent, with clear blue skies and the breathtaking backdrop of Mount Vesuvius. There were no organised tours of Naples on offer, but we were free to wander the city. Naples already had a reputation as a dangerous, Mafia-ridden town and we were warned about pickpockets. We were also urged to change our money into Italian currency, lira[28], only on board the ship or at official moneychangers. The official exchange rate was nearly 2000 liras to the pound. On disembarking, we were assailed by hawkers offering a much better black market rate, a temptation we managed to resist. Some passengers succumbed and, when they unravelled the large bundle of lira notes, the core contained cuttings from old newspapers.

Ian and I accepted the friendly offer of a brief tour from a passenger who claimed some knowledge of Naples. It was indeed an interesting experience. Much of the city was very poor, with run-down buildings and washing hanging on poles sticking out of windows. Hawkers were everywhere, trying to press upon us all manner of merchandise. Wandering the streets reminded us of scenes from Vittoria de Sica's excellent film, *Bicycle Thieves*, which we had seen in the basement theatre at the Australia Hotel in Collins Street, which showed 'Continental' films.

Our next destination was Marseilles in southern France. We were looking forward to exploring the city and taking one of the tours of the nearby Riviera. However, when we sailed in early on a Saturday morning, we found a city covered in snow and ice. An unseasonal cold snap had paralysed the city as the authorities had been totally unprepared for the arctic weather. As we docked in the old port district, there was total chaos with traffic at a complete standstill. The planned tours were cancelled, and passengers were strongly discouraged from venturing into the city. Spending the day in the warmth of the ship's public rooms was the only

---

[27] In 2002 the lira was replaced by the euro.

option and most people were resigned to it. In fact, some were looking forward to draining the contents of the ship's various bars. Ian, too, was happy to spend the time with Jane and her girlfriends.

I didn't want to stay on board and, as it was still early on a Saturday morning, I decided to try to find a synagogue. After checking a map, I rugged up, took my *kippah* and *talit*, and proceeded to walk to a building that was more like a *shtible*, a basic religious meeting place of the poor Eastern European Jews in the prewar era. There, I found nine elderly Jewish men huddled together and waiting for a tenth Jewish male to form a *minyan*, the minimum number required to pray collectively and read the Torah. Some of the other elderly congregants had been unable to make the trip to the synagogue because of the freezing conditions. When I turned up out of the blue and explained that I was from the cruise ship travelling from Australia, it was as if a miracle had occurred. They welcomed me warmly, and my knowledge of Hebrew prayers and the Sabbath service made it a particularly wonderful occasion. After the service concluded, the *kiddush* prayer was recited over the kosher wine and the challah bread. Then, in honour of the special occasion, they brought out salted herring, black rye bread and vodka. The congregants were originally from Eastern Europe, mainly Russia, and we managed to communicate in Russian and French. They enjoyed hearing about my family's history in Odessa, Vladivostok, and Shanghai. We drank, ate, and talked for hours, and it wasn't till mid-afternoon that I staggered back to the ship. I went straight to bed and was out like a light. The experience was undoubtedly a highlight of the trip.

After a brief stop in Gibraltar, the *Orcades* headed out into the Bay of Biscay and turned north for London. Being winter, the sea was quite choppy and much of the social interaction on board took place indoors. During one afternoon tea, Ian finally 'cracked the code' as to whether Jane was Protestant or Catholic. The conversation revolved around a social gathering organised by Jane's church in Molong in New South Wales. As he later recounted to me, "quick as a flash", Ian jumped in and asked for the name of the church. The name was obviously Church of

England, so he finally knew that she was Protestant. For the remaining few days of the journey, Ian devoted himself wholeheartedly to the pursuit of Jane Carroll.

As we approached London, passengers started to talk about their plans. To take advantage of the extraordinarily low duty-free prices, I decided to invest in big cartons (containing 10 packets each) of Senior Service cigarettes to tide me over the following months. Ian did the same with his preferred brand. However, we were told by the ship's purser that there was a limit to how many cartons we could bring into the country. So we hit upon the idea of asking some of the girls who did not smoke, to bring in the excess cartons for us.

———◆———

On a cold and gloomy morning in late January 1960, the *Orcades* sailed up the Thames and moored at Tilbury Docks, London's only deep-sea cruise terminal. We disembarked and were cleared by customs in a speedy, almost perfunctory way. Our passports were still marked as 'British', with 'Australia' printed in brackets underneath. In fact, many Australians travelling to England back then would say they were "going home".

A typical London black taxi took us to our bed & breakfast, a quaint three-storey terrace house in Tottenham Court Road. It had no lift and a creaking staircase, but it was cheap and clean, and certainly suited us. We each had a bedsitter with a small gas fireplace activated by inserting a two-shilling coin, which gave about half an hour of heat. In the mornings, we were woken by the smell of frying kippers, which we were served for breakfast.

During our first few days in London, Ian and I travelled all over the city to collect the cigarette cartons our friends from the boat had brought into the country on our behalf. One such expedition was quite embarrassing, as the girl in question had given them to her father, a senior official at the Australian High Commission. He handed them over with a disapproving look.

Our Continental Tour

Our main objective in London was to purchase a small car, like a Morris Minor, to tour Europe and the UK. The idea was to buy the car in the depth of winter when prices were low, and to resell it in spring, the tourist season, when the price might be higher. However, Ian now wanted to purchase a four-seater car so we could possibly transport Jane and her friend Elizabeth for part of the journey. We finally settled on a 1958 Ford Anglia in very good condition, with 7000 miles 'on the clock', for 450 pounds. The car served us well and, over the following five months, we drove almost 12,000 miles. Fortunately for our dwindling finances, we were able to resell the car to the same car yard we had purchased it from for almost the same price.

London was exciting. Despite his French origins, as a Scotch College boy, Ian considered himself to have British heritage, so London felt like an extension of home to him. London also strongly resonated for me as a result of my British education in Shanghai, and the influence of Britain on Shanghai's cultural life. We marvelled at Hyde Park, Marble Arch, Buckingham Palace and Piccadilly Circus, and we found Soho especially interesting with its bizarre shops and restaurants serving cuisines from all over the world. I particularly enjoyed the not-very-British pickled cucumber and herring rye bread sandwiches I bought from one of the local delis. There were also quite a few elaborately decorated Chinese restaurants that served a greater variety of regional dishes than we were used to in Melbourne. One night we invited Jane and a few friends to dinner at a Chinese restaurant to celebrate our time in London. We were in a jovial mood, and, because of my background, they asked me to do the ordering, which I did, showing off my Chinese knowledge. I regaled them with stories of Shanghai and, when the Chinese waiter started to serve the food, I could not resist saying a few words to him in the Shanghainese dialect. When he said he could not understand what I was saying, I asked where he was from, expecting him to say that he was from another province. Instead, in a clipped English accent, he told us that he was from Liverpool. That put me in my place.

One of the highlights of our time in London was an invitation to attend a lunch at the National Bank from Geoff Smith, our friend from the *Orcades*. We dressed up in our suits and hats and made the trip to 'the city'. We were served drinks before entering the boardroom, where we were attended by uniformed waiters in the club-like surroundings and enjoyed a lively discussion on worldly topics and economic matters over our meal.

In accordance with Alan Dick's suggestion, I paid a visit to the London office of Arthur Andersen to find out more about my forthcoming program at the Chicago office. I was received by the managing partner, who was extremely welcoming. He gave me a tour of the office in a high-rise building in the centre of London and drew my attention to the solid oak double doors (which I had seen on the cover of the firm's magazine), telling me that it was firm policy to have the identical doors in every office worldwide. He informed me I should plan to arrive at the firm's head office at 120 South Lasalle Street in Chicago by 1 July and report to Carl Boehne, the partner in charge of training. After the meeting, I went directly to the nearest travel agent to book my boat to New York and the train to Chicago. I was heady with excitement.

Encouraged by Joel Crowe, the Australian managing director, I contacted his associates at Minet's London office. They invited me to dine with them at top-end restaurants and I was lucky enough to be taken to a theatre show in the West End.

Amongst all the touring and festivities, I made a point of fulfilling the promise I had made to Maurice Cohen to meet with Henry Shaw, the director of Hillel House. So, one Friday evening, I made my way there to join a warm gathering of students welcoming the Sabbath. I sought out Henry and his wife Sybil, who were mingling with the students. They invited me to participate in programs at Hillel House over the next few weeks, which I gladly accepted. I formed a very favourable opinion of the work the Shaws were doing and wrote as much to Maurice. By the time I returned home 18 months later, Henry and Sybil Shaw were living in Melbourne and had successfully started the Melbourne Hillel program.

Above: The *Orcades* moored in Gibraltar
Below: Elijah (holding a camera), Grandmother, Father, Eva & Nathan

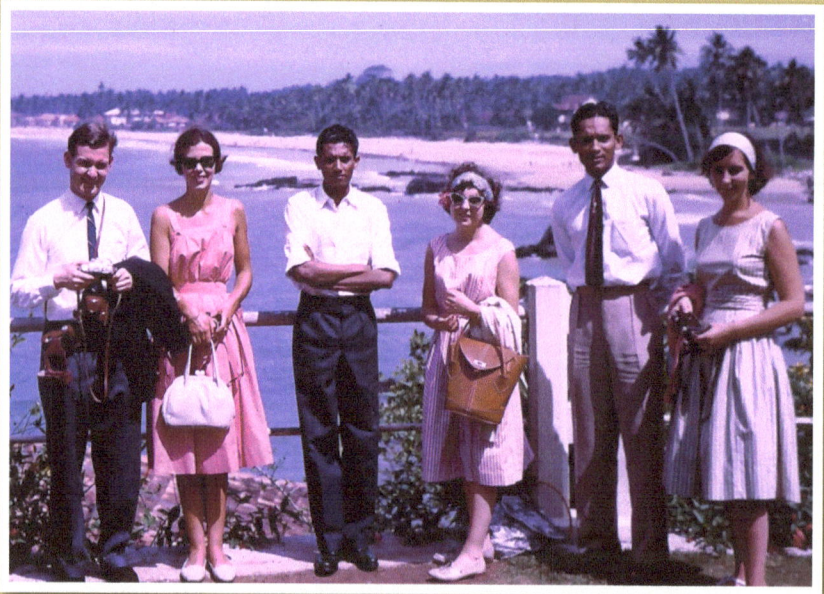

Above: In Colombo. My first rickshaw ride since Shanghai
Below: On a guided tour in Ceylon. Ian & Jane are on the left

Our Continental Tour

At the end of January, Ian and I set off on our Continental tour with a plan to meet Jane and Elizabeth in southern Spain. We drove to Dover and, rather than taking the overnight ferry, we decided to cross the English Channel by air with Silver City Airways, on its recently established freight and passenger service. It cost three pounds for the car and four pounds 10 shillings each. We arrived in Dunkirk in the late afternoon and drove to a small, picturesque town called Beauvais, where we enjoyed our first of many delicious meals featuring soupe à l'oignon.

We arrived in Paris the following morning and found a reasonably priced hotel in Rue Bonaparte on the Left Bank. Our first commitment was to meet Ian's Paris-based cousins, so we made our way to their spacious apartment. The family were welcoming but didn't speak English and Ian didn't speak any French. So, with my conversationally passable French language skills, I was left to tell them about life in Melbourne and pass on news from Ian's family in Australia.

We toured the city on tourist buses to avoid the freezing temperatures. Despite the dreariness of the weather, the grandeur of the buildings and the boulevards lived up to our expectations, as did the city's many wonderful galleries. Ian was keen to move on, to ensure he could spend as much time as possible with Jane in Spain, but I insisted on spending an extra day touring the palace of Versailles and its magnificent gardens.

We eventually packed the car and headed south to Lyon to meet more members of the Permezel family. Upon arriving, we attended a Sunday lunch with a large gathering of curious relatives. Once again, I acted as a translator. This time I had to exercise considerable tact as one of the relations was a Catholic priest who became quite aggressive while questioning Ian's faith. Knowing Ian's attitude to Catholicism, I had to summon all the resources of my limited vocabulary to delicately deflect the tone of some of the priest's questions and Ian's replies. Apart from that fraught discussion, we enjoyed a long lunch with delicious food and much wine and cheese.

The next morning, we started our long journey to southern Spain. As we traversed the narrow winding roads of the Pyrenees, the great mountain range separating France and Spain, we had to remain particularly alert because our lefthand-drive English car was not designed for driving on the right side of the road.

We arrived in Madrid at dusk and headed to a bar that featured Flamenco dancing. Spain was still under the rule of Franco, the fascist general who initiated the Spanish Civil War in 1936 and, with the help of Hitler and Mussolini, defeated the democratically elected republican government. It was sickening to see the city, though filled with opulent cathedrals, so neglected and poverty-stricken. We decided to proceed directly to Toledo.

For 400 years, until they were expelled in 1492, Toledo was a centre of Jewish life and learning in Moorish Spain. I particularly wanted to visit an ancient, and largely intact, synagogue, which had been converted into a church. The vestiges of the synagogue were plain to see, particularly in the overlooking balcony, which allowed for the segregation of men and women, typical of Orthodox services. In a square nearby, we also saw the house of the Greek artist and architect of the Spanish Resistance, known as El Greco. I would have liked to spend several days wandering the historic city, but Ian was restless and determined to see Jane as soon as possible.

Finally, after a few days of frantic driving through Spain, we arrived at Torremolinos, where we had arranged to meet Jane. It was a quaint seaside resort not yet ruined by hordes of British tourists. We settled on a small hotel and, feeling exhausted, I decided to get some sleep. Ian dumped his bags and announced that he was going to look for Jane. He had no meeting place arranged and no knowledge of where she was staying so his only option was to scour the streets. Later that night, he excitedly woke me to say that he had somehow discovered the name of Jane's hotel and found her there.

Jane and her friend, Elizabeth, were staying at an up-market establishment with nicely appointed lounges and a bar overlooking the sea. Coincidentally, a friend of Jane's father, Mr Robson, was also staying there and, over the next few days, he generously paid for us all to enjoy drinks and dinners with him. He knew the area well and led us on excursions to local sites including the Caves of Nerja and the town of Guadix, where cave dwellers, called troglodytes, had lived in underground houses for hundreds of years. We also visited Roman ruins near Cadiz and graceful palaces dating back to the long presence of the Moors in Spain, who, like the Jews, were expelled by ascendant Christians in 1492.

After a week of touring and enjoying the warm sunny weather, Ian and I decided to keep moving. Elizabeth was returning to London, but we agreed to meet up with Jane in Genoa in a few days' time.

Ian and I drove to the Riviera, stopping in Nice, where we witnessed the famed floral parade called La Bataille de Fleurs. We arrived in Genoa on a gloomy morning and as soon as we had checked into a small hotel near the railway station, Ian went to the American Express[27] office where Jane had planned to leave him a message detailing where in Genoa she was staying. Half an hour later, a downcast Ian returned to our hotel, empty-handed. There was no message from Jane.

When, the following day, there was still no message, Ian was mystified. For the next few days, twice a day, he would go to the American Express office only to return disappointed. We struggled to while away our time in Genoa, a grim industrial port city with few tourist attractions. And, of course, there was the underlying fear that Jane had changed her mind and had decided to end the budding relationship. We had to set a time limit and on our last day we sadly packed our things. I sat in the car while Ian made his final visit to the American Express office. After what seemed a long time, I heard a tapping sound on the car window and looked up to see the beaming faces of Ian and Jane. As it turned out, the clerk had misfiled Jane's letter under 'C' for Carroll instead of 'P' for Permezel. Jane had also been about to abort the rendezvous and return to London. She had spent the past few days staying at a hotel and aimlessly wandering the streets. It was a wonder that we hadn't run into her.

From Genoa, the three of us drove to Rome and, because of the time lost in Genoa, we did as much sightseeing there as we could squeeze in. The city was bedecked with banners to mark its hosting of the summer

---

[28] American Express was, in those days, one of the largest travel organisations, with offices in cities around the world. Its travellers cheques were widely used by travellers in the era before the ubiquitous money dispensing machines and various credit and debit cards. The offices also provided a convenient message depository service for travellers in the days before mobile phones and the internet.

Olympic Games, due to open in August. Having helped with the Melbourne Olympics as part of his Jaycee involvement, Ian was keen to tour the impressive new stadiums.

Ian and Jane planned to return to London together, but Jane hadn't realised that I would not be chaperoning them. She was concerned that her parents would be upset about the arrangement, so she insisted on ringing them in Molong, New South Wales, to seek their permission. This was not easy as our hotels did not handle international calls to Australia, so Jane went to the post office to book a call in advance. After several attempts, she managed to get through and, to Ian's immense relief, Jane's parents reluctantly agreed.

I still had a few days in Rome before going to Naples to catch the ship to Haifa, Israel, where I planned to spend a few weeks before travelling to America. As the following day was a Saturday, I decided to go to the main synagogue. The Jews of Rome were one of the oldest communities in Europe, and, over the centuries, they had endured much persecution. Many congregants turned up that morning to attend a commemorative service to mark the Ardeatine massacre, a Nazi operation which claimed the lives of 335 civilians and political prisoners at the Ardeatine caves in 1944. At the *kiddush* afterwards, I met some worshippers who were also members of the local B'nai B'rith lodge. When they learned of my association with the organisation in Melbourne, they invited me to join them at the official remembrance function to be held at the caves where the massacre had occurred. After the moving service, a few of the members took me on a tour of the Jewish sights of Rome, including the Arch of Titus, with its depiction of the treasures from the Temple in Jerusalem following the Roman victory in the Judean War of AD70. Being particularly interested in Roman history from my school days in Shanghai, I thoroughly enjoyed spending my last day walking through the ruins of the old Roman Forum.

After a pleasant two days, spent wandering around the historic parts of Rome, I caught the train to Naples and boarded the *Theodore Herzl*, a passenger ship belonging to the Israeli-owned Zim Shipping Line.[30] The company was founded in 1945 with the help of the Jewish Agency to transport Holocaust survivors from the European refugee camps to Mandated Palestine.[31]

The atmosphere on the ship could not have been more different to that on the *Orcades*. It was a one-class ship and its Israeli rules (or lack thereof) contrasted sharply to the formality of the British liner. The passengers were drawn from a wider background and the food was more cosmopolitan. I marvelled at the adroitness of the drink stewards in their handling of the multiplicity of currencies. You could pay for drinks in one currency and get change in several different currencies, all mentally computed by the steward while mixing cocktails.

On board, I made several Israeli friends who generously invited me to stay with them while in Israel. One new friend was an impressive young man, Dov Shomroni, who had boarded the ship in Marseilles. The Israeli government had sent him to France to study port construction engineering. He was returning home, tasked with developing Eilat, the small port on the Red Sea, which was awarded to Israel as part of the 1949 Armistice Agreements following the War of Independence.

We entered the Bay of Haifa on a clear and warm morning, and we all went out on the deck to witness the entry. It was a majestic sight, with Mount Carmel towering over the city and the deep blue waters of the bay. Although 12 years had passed since the Jewish state had been established, I still felt great excitement at being processed by Jewish port officials and treasured the first Hebrew-lettered arrival stamp in my passport. My Zionist leanings, nurtured by membership of the Betar youth movement in Shanghai, had taken a back seat during my demanding first years in Australia. Here in Israel, pride in the Jewish dream was rekindled.

---

[30] It is now called Zim Integrated Shipping Services Ltd, and is still an Israeli-owned company, with headquarters in Haifa. It is one of the top 10 global carriers.

[31] Later it was involved in running the gauntlet of the Royal Navy when the British government imposed severe restrictions on immigration to a Palestine already heavily embroiled in a war against British rule. Following the creation of the State of Israel, it continued to legally bring thousands of Jewish immigrants to their new country. With funding from German reparations, the shipping company upgraded its fleet and branched out into a more conventional passenger liner. In the late 1950s and early '60s, it had several ships plying the Marseilles/Naples/Haifa route, before air travel became cheaper and mostly replaced sea travel.

Not knowing anyone in Haifa[32], I proceeded south directly to Natanya, a seaside town on the way to Tel Aviv where several of my Shanghai friends had settled.[33] Eva had sent letters to the Rosenstein and Grohovsky families notifying them of my arrival; they were all pleased to see me and insisted that I stay with them. It was great to see my close friends from Betar, Arik Rosenstein and Bobby Grohovsky. I heard their parents' many stories about the difficulties of those early days of the state's existence, as it attempted to cope with the flood of Jews either fleeing or expelled from Muslim countries, and the military conflicts with its hostile neighbours. Their financial difficulties were exacerbated by the partisan politics of the day. The centre-left Mapai-dominated government, headed by David Ben-Gurion, discriminated against followers of the Jabotinsky-inspired right-wing Herut party, which included most of the Russian Jews from Shanghai.

Natanya was a good place for me to rest and familiarise myself with the culture of this new Jewish state. After a few days, I contacted Dov, my friend from the ship, and he invited me to lunch with his parents at their apartment in Rehov Rothschild, a tree-lined boulevard in Tel Aviv. Their spacious, tastefully appointed apartment gave me a glimpse into the lives of the more established stratum of Israeli society. Dov's father was a director of Bank Leumi, Israel's largest financial institution. He and his wife had fled Nazi Germany early, in the 1930s, with like-minded immigrants seeking to escape the growing antisemitism. Dov proudly called himself a '*sabra*' (prickly pear), a term used to describe native-born Israelis who are tough on the outside, but sweet on the inside.

I drove with Dov to Eilat, which looked nothing like the busy port and tourist resort it would later become. There was only one wooden pier and a few inhospitable buildings. The Suez Canal was closed to shipping to and from Israel, so Eilat was the country's only maritime outlet to the Red Sea and, from there, the promising markets of India and Asia. It was clearly vital that the port be developed to allow for trade and associated economic prosperity.

---

[32] Years later, I would become a regular visitor to Haifa when Ada and I would accompany my father-in-law, Mietek Gringlas, to his meetings at the Technion, where he was a member of the board of governors.

[33] Natanya became a favoured place to settle for successive waves of immigrants from the former Soviet Union.

My good friend from Melbourne, Maurice Burstin, invited me to celebrate Passover with him at Kibbutz Gvat near the city of Afula in northern Israel. In the 1960s the kibbutz movement was strong, and most were ideologically or religiously aligned. The members of Kibbutz Gvat were followers of Mapam, a left-of-centre political party inspired by the Soviet Union (despite the Soviet Union's antisemitism), who strongly believed in the socialist principle of eschewing private possessions in favour of communal ownership. When we arrived, the members were involved in an intense discussion about whether a small refrigerator, gifted by an American relative of one of the members, should be kept in his unit or in the communal dining hall.

Being accustomed to the traditional celebration of Passover, the modern kibbutz approach was a real eye-opener for me. The kibbutz was festooned with banners and red flags, alongside the Israeli flag, to symbolise the liberation of oppressed workers from capitalist masters. A ceremony in the fields was followed by a politicised *seder* unlike any other I had ever attended. The experience, whilst bizarre, was an interesting lesson in my evolving education about the diversity of the Jewish people.

As I did not need to return to Europe till early May, I decided to travel throughout Israel to learn more about this intriguing country. Leaving the bulk of my belongings with the Grohovskys, and with a map of the Egged[34] bus network in hand, I started my journey. My first stop was the new city of Jerusalem (the Old City was still in Jordanian hands). I first made my way to the famous King David Hotel to see the section that had been bombed in 1946 by Irgun Zvai Leumi, the military wing of the Revisionist Movement[35], killing 91 people. In Israel, I found that there were mixed feelings towards the Irgun and its extremist actions. This was compounded by the Altalena Affair in June 1948 when the Irgun attempted to take delivery of an independent shipment of arms and was involved in a violent confrontation with the newly established Israel Defense Forces (IDF). Following the incident, the Irgun was formally disbanded as a separate military entity and its remaining members enlisted in the IDF.

---

[34] The word 'egged' in Hebrew literally means 'union'. The great Israeli poet, Hayim Nahman Bialik, gave the bus operator this name on its creation in 1933 as a worker co-operative. [35] The Revisionist Movement was founded by the late Vladimir Jabotinsky (a native of Odessa, like my grandmother) and was later headed by Menachem Begin.

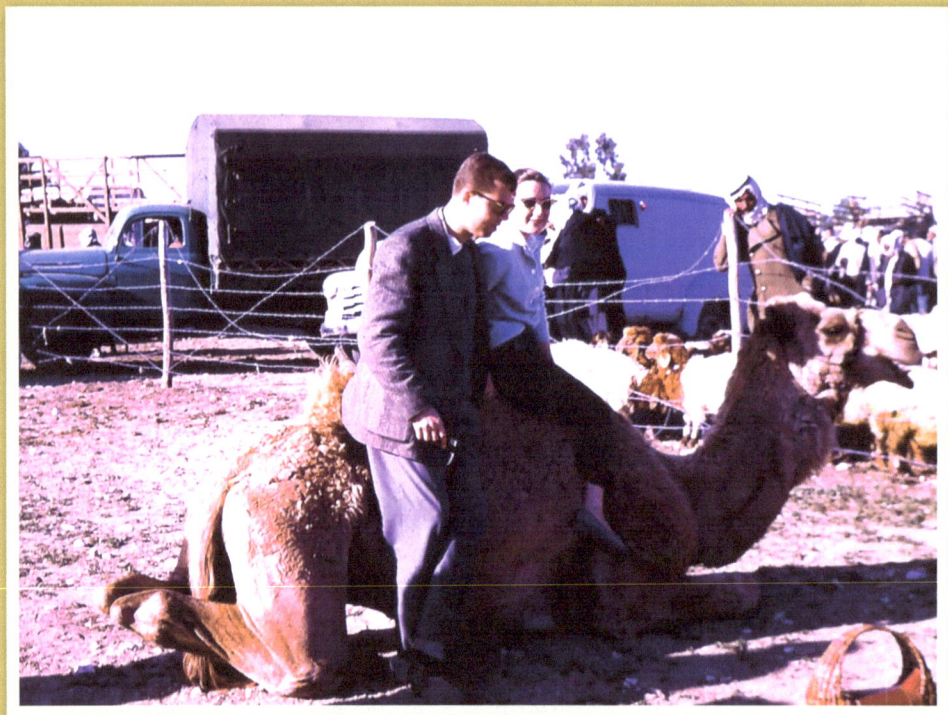

At the Beersheba camel market in the Negev

From the King David Hotel, it was a short walk to the Mandelbaum Gate, the famous checkpoint between the Israeli and Jordanian sectors of Jerusalem (until 1967 when, during the Six Day War, the IDF recaptured and reunited the Old City). I then met up with Ellis (Ika) Joffe[36], a close friend from Shanghai who had been my sparring partner in Betar boxing events. It was wonderful to see him and to be shown around the other sights of Jerusalem.

Travelling by bus alongside city workers, Arabs, and, in rural areas, farmers (sometimes carrying chickens) was an interesting and egalitarian experience. I visited the town of Safed with its beautiful synagogues, the Dead Sea, and the ruins of Kfar Nahum (also known as Capernaum), which I was familiar with from studying the Gospel of Matthew at St Xavier's in Shanghai.

On my travels, I learned that the central issue concerning most Israelis was how the young nation could integrate the thousands of Jews who were being expelled en masse from Muslim countries where their ancestors had lived in relative peace for millennia. The people I spoke to believed that the cultural and ethnic gulf between these newly arrived Sephardi migrants and the Ashkenazi citizens of Israel was immense and unbridgeable. From my perspective as a diaspora Jew, I remember finding it surprising that their main concern was not the threat posed by the rabid hostility of Israel's neighbouring states, particularly Egypt under its leader Gamal Abdel Nasser.

◆

After two weeks of touring, I returned to Natanya, collected my things, bade farewell, and headed for Haifa, where I boarded the *Theodore Herzl* for my return trip to Naples. Because I had stayed in Israel longer than originally intended, I needed to get to Paris as quickly as possible to meet Ian on the agreed date. To save money, I travelled second class on the various trains north, which meant sitting upright on the overnight trips. By the time I reached Vienna, I was so tired that I interrupted my journey and checked into a small hotel near the station. Before going to bed, I took the opportunity to walk through the city's stately streets but, unfortunately,

---

[36] Ika went on to enjoy an illustrious academic career as a professor of Sinology (the study of Chinese language, history and customs) at the Hebrew University's Truman Institute. We remained in touch until he died in 2010.

my dwindling finances meant I could not visit the renowned coffee and cake shops.

After another two days of uncomfortable travel, I finally arrived in Paris and made my way to the Left Bank to find Ian. I cursed myself for the looseness of our meeting arrangement and tried to find the pension where we last stayed. I was tired from my journey and from lugging around my suitcase when, miraculously, we bumped into each other on the street. Ian and Jane had just checked into the same pension, and he had left Jane there to wander the neighbourhood in the hope of finding me. That night we treated ourselves to a delicious leisurely dinner in a nearby bistro.

We returned to London via Belgium, Holland, Germany, Norway, Sweden, Scotland and northern England. While traversing Germany, we stopped in Hamburg for a brief rest. Although heavily destroyed by bombing during the war, Hamburg had largely been rebuilt and was once again a bustling city with new office buildings and colourful neon lights. Ian was amazed by how much better Hamburg looked than London where, so many years after the blitz, you could still see potholes and ruined buildings. After all, Germany had lost the war! My mood deteriorated further when I discovered that our accommodation, run by a middle-aged couple, was in a spacious apartment adorned with several framed photos brazenly depicting a young man in a Nazi uniform. I could not get out of the place fast enough.

The next morning, we went to a nearby travel office to purchase a touring map. Still upset by the photos of the Nazi at our accommodation, I asked an attendant to mark out the Bergen-Belsen concentration camp. At first, she pretended that she didn't know where it was, but after I asked again in a raised voice, she circled the nearby township of Bergen and said to follow the signs to "the site". Sensing my agitation, Ian agreed to accompany me on the journey. I wanted him to get a different perspective on the Germany he seemed to be admiring.

The township of Bergen was totally unscathed by the ravages of war and presented the typical German *gemutlich* atmosphere of pleasant cheerfulness, even though it lay in the shadow of terrible evil. Bergen-Belsen was established by the Nazis as a prisoner-of-war camp. In

1943, parts of the complex were converted to a concentration camp to accommodate the thousands of Jews herded in, after terrible death marches, from eastern death camps that were under threat from advancing Soviet armies. Countless thousands died there, 35,000 alone in the first few months of 1945. When British soldiers liberated Bergen-Belsen on 15 April 1945, they discovered approximately 13,000 unburied corpses lying around the camp, as well as about 60,000 prisoners half-starved and on the verge of death. When we drove through the front gates, the camp had already become a memorial, with an exhibition hall at the site. Greeting us, as we drove through, were mounds with placards stating that beneath the dirt lay the remains of thousands of bodies.

Later, we found a small clearing in the nearby woods to stop for a picnic lunch. As we sat on the blanket, it was clear that we had lost our appetites. Jane broke the silence by saying that we should pack up and get out of Germany as quickly as possible. Before long we were headed towards Scandinavia.

It was May, and the days had started to get warmer and longer when we arrived in the 'land of the midnight sun'. The hotels were models of cleanliness, and the breakfasts featured an astonishing variety of seafood and other delicacies laid out in a Scandinavian smorgasbord—all for a flat price! We did not venture as far east as Finland, but we enjoyed the pleasant and civilised atmosphere in Denmark, Sweden and Norway. When we got to Oslo, we were left breathless by the grandeur and beauty of Vigeland Park, inside Frogner Park, which boasts more than 200 sculptures of naked figures made from bronze and granite by the celebrated Norwegian artist Gustav Vigeland.[37]

While in Oslo, Ian wanted to see the 60-metre ski jump located in nearby Holmenkollbakken, which had hosted the 1952 Winter Olympics. It was indeed an impressive site, and very popular with tourists. I also paid a visit to the head of the Oslo Jewish community, who told me the history of the Jews in Norway dated back to when the Spanish and

---

[37] The central sculpture in this amazing collection is *The Monolith* situated on a plateau raised high above the surrounding park. It is carved out of one enormous piece of granite, 46 feet tall, and depicts 121 figures climbing in and around each other, all fighting their way to the top. Gustav Vigeland, who was born in 1860, began the project in 1931 and died in March 1943 during the German occupation, and did not live to see the park's completion. That visit created an indelible mark in my memory, so when Ada and I travelled with Mark in Scandinavia years later, I made sure we visited Frogner Park. The sculptures were as grand and sensitive as I had remembered them.

With Ian & Jane, outside Hamburg

Portuguese Jews were expelled from Spain in 1492. He also told me about the persecution of local Jews during the Holocaust. On 9 April 1940, Nazi Germany occupied Norway while the Nazi collaborator, Vidkun Quisling[38], nominally headed the government. The Norwegian police helped in the arrest of Jews and deportations began, mostly to Auschwitz. A Norwegian resistance movement helped to save some Jews, but few survived and even fewer returned after Germany's defeat. The man I spoke to was pessimistic and questioned whether the Jewish community in Oslo had the numbers to survive.

May was slipping past, and as we needed to be back in London by mid-June, we booked passage on a ferry travelling to Newcastle in northern England. With the onset of the northern summer, the crossing was mercifully smooth.

Before heading south for London, Ian wanted to pay a quick visit to Glasgow, where he hoped to attend a service at the leading Presbyterian church or 'kirk' as it was known in Scotland. Jane and I accompanied him, and we sat through a bewildering sermon delivered in such a strong Scottish accent that it was almost incomprehensible. I also went to a kosher restaurant, and it was wonderful to hear 'gelfilte fish' and 'chicken soup with knaidlach' ordered in the Scottish burr.

Time was running out, so we drove on to London, with brief visits to Carlisle, Edinburgh (a much more beautiful city than Glasgow), Loch Lomond, Loch Ness and Aberdeen. Finally, back in London, we checked into the same B&B that we had stayed in when we had first arrived. We sold the car back to the original dealer and I touched base with the partner at Arthur Andersen to let him know I would soon be departing for New York. Next, I cashed in the return component of my 'boomerang' ticket and was disappointed to receive only a small fraction of the purchase price. The money did, however, help cover the cost of my trans-Atlantic crossing on a small Dutch passenger ship leaving Southampton on 22 June.

Ian was staying on in London for another few months to work at a stockbroking firm, so, on the appointed day, he and Jane drove me to Southampton, and I bade farewell to a wonderful and eventful six months.

---

[38] The word *Quisling* later became part of the Norwegian and English vernacular, a synonym for traitor.

Chicago

The crossing of the Atlantic was smooth and shipboard life pleasant enough. I had booked an economy-class ticket, which meant sharing with a young Englishman going to work in the United States. Undoubtedly, the highlight of the journey was our entry into New York on a warm and sunny morning with the spectacular skyline as a backdrop.

From London I had written to Stasia and Alec Feldman, who met me at the docks. Stasia was Eva's childhood friend from Harbin, and her husband, Alec, was from Shanghai. They had migrated to America shortly after the war and settled in Queens, one of the five boroughs of metropolitan New York. I can't recall what Alec did for a living, but I do remember Stasia had an unusual job as a necktie designer.

After I cleared customs, they drove me to their house, where I was invited to stay for a few days before travelling to Chicago. That night they took me to a Chinese restaurant, and over dinner I filled them in on our life in Australia. They also gave me mail from my family. I had not heard from home for some time and was relieved to read that all was well and that Grandmother was in good health.

The following day, I made my way into Manhattan and located the offices of Arthur Andersen in one of the many skyscrapers. I was greeted by a partner who told me that his secretary had booked me on a train to Chicago, leaving the following evening. I then headed to the Empire State Building, then the world's tallest building. I can still recall the marvel of travelling at high speed on the express lift from the ground to the observation deck on the top level.

When I boarded my assigned railway car and sleeper, to my horror, I realised that I had accidentally overpaid the taxi driver and had hardly any money left to tide me over until I could get to a bank. It was an easy mistake to make, given that in the United States the various denominations are all green, unlike the more sensible system in Australia. There wasn't even enough to spend on dinner or breakfast in the club car of the train. By the time I dropped my bags at my accommodation at the city campus of Northwestern University and arrived by bus at the Arthur Andersen office in the central business district, I was famished.

I entered the office building at 120 South Lasalle Street and hoped that Carl Boehne, the partner in charge of training, would be there and would agree to loan me some money for lunch. To my disappointment, according to the receptionist, he was not expected back in the office until later in the afternoon. I had no option but to wander the streets of Chicago, ravenous. I had never experienced hunger in my life and, looking at the plentiful food on display, I was reminded of the suffering endured by the poor and hungry Chinese beggars in Shanghai.

Fortunately, when I returned, Mr Boehne was there to receive me in his office. He was tall, thin and more laconic than the two friendly partners I had met in London and New York. Not one for small talk, he immediately launched into a description of the two-week intensive training course. Finally, he asked me about my financial situation. Appearing as nonchalant as I could, I answered that I was low on money and could do with an advance. He immediately rang his secretary and asked her to give me $300 in cash. I nearly fainted at the prospect of receiving such a large sum.

Mr Boehne introduced me to a young man named Arnie Barnett and asked him to look after me. Arnie invited me to dinner that night, which I gratefully accepted. At the restaurant I learnt that Arnie was Jewish, and, over the course of the evening, he told me what to expect at the firm. Arnie ended up being a great contact for me. Later, when it was decided that I would stay on in the Chicago office, he helped me find accommodation and introduced me to his friends. That night, however, I overate, and I had to excuse myself to get to the bathroom to throw up. I returned to my room that night feeling quite wretched. Fortunately, things improved after that challenging start.

Established in 1851, Northwestern University is one of America's most prestigious private universities. The main campus is in Evanston, just north of Chicago, but the business school, known as the Kellogg School of Management, is in downtown Chicago. During the northern summer holidays, the facilities are leased to businesses and other organisations for training purposes. The association between Arthur Andersen and Northwestern University dates back to the 1920s when the firm's founder, Arthur Edward Andersen, became a professor and head of the accounting faculty. The focus on rigorous professional training at the firm has its roots in the educational career of its founder.

I was allocated a student dormitory room, which I shared with another recruit. The accommodation was basic but clean. Shared bathroom and washing facilities were down the passageway and we enjoyed tasty meals in the student dining room. My roommate was from Atlanta, Georgia, and I had difficulty understanding his broad southern drawl. He also struggled with my strange Shanghai/Australian accent. I was reminded of George Bernard Shaw's saying, that England and America are "two nations divided by a common language". The man was also an unabashed racist when it came to African Americans. It was an introduction to the widespread racial divide I was to encounter in America.

On the first day of the two-week intensive course, we were told that every year the firm took on 500 young men—no women—with university degrees spread over a number of disciplines. To me this was a mind-boggling example of the vast scale of American business, relative to what I was used to in Australia. I was also surprised by the candidness of the questions asked by students, which seemed symptomatic of the openness of American society when compared to my more formal British-influenced education.

The managing partner of Arthur Andersen, Leonard Spacek, emphasised that a central principle was that the firm was a meritocracy and that reaching the top was within the grasp of everyone there. This was based on a comprehensive rating system designed to ensure that the most deserving would receive promotions. He then asked for questions and one of the attendees asked what he earned as partner. Without batting an eyelid, Spacek answered "$100,000", which was then an enormous amount of money. Asking such a question and answering it so directly would have been unheard of in Australia!

The course was designed to prepare us for working at Arthur Andersen. The morning lectures dealt with the history and philosophy of the firm, as well as an introduction to the afternoon's accounting topics. Our first 'professional assignment' was to audit the fictional accounting records of the XYZ Corporation. We were told that the Arthur Andersen approach involved preparing detailed working papers. This 'evidence' was required in case of litigation because in the United States auditors were regularly sued for negligence. The final afternoon of the course was devoted to review and wrapping up. Our working papers were handed in and we were each rated by our respective supervisors.

After that, I experienced another American tradition: playing hard after working hard. The American participants, who formed a large majority of our group, had planned the celebrations for the course's completion, which involved a visit to Calumet City or 'Cal City'[39], a southern suburb of Chicago notorious for its nightclubs and red-light district. I went along with a few of the recruits for what should have been a night of carousing, but soon tired of the hard drinking and retired early.

Another new American experience was the obligatory salad served to diners upon being seated at a restaurant, with a choice of dressings, including one with the exotic name of 'thousand island'. I recall a reunion dinner with visiting Australians from the Melbourne office. We sat down, ordered our meals, and the plate of assorted greens was served to each of us. We expected the other dishes to readily follow, so we waited. The waiters, hovering nearby, were also waiting for us to consume the salad, before proceeding with the orders. A classic standoff, for a full ten minutes, ensued until the headwaiter eventually came along and asked if there was anything wrong. We also had some initial misunderstandings

---

[39] Like many American municipalities, Calumet City had its own independent administrative authority. It relaxed the strict public entertainment prohibitions in Chicago, so it had many nightclubs, a red-light district and even havens for organised crime, earning it the name 'Sin City'.

with terminology, as the Americans called the main course the 'entrée' and our entrée, the 'appetizer'.

Apparently, I had done very well in the course as, for some time afterwards, several people in the Chicago office stopped to congratulate me. I was invited to join the merchandising audit team and to participate in several more courses over the next few months. This involved extending my work visa, which the firm took care of.

With Arnie's assistance, I located a fully furnished and serviced bedsitter, with a Pullman kitchenette, in a five-storey apartment building in Surf Street, one block north of Diversey, abutting the beautiful Lincoln Park. The area clearly catered for young single people like me and featured an iconic drugstore that was a popular meeting place, particularly for breakfast on Saturday and Sunday mornings.

The merchandising division of the Andersen audit practice was a major component of its 'industry competence' approach. This concept, quite different to our practice at that time in Australia, involved the consolidation of clients in one industry and additional training for auditors so that they developed expertise in the business issues and terminology of that particular industry, in order to provide a superior service.

The Chicago office had several significant retail clients, including the Marshall Field Group, Carson, Pirrie, Scott, the Montgomery Ward mail order group, and the very large drugstore chain, Walgreens. With exposure to that industry, I could pioneer the approach when I returned to the Melbourne office, which also had several prominent retailers as clients.

I was promoted to the position of 'senior', the next category above the four levels of 'assistant', the lowest in the Andersen hierarchy. I was then enrolled into my next training course, held over a long weekend at the Union League Club, an exclusive businessmen's club, with dark-panelled walls and Chesterfield couches. These clubs had started to become an anachronism but, with typical American ingenuity, surplus availability allowed for short-term use as training and conference venues.

Chicago

There were only about 40 participants in the course and the format comprised of lectures on working paper reviews, design of audit programs, and an introduction to the Andersen philosophy of rating both subordinates and supervisors following completion of each assignment. This approach was in line with the firm's principle of merit as the basis for promotion and advancement. While meritocracy was already an important element in most advanced societies, the approach at Andersens exemplified it to the 'nth degree', at least in theory.

The Chicago office was known as 'home office', where the managing partner, other partners in charge of operations, and the central administration of the firm were located. It was the largest office in terms of numbers of professional staff, attesting to its strong presence and reputation in its founding city. It was located over several floors, the various divisions occupying their own separate floors. In addition to the mainstay audit division, there were two other divisions: tax and administrative services, whose raison d'etre were to provide specialist support to the clients of the audit division. There was no point in my getting involved with the tax division, as the difference in laws between the US and Australia precluded the need for co-operation between the tax practices of the American and Australian firms. However, the administrative services division was of interest as it had similar aims to the department that Alan Dick was working to establish in Melbourne.

The first thing I noticed on entering each floor of the Andersen office in Chicago were the racks of hats. There were literally hundreds of hats, as the dress code was suits with white shirts, conservative ties, leather shoes and straw hats in summer or felt hats in winter.

Although Chicago's population featured a fair proportion of African Americans, all the professional and secretarial staff of the firm were white. The only non-whites were the shoeshine boys who swarmed in first thing each morning to shine the shoes of partners and managers in their respective offices. The justification I was given, was that difficulties would arise if 'coloured' external auditors were to demand paperwork from white client executives.

I should not have been as surprised by this divide as I was, as Australia had its White Australia policy and, apart from a few young Asian people who arrived in Australia under the Colombo Plan, the composition of the Melbourne office was equally white.

I spent a few days in the office before being assigned to a client, Marshall Field's, Chicago's leading department store. The audit team was preparing for the closure of the annual accounts on 31 January. Although most companies in America balanced their books at year end, the retail industry did it a month later, as stocktaking on New Year's Eve would be difficult. The junior members of the audit team were tasked with supervising the packing of a large black trunk containing the previous year's audit working papers, the audit plan, and a plentiful supply of yellow paper pads. This trunk was to be delivered to us in the assigned Andersen's office at the store.

The Marshall Field's store on State Street was the flagship of a publicly listed chain of stores, founded in 1852. Its opulent building and luxurious merchandise differentiated it from other department stores. The company introduced merchandising concepts that were revolutionary at the time and placed strong emphasis on the customer experience. It pioneered the concept of the bridal registry and provided in-store restaurants for shoppers. As many told me, I was lucky to start my grounding in merchandise management in a store like that.

Marshall Field's prowess in merchandising was matched by the rigour of its accounting and management information system. The ready knowledge of margins earned, stock levels and expenditure were the drivers of the system. In the days before computers, the company engaged extra resources to achieve this outcome. Every working day after 4pm, a small army of people would appear in the general office and work till late in the night to compute the key results of trading across the whole range of products sold, so that the information would be available the following morning on the desks of the relevant managers for analysis. I later found out these night workers were teachers from nearby schools who were keen to earn extra income.

Chicago

The Andersen audit team also worked to a tight timetable, one that would still be unheard of in Australia. By 10 February, the accountants at Marshall Field's would produce the financial results for the fiscal year ending 31 January and deliver them to the auditors for verification and sign-off 10 days later so that the results could be publicly released by the end of February! This required a titanic effort and staff were expected to put in whatever hours were necessary. Some of the Andersen people who lived in the outer suburbs would have to book into local hotels to snatch a few hours of sleep. I was also expected to participate in this gruelling schedule but, fortunately, my apartment was only a short bus trip away. The firm was very fair in remunerating its staff for the overtime they were expected to work and some of the younger auditors welcomed this opportunity to earn the extra money.

The use of random statistical sampling was a new audit technique employed by the division and, of course, I was happy to learn all about it. The basic audit process involved rigorous cross-referencing and the creation of detailed, flawless working papers, which had to be personally signed off with the opinion that the outcomes were valid and could be relied upon.

My relationships with fellow audit team members were very good. The Americans, who were mostly from the mid-west, were intrigued by my background and I was continually peppered with questions. Some of them invited me for dinner to meet their families. I recall being impressed by how proudly they shared details of their achievements and their candidness about personal money matters.

My life started to develop a very pleasant tempo. On the weekends, I would shop at the newly opened supermarkets and marvel at the plethora of choices. My favourite was the newly released Sara Lee cheesecake, in which I over-indulged to the point that I had to start taking a popular new diet product called Metrecal. I will always associate that product with a famous quote from *Time Magazine*: "During the 1960 campaign, Senator Kennedy remarked that 17 million Americans go to bed hungry every night—most of them are on Metrecal."

On Sunday mornings I would catch up with some of the local people I had befriended, and we would enjoy a typical American breakfast of pancakes with maple syrup at the local drugstore. Often, we would go for a walk in nearby Lincoln Park, an oasis of calm and beauty amid the high-rises and constant traffic. I had never seen so many squirrels, and the changing of the leaves with the onset of autumn was magical. In the afternoons, I would either work or go with friends to the wonderful galleries and museums. I also spent time with Bill Hibble, a Melbourne partner who was posted to Chicago to study data processing in order to help establish a consulting team in Australia. He and his wife, Bette, were particularly kind to me.[40]

Arnie Barnett introduced me to several of his Jewish friends. They were a great conduit to a vibrant social life, and like many Americans I met, generously included me in whatever they were doing. Some were members of the local B'nai B'rith Youth (BBY) and, when they found out about my Melbourne connection with the organisation, they invited me to join in. I was also welcomed to the Hillel House social events at the main campus of Northwestern University. It was there I first saw Samuel Beckett's perplexing play *Waiting for Godot*.

I particularly enjoyed visits to the jazz bars and cocktail lounges in nearby Rush Street, where I was introduced to drinking Scotch, listening to smooth jazz and the uniquely American concept of stand-up comedy. I was lucky enough to see Mort Sahl who was known for his biting tongue. He pioneered a style of social satire, which poked fun at political and current events. It was risqué and the audience loved it.

One day, at the end of August, I decided to search for Grandmother's relatives, the Caismans, who had immigrated to the United States from Odessa, and settled in Chicago. I struck it lucky with the first telephone call, which was answered by an elderly relative who recalled meeting my father when he visited in the 1920s. The family was excited to meet me, and hastily organised a gathering to hear news about our family's life in Shanghai and Melbourne. Thirty members of the extended Caisman family, spanning several generations, gathered in one of their homes

---

[40] A few years later, Bill died prematurely from a sudden heart attack. It was a loss I felt keenly.

in Skokie, a town north of Chicago that was popular with younger middle-class Jews. They asked me to join them for synagogue services and a family dinner during the approaching High Holidays. I gratefully accepted their invitation.

Al Winnick was a young partner in the office, whose family was originally from Europe but had settled in America several generations ago. Al told me there were very few Jews in the Chicago office, mainly because the staff were recruited from hinterland states, like Iowa, which had small Jewish populations. He was adamant that there was no discrimination against Jews, nor did I encounter any antisemitism whilst there. American Jews were largely assimilated and hard to distinguish from the average American. One evening, when I was a guest at his house for Friday night dinner, Al showed me an Andersen publication I had not seen before. It was a listing with photos of the firm's partners and managers, featuring a summary of their backgrounds, including education, family details and faith. The management team publication was issued annually following the appointment of new partners and it became an excellent source of information for me over the years.

By the end of September, the tempo of the forthcoming elections started to quicken. I was surprised at how grassroots the American election process was. Particularly surprising were the elections for local judges and police chiefs, a very different system to that in Australia. The contenders for president were the charismatic young Catholic senator, John F. Kennedy, the Democratic candidate, and the incumbent Republican vice-president, Richard Nixon, who was not as popular as Kennedy, but obviously more experienced. I was surprised by how polarising the issue of religion was — no Catholic had ever been elected to the office of president.

For the first time, there would be a series of public debates on television. Many of us did not own a television set, and I was invited to several parties to watch the debates, which were a great introduction to American politics. Kennedy was the clear favourite among young people.

Election day passed without incident. By Australian standards it was a non-event as it was held on a normal working day (the first Tuesday of November) and it was not compulsory to vote. But that night we were again glued to the TV and radio, following the counting and announcement that Kennedy had won.

The next morning at Marshall Field's, everyone was talking about the close election results. The main local newspaper, *The Chicago Tribune*, owned and run by a die-hard Republican, Robert 'Colonel' McCormick, alleged that the elections were rigged by splashing, on the front page, news that in several precincts more votes were cast for Kennedy than there were registered voters! I was shocked by how sanguine everybody was about this. Little did I know that the mayor of Chicago, Richard Daley, had done a secret deal with John F. Kennedy's father, Joseph Kennedy, to 'deliver' Cook County, which included Chicago, to Kennedy.

By the end of November, we had completed our preliminary work at Marshall Field's. We still needed to check the year-end stock and verify the year-end accounts by the end of January. Much ground had to be covered in a short space of time. However, for our non-retail clients, all the stocktakes had to be completed by 31 December. In true Andersen tradition, nothing was left to chance so there were seminars in the office on stocktaking practices and their audit implications. I recall being enthralled at one session, listening to a manager describe stocktaking at a large paper manufacturing company that also owned forests. After the felling of the trees, the logs were floated down the river to the factories. The problem was how to count the inaccessible logs, which were still floating downriver on 31 December? The manager proudly revealed that a helicopter was employed to fly slowly over the logs and photograph them. He was also pleased to say that the photos made excellent working paper evidence.

I was enlisted to assist with these stocktakes, but none were particularly interesting. I was assigned to a team doing surprise counts of the cash-in-hand at various branches of the firm's banking clients. On a freezing December night, or very early on New Year's Day, we would meet in secret and then pounce on surprised tellers to verify their earlier counts of the same bundles of notes. All this had to be done in a great hurry and I recall again being confused by the uniformly green colour of the notes, irrespective of their denominations. When it came to Marshall Field's stocktakes at the end of January, I was given the pillow department. I had never seen such a range of sizes, colours and shapes of pillows. The immense number of choices seemed emblematic of American consumerism at the time.

In September, I was selected to participate in the basic systems course for those going into the administrative services division, the firm's up-and-coming management consulting practice. The name was chosen to underscore that the practice area was restricted to quantitative issues, rather than organisational management, which was then considered to be within the human resources area and outside the expertise of accountants. I was pleased to be selected as I sensed Alan Dick was positioning to recruit me into the consulting practice he was developing in Australia.

The intensive course was held in the Bismarck Hotel, a comfortable establishment in the Loop area, and we were expected to live there for the two-week duration of the course. Joseph Glickauf, the charismatic firm-wide partner in charge of the administrative services division, addressed the opening session and told us that the division's aim was to support the main business of the firm, which was its large and prestigious audit practice. It was not until several years later that the division developed the expertise and confidence to present itself as a serious, separate offering in the wider management consulting market.

We were fully engaged over the next two weeks with lectures in the hotel's spacious convention facilities. We were also given practical exercises that were reviewed and rated each morning. Subjects ranged from elementary flow-charting to operations research, which was the relatively new approach of using mathematical modelling in business operations. Underlying it all was the introduction of electronic data processing, which by today's standards was still quite primitive, being limited to punched cards and the early IBM machines.

After the course, I returned to my flat and resumed my social life with Arnie Barnett and his friends, members of the Chicago BBY, and friends I had made at Hillel House at Northwestern University. I got on well with several faculty members who invited me for dinner at their homes on campus. The university was located on the crime-ridden south side of Chicago, an area which had fallen into disrepute, as it was largely populated by poorer people, mostly black, who lived in derelict public housing. When I told my colleagues that I had travelled from there by train, alone and late at night, they were horrified. Despite their admonishments, I continued to travel there by train without mishap.

I was also invited for dinners at the homes of some of my work colleagues. Invariably, they lived in spacious modern houses in outer suburbs. Many hailed from the farming states, like Iowa, and being able to afford such a home was considered a great achievement. They had relied on low interest tax-deductible loans to acquire the houses, and after a few years of receiving the substantial overtime cheques for the insane hours they were expected to work, they were able to furnish them. They took great pride in their homes and would lead me on detailed tours, including a survey of their prized basements, equipped with billiards or table tennis tables.

After a hot and steamy summer, the welcome autumn coolness gradually gave way to winter and the legendary icy blasts coming in from Lake Michigan. By December, snow had fallen, on some days quite heavily. I went to the Marshall Field's menswear store and bought myself an overcoat and warm shoes to navigate the snow and ice.

My apartment was centrally heated and far too hot by Melbourne standards. I was used to sleeping with the window slightly open, a habit I continued as the weather cooled. One morning, early in winter, I woke up to a large pile of snow that had blown in through the gap in the window— the result of a snowstorm during the night. I got rid of the snow as best I could before I went to work and left a note for the cleaning lady. By the time I left the building and walked to the bus stop, the snow on the roads had been largely cleared, another marvel of American efficiency.

Chicago

In early January, I was asked by the manager heading the Walgreens audit whether I would be prepared to go to Beaver Dam, a town in Wisconsin, to conduct an audit at the Walgreens regional distribution facility. The senior originally assigned to carry out this solo operation was unwell and the powers-that-be thought that it would be a good experience. Needless to say, it would read well in my rating form. I went by train to Milwaukee and then by bus to Beaver Dam, where I was met by the Walgreens manager and ensconced in a modern motel.

If I thought Chicago was cold, that was nothing compared to Beaver Dam, where the temperature was at least 15 degrees Fahrenheit lower. After an early breakfast at the motel, the manager took me on a quick tour of the snow-covered township. He explained that it was the principal city of Dodge County and was first settled in the mid-nineteenth century. Its name was derived from an old beaver dam located in a stream flowing into the Beaver Dam River. Staff at the facility were extremely friendly and cooperative and I experienced no problems when checking out the stocktaking procedures, which I committed to the working papers that night back in my motel room.

While there, I turned on the television one night to watch the inauguration ceremony in Washington of the newly elected president John F. Kennedy. I can still recall being moved by his famous line exhorting Americans, "Ask not what your country can do for you, but what you can do for your country."

My return to Chicago coincided with preparations for Marshall Field's stock counts on 31 January and assisting with the completion of the audit work so that the final accounts could be signed off and publicly released by 20 February.

I was then enrolled in a seminar to introduce Andersen employees to a novel piece of research that was to be undertaken by the merchandising division in conjunction with various universities. In charge of this industry research program was John R. Jones, a highly respected partner, who was credited with creating several original solutions to existing business problems. Merchandise Management Accounting, or MMA for short, was one such example. It was designed to promote profitability by finetuning the incentives given to the sales force of 'big ticket', high-value items like furniture and appliances. This methodical approach to isolating the key differential advantage between various similar products, was embraced by businesses as a very useful tool. As the Melbourne office had a similar client mix, MMA could also be applied there and, unbeknown to me, efforts were already being made to promote this system. Hence the call from the Melbourne office to accelerate my return.

And so, with the return of spring, the melting of the snow and the resulting dirty slush in the streets, I started to wrap up my activities and say my goodbyes. In a way I was sorry to leave, as I was learning a lot and felt appreciated by my work colleagues. The culture of the organisation promoted self-confidence and I felt that I was leaving the US a more assured individual. I was still a great admirer of the United States, although no longer oblivious to the inherent contradictions of its complex society. I too was a beneficiary of its meritocracy, its 'can-do' culture and the absence of a stultifying class structure. However, in its driving quest for achievement, I felt it to be a harsh society. Even during the prosperity of those times, the wretchedness of the lower echelons of society was widely evident. I continued to be puzzled by the blind spots—how this sense of equality and inclusion was not extended to the African Americans, despite the explicitness of the cherished constitution. The other anomaly was the tolerance of organised crime. During my early days in Chicago, I was taken on a tour of a neighbourhood where Mafia crime bosses lived in huge mansions. In my naivety, I asked why, if their illegal activity was so widely known, hadn't the police arrested them? I was met with a knowing grin. When I asked some of my colleagues for ideas for souvenirs to take home, they suggested a submachine gun, a symbol of the Al Capone days. And yet, in everyday life in Chicago, I found the general atmosphere to be one of punctilious honesty and probity.

Just before I booked my trip home, a partner in the merchandising division, Harvey Kapnick[41], asked me to visit some department stores in other cities where an MMA system was either being installed or

---

[41] Kapnick, who possessed the rough mannerisms of a Chicago mobster, was later to become a controversial managing partner of the firm, overseeing a period of rapid growth during the 1970s.

was already operating. This was typical of the thoughtfulness and thoroughness of the Andersen management, given the prospect of MMA being introduced to the Melbourne office's substantial department store practice. Foremost in his mind was a visit to Detroit, then a vibrant city and the centre of American automobile manufacturing or Motown as it was fondly called. I was booked in for several nights at the Cadillac Hotel, the appropriately named leading hotel of the city, and asked to contact the partner in charge of the Andersen office located nearby. In true American tradition, he proudly took me on a tour of the office, which he had established.

The purpose of the trip to Detroit was to familiarise myself with MMA at the leading department store, J.L. Hudson, which was a showpiece for the benefits of the system. The store bore the name of its founder, Joseph Lothian Hudson, who opened it in 1911 and gradually built it into the dominant merchandising institution of Detroit. J.L. Hudson also pioneered the establishment of satellite stores, which became malls, in the burgeoning suburbs of Detroit. After the office tour, the partner introduced me to the team working on the system and invited us all to lunch at his club on the top floor of a high-rise office building. From that vantage point, they delighted in pointing out that to the south was the city of Windsor in Canada, which surprised me given that Canada is, for the most part, north of the United States.

On one of my free afternoons, I was taken on a tour of Greenfield Village in Dearborn, just outside of Detroit. The historic village was established in 1933 by Henry Ford, one of the country's leading industrialists, who harboured a passion for preserving significant Americana. The 80-hectare site included about 100 buildings which housed iconic items such as: Thomas Edison's laboratory; the chair Abraham Lincoln was sitting in at Ford's Theatre when he was assassinated; and the Wright Brothers' bicycle shop. The tour provided a lasting impression of the comprehensive sweep of American inventiveness before my departure for home.

Outside the Arthur Andersen office in Chicago
Right: State Street, Chicago. The Marshall Field's store is in the background

PART TWO

1961 - 1982

Ada, 1962

Meeting Ada

I returned to Melbourne in May 1961. The social scene had changed significantly since I had left 18 months earlier for an exciting life of travel and work in Europe and the United States.

I discovered that the 'study group' had been disbanded and that many of the young Jewish people I had met through the group had either married or moved overseas. Similarly, most of the young women I knew through B'nei B'rith Youth (BBY) were either engaged or already married.

I called Nathan Fink to let him know I was back, and he filled me in on all the Melbourne news. He told me that he had been dating Elly Symons and confided that they planned to become engaged shortly. In due course the engagement was made public in the *Jewish News*, and the party was set to be held on 12 August. I looked forward to the event and the opportunity to catch up with old friends and meet new people.

On that night, I drove in my family's Humber Hawk to Nathan's parents' gracious two-storey home in Berkeley Court, Kew. I congratulated his parents, Mina and Leo Fink, who seemed genuinely pleased to see me again and made me feel welcome. I had always been impressed by their active support of Jews who settled in Melbourne after the war, and the fact that Mina headed the National Council of Jewish Women.

I entered the crowded lounge room and circulated among the guests, stopping to have a chat with Vita Hasen, with whom I had studied commerce at university. Whilst we were talking, a slim and pretty young woman joined us, and Vita introduced her as Ada Gringlas. After a few minutes, Vita excused herself and I continued talking with Ada, who I learned was studying law at the University of Melbourne. I attempted to find common ground by mentioning all the Jewish organisations I was involved with, and was taken aback when Ada unabashedly stated she hadn't heard of any of them—not even the popular BBY youth group. When I expressed surprise, she said that organisations were not her thing! When she said she didn't know many people at the party, I asked how she was there, and she replied that Nathan had taken her out a few times. She seemed different to other women I knew, and I found her self-confidence and direct manner intriguing.

As the party was ending, I decided to be forward enough to ask if I could drive her home. I was relieved to hear that her mother had dropped her off at the party, so she did need a lift. Later I learned that her mother, fearing that Ada would make a brief appearance and leave, insisted on driving her, in the hope that she would meet someone nice who would drive her home. Apparently, her mother felt vindicated and relieved when this event transpired.

While dropping her off, I asked if I could see her again, but she said she was going to Surfers Paradise with her parents for two weeks. Diffident as she was, fortunately, I managed to extract her home phone number and the date of her return.

Two weeks later, I called, and despite having to remind her who I was, she agreed to an 'after eight' date at a dimly lit Hawaiian-themed coffee shop in Toorak Village called The Hut, which would soon become one of our favourite haunts.

I later learned that when I arrived to pick Ada up, her mother, Lida, nearly fainted when she saw me standing there. Asking me to wait in the entrance hall while she went to get Ada, she apparently blurted, "It's him, it's him—the young man who spoke at the Warsaw Ghetto evening at the Melbourne Town Hall!" It seemed that I had made a favourable impression when, before leaving for overseas, I had spoken, in my capacity as youth chairman of the Victorian Jewish Board of Deputies, to a packed gathering at the town hall, on the Warsaw Ghetto Uprising Commemoration evening. Sharing the platform with me that night was

Meeting Ada

Rabbi Dr Herman Sanger of Temple Beth Israel, widely regarded as a brilliant orator. It was a major annual event in the Melbourne Jewish calendar and, at the time, the principal way for the Polish Jewish community to mark their tragic experiences under the Nazis. Ada's parents had apparently voiced their hope that, one day, Ada would "meet a young man like that". And there I was at the door—tall, presentable, and polite. For the rest of our courtship, I felt that I had Ada's parents, and particularly her mother, on side.

Looking back, those evenings at The Hut, when I would pick her up after dinner and we would spend a couple of hours over a modest coffee and raisin toast, cemented our budding relationship. I had not expected to fall for someone so different to me. I had assumed that I would make my future with somebody more like the women I had previously dated; women who were involved in community organisations, who valued my communal roles and contributions, and who looked up to me and my achievements. Further, unlike me, Ada was not interested in talking about her heritage—I had to glean all of that from discussions with her parents, with whom I got on very well.

Gradually our dates progressed from coffees to dinners. Ada seemed to like unusual restaurants and was particularly pleased when I took her out to a French restaurant, replete with red and white checked tablecloths and dripping candles, called Le Coq au Vin.

Our new relationship was soon tested. Surprisingly to those who knew me later, I was a squash player, and had a regular after-work game with Bill Charlton, the tax manager of the Melbourne office of Fuller King/Arthur Andersen. During one game, I fell and broke my ankle. My lower leg was put into a plaster cast for a few weeks, which put paid to my driving. It was early in our courtship, and I was worried about how we could continue going on dates; public transport or expensive taxis were both out of the question. However, I soon learned that whenever a problem emerged, Ada was quick with a solution. She resolved to drive me around in her family's car until my leg healed. Looking back, I can see that the arrangement had a bonding effect. Ada got to know my parents when she came to our house and her breezy nature endeared her to them.

When the plaster finally came off, by way of thanks, I invited Ada to a live performance at the Princess Theatre, followed by supper. It was a new Neil Simon comedy called *Come Blow Your Horn* and Lida insisted that Ada wear her mink stole for the occasion. After that, we started to feel like an official 'item' and we were invited together to parties and social occasions.

By current standards it seems amazing that, after only a few months of dating, we were contemplating marriage. But in the atmosphere of those times, the timing was not unusual. With our new status came the attendant rituals. Initially, I was regularly invited to informal dinners at the Gringlas' kitchen table. Later, when my parents were invited for dinner, we ate in the dining room. The experience was mirrored when the Gringlas family came to our home.

My grandmother did not meet Ada on these occasions, as she was no longer living at home. The previous year she had slipped and injured herself. Unable to walk, Grandmother could no longer be left at home on her own, and we arranged for her to move into a private room at the Montefiore Homes for the Aged. Because of our special relationship, I visited her often. Although looked after very well, she was quite lonely because her English was so poor. In those days, before the influx of Jews from the Soviet Union, hardly any of the residents spoke Russian and I would have to interpret her needs for the staff.

After a while, I realised the time had come for Ada and Grandmother to meet, which would also require my skills as a translator. By then, Ada appreciated the importance of my relationship with Grandmother and, luckily, their first encounter went well. The following day I visited Grandmother to get her feedback and I was relieved to hear that she approved. "You've done well," she told me, and wished us all the best.

Then Grandmother asked if Ada intended to continue studying law. I replied that I did not know, as we had not discussed the topic, adding that many young women did give up their studies once married. Grandmother drew me close and said that under no circumstances should I allow this. On the contrary, I should encourage Ada to continue studying and then work as a lawyer so that she could earn money in her own right. "That way," she said, "she will stay with you because she wants to, rather than because she has to!" I was totally floored by this statement. My grandmother had certainly retained her wits and sagacity, despite the challenges she had faced and her deteriorating health.

Ada's parents held the same view; they too wanted Ada to complete her law degree and become a professional woman. Taking my grandmother's words to heart, I started encouraging Ada's studies and, over the next few years, I helped her by cooking and ironing, and by rewriting her lecture notes, which were illegible.

I had kept my parents and brothers informed regarding the progress of our romance and they were thrilled for me as they liked Ada very much. In December 1961, I arranged to meet with Ada's father, Mietek, or Ken as he was known, to ask for his daughter's hand in marriage. I arrived at their home in Frater Street, Kew, just after dinner. Ada and Lida had arranged to be out of the house with Ada's young brother Jack for a few hours (which seemed like an unreasonably long time under the circumstances). I must have appeared nervous, because Mietek took the initiative and told me that he and Lida were delighted to welcome me as a son-in-law, and he wished the two of us a long and happy life together. In a nod to my heritage, he pulled out a bottle of vodka that he had bought for the occasion.

Unsure of how long the two of us would be spending together, and to avoid any awkward silence, I asked Mietek about his wartime experiences. Not surprisingly, he was happy to have an audience. By then we had drunk a few small glasses of vodka, and Mietek launched into his fascinating life story, including his part in the Battle of Stalingrad.[42] He was surprised by my knowledge and interest, and

---

[42] In 1989, Mietek's life story was preserved in a biography written by our eldest son, Mark.

this fuelled the conversation and the drinking of the vodka. If he had harboured any doubts about me, my fascination certainly won him over! Just as he got up to show me the medal he had been awarded, the others returned home to find us with two empty bottles of vodka on the table. Lida, seeing the happy state we were in, asked in Polish whether we had managed to discuss the marriage. Mietek assured her that he had given his blessing. I took my leave shortly after and drove home quickly, fearing that I would be picked up by the police. The medal that Mietek showed me that night was later gifted to me, and is now proudly displayed in my study, a reminder of that special evening.

Ada and I announced our engagement in the *Jewish News* and started planning an engagement party to be held at the Gringlas' home the following month. Most of our friends were not surprised by our news. We received an avalanche of flowers, congratulatory telegrams and messages, and enjoyed a seemingly endless number of celebratory dinner parties.

За нашу Советскую Родину

СС СР

★ УДОСТОВЕРЕНИЕ ★

За участие в героической обороне

СТАЛИНГРАДА

Грингляс

Хаиму Янкелевичу.

Указом ПРЕЗИДИУМА
ВЕРХОВНОГО СОВЕТА СССР
от 22 декабря 1942г. награжден
медалью

«ЗА ОБОРОНУ СТАЛИНГРАДА»

★

От имени ПРЕЗИДИУМА
ВЕРХОВНОГО СОВЕТА СССР
медаль «За оборону Сталинграда»
вручена „30" октября 1944 г.

Л № 46978

Начальник 26 Управления Оборонительного

Строительства РГК.

ГЕНЕРАЛ-МАЙОР ИНЖ. ВОЙСК   Горбачев.

М. П.   (должность, военное звание и подпись лица, вручившего медаль)

Mietek's medal from the Battle of Stalingrad

Early Married Life

The Gringlas family were members of Kew Synagogue, but they were happy to defer to my wish to be married at Temple Beth Israel. Lida admired Rabbi Dr Sanger very much and was thrilled that he had agreed to preside over our wedding.

As was customary, Ada and I went to see Rabbi Sanger in his modest office at Temple Beth Israel in Alma Road, St Kilda. The relatively new building had been designed to accommodate the rapidly growing Liberal Jewish congregation in time to hold the 1958 High Holidays. It replaced the original temple, whose foundation stone was laid by the Jewish former governor general, Sir Isaac Isaacs in 1937. Many years later, I would chair the fundraising effort to build a new, even bigger synagogue in its place.

The rabbi made us feel welcome and took great interest in our lives. He asked after my parents whom he knew because he had officiated at the bar mitzvahs of my brothers, Nathan and Elijah. We settled on a date for our wedding—Saturday 2 June at 6.15pm after the end of the sabbath. He then gave us special advice for our married life, which we have never forgotten. He said that although there would be days when there were disagreements, and even irritation and anger between us, we should always make up before going to sleep.

At the time, the rabbi was a bachelor, but soon after our wedding he married Winifred Nathan, a widow from a respected Temple Beth Israel family.

We were pleased with the 6.15pm time as we wanted to hold the black-tie reception (quaintly known as 'the breakfast') immediately after the ceremony, so that everyone would come to the synagogue dressed in their finery. For the reception, we decided not to adopt the customary format of hosting two sittings: a formal dinner and speeches for our parents' friends and bridal party, followed by 'the supper' for our friends. I still recall the many wedding suppers I was invited to, and the tedious wait outside while lengthy speeches ran overtime. Both Ada and I thought it a ridiculous practice and so did our parents, so we invited everybody on our guest list for the dinner. I believe our wedding was one of the first to do away with the traditional format, and this quickly became the new norm.

We had our hearts set on hosting our dinner at the stylish Bamboo Room at the Chevron Hotel, so we were relieved that it was available.[43] We then arranged the invitations and booked the band and the photographer, Izzy Rosenfield. Ada took time out from her studies to have her beautiful wedding dress made, and Lida happily looked after everything else.

Ada chose two close girlfriends to be her bridesmaids: Rosie Black, who threw us a great pre-wedding party at her home; and Megan Sanders, a close school friend. I chose my brothers, Nathan and Elijah, to be my 'best men'. To complete the wedding party, we asked Ada's brother, Jack, who was 11, and Janie, the Sklovskys' youngest daughter, to be the pageboy and flower girl.

A Women's International Zionist Organisation (WIZO) volunteer, Klara Lane, hosted a pre-wedding party for the friends of our two mothers. Such functions were popular fundraising events for Israel.

My bucks night was a conservative affair—Sasha invited Ada and me, together with our parents and a few mutual friends, to a dinner at his small house in Fitzroy.

In the week leading up to the wedding, it was customary to set up a large table in the entrance foyer of the bride's parents' home to display all the presents for the admiration of family and close friends. There was no such thing as a wedding registry yet in Australia and duplications were inevitable—we later exchanged the numerous extra toasters, teapots and frying pans we received. The task of being available when friends would drop in with their gifts, and to admire

---

[43] The Chevron, on the corner of St Kilda Road and Commercial Road, was built in 1934. It was designed by leading Melbourne architect, Leslie M. Perrott. His son, Les Perrott, Jnr., was also a leading architect and a president of the Melbourne Junior Chamber of Commerce, who I knew very well from my active years in the Jaycees.

the display, fell largely to me as, a few days before the wedding, Ada came down with a cold and was staying in bed to shake it off. I suspected it may have also been an attack of nerves. Fortunately, by the Friday before the wedding, she felt well enough to get up and greet some of the last-minute visitors.

The best gift was from Ada's parents: a near-new Simca Aronde. At a time when most Australians drove Holdens and Fords, this was indeed a chic purchase. We loved its modern lines and driving the car made us feel young and 'with it'. It was only later, when driving in the countryside, that we experienced the problem of finding a mechanic who could get spare parts and service a 'continental' vehicle with components manufactured according to the metric system.

Saturday 2 June 1962 dawned sunny and clear, which was a great relief. However, it then rained intermittently all day, stopping only as we entered and then left the synagogue. We were told that the rain was good luck. As our wedding film reveals, the afternoon was devoted to Ada getting ready and being attended to by our mothers, the bridesmaids, flower girl and pageboy. I had organised for a Humber Super Snipe and other limousines to transport the wedding party to Temple in the late afternoon.

Once the signing formalities were completed in the rabbi's office, Mietek was ready to lead Ada to the *chuppah*, which was set up on the *bimah*. His face was beaming as he led her down the aisle, accompanied by traditional wedding music. He must have reflected on the wonderful change in their lives since the war and their early years in Melbourne. Here he was, escorting his daughter at a stylish wedding attended by a large gathering of friends and family members.

I was waiting under the *chuppah* for Ada. I stood there with Lida and my parents who, no doubt, were also contemplating that it had been 10 years since they had arrived from Shanghai. Once again, I was the vanguard of the family, marrying and settling into this new and accepting country.

The reception, dinner, speeches, and dancing were an outstanding success, and the photo album and colour film of the evening show how much everybody enjoyed themselves.[44] I still think of my grandmother sitting at the head table. I am sure that she must have been missing my grandfather, who had died prematurely in Shanghai in 1944. Despite the eloquence of Rabbi Sanger, it was Mietek who stole the show with a very funny speech. There was also an avalanche of telegrams and letters, some of which were read by a very nervous Elijah, whose hands were visibly shaking. Ada's brother Jack also provided great entertainment with his lively dancing with Ada's friend, Pauline Serry.

After the traditional cutting of the elaborate, multi-tiered wedding cake, it was time for Ada and me to take our leave. We went to a room reserved for us to change from our formal wedding attire. I put on a newly tailored suit and Ada changed into a beautiful 'going away' outfit featuring a fashionable pillbox hat, à la Jackie Kennedy. When we returned to the party, our parents and all the guests formed a large circle and, to very lively music, we went around thanking them for celebrating the occasion with us. For our parents, it was an emotional moment that symbolised the fact that we were leaving our family homes.

After the last goodbyes, my closest friends, Sasha and Ian, picked me up onto their shoulders and carried me out, with Ada in tow pleading with them not to drop me. They had retrieved our Simca from the garage and tied a 'just married' sign and empty cans to the rear bumper bar. We drove off to the sounds of clapping, *mazal tovs* and the loud rattling of the cans.

Our destination was the Park Royal Motor Inn in Parkville, recently built by Irvin Rockman, the young scion of a leading Jewish business family.[45] Our lavishly appointed, teak-panelled suite featured Japanese wallpaper and stylish, contemporary furniture, including ceramic ashtrays designed by the noted potter, Guy Boyd. Ada loved the room so much; she was reluctant to leave after only one night.

---

[44] It was one of the first weddings filmed in full colour, but unfortunately there was no soundtrack and we did not think of recording the speeches. The film has since been transcribed to DVD.

[45] Irvin Rockman was to become a leading hotelier and businessman and the lord mayor of Melbourne. His family operated a very successful chain of clothing stores, which they sold before diversifying into real estate and the rapidly emerging travel business. Apparently, Irvin and a friend, Jessel Rothfield, travelled throughout the United States, staying at every upmarket motel and they incorporated all the latest trends into the Park Royal Motor Inn.

My bucks night at Sasha's house

Kissing Ada on the way to the reception

Above: Our bridal party
Below: With our proud parents

Above: The Moshinsky men
Below: With Grandmother

Being carried by Ian & Sasha

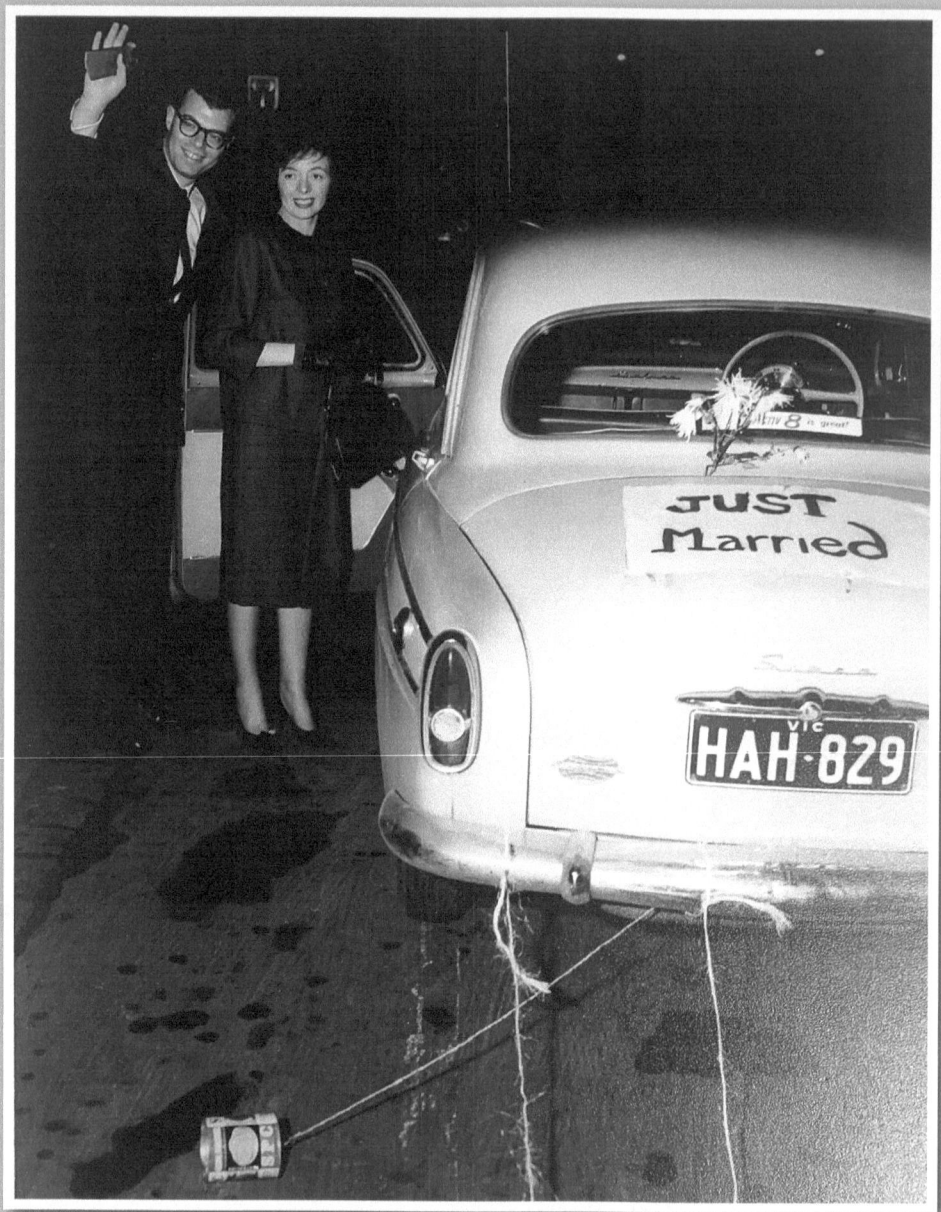

Just married

Our honeymoon plan was to slowly make our way, by car, to Sydney, where we aimed to live while I worked on an MMA study at the NSW department store, Farmers. As it was winter, we decided to head to snow country—Kosciusko, New South Wales. Although neither of us were skiers, we had heard of a beautiful new hotel there named The Man From Snowy River. It was an easy drive to Cooma, but as we got closer to Tumut we realised that the roads shown on the map had not been finished. In fact, bulldozers were still completing paths and, as it had rained heavily the previous night, the way to Kosciuszko looked like an impassable swamp. We sat in a long line of cars for several hours before finally receiving the go ahead to inch our way forward. At dusk we could finally see the welcoming lights of Kosciuszko and we eventually found our way to our hotel in Perisher.

It was a magnificent hotel.[46] The glass entrance glowed from the open fireplace that guests sat around whilst looking out onto the snow. Perhaps because it was a ski lodge, our room was small and had single bunk beds, rather than the double bed we had expected. We headed straight to the noisy bar and ordered the house specialty, an Italian drink called Fiori Alpini, served with the alcohol still flaming. At dinner, we were seated with another couple from Melbourne, also on their honeymoon. They asked what part of Melbourne we were from and laughed when I said that Ada was from Kew and I was from Camberwell. I explained we had both been living with our parents and were yet to move in together. After dinner we returned to our room and squeezed onto the bottom bunk.

We spent the next six glorious days walking, building snowmen and taking photos. We befriended other holiday makers over meals at the hotel, and each night we indulged in our favourite new cocktail.

In Canberra we stayed at the luxurious Rex Hotel. We had a spacious room with a generous balcony, and we enjoyed the silver service breakfast, which was wheeled in on a trolley that converted into a table.[47] In the 10 years since I had last been there, Canberra had grown to achieve the vision of its founding architect, Walter Burley Griffin.

---

[46] Regrettably, it was burnt down some years later.
[47] In all our years of travelling and staying in luxurious hotels, nothing surpassed the Rex Hotel.

New architecturally appealing buildings had been erected, as well as several modern sculptures. Ada was interested in modern art, and we took numerous photos with my Minolta camera. We also did some filming with the 8mm Bell & Howell movie camera that my father had bought for me on his trip from Shanghai to America way back in 1947. I took Ada to Parliament House, where Sasha and I had seen the prime minister, Robert Menzies, announce the death of King George VI and the accession of Queen Elizabeth II.

In the evenings we dressed up for dinner, enjoyed a pre-dinner drink at the bar and then went to the hotel's elegant dining room. One night, for fun, we decided to go for flambé, so enjoyed steak Diane followed by crêpes Suzette. Both dishes were prepared at the table by the formally attired waiters who set our food alight with flaming brandy.

Our final destination was Sydney. We stayed in a motel in Bondi, which, although comfortable, was not a patch on the Park Royal. We paid a visit to Eva's sister, Nusia Shergoff, and her husband Boris at their new apartment overlooking Bondi Beach. And we continued to take photos of the modern sculptures Ada noticed around the city.

We spent time in Kings Cross, then a fashionable area favoured by Central European Jews. The delicatessens gave the area a cosmopolitan atmosphere that we had not experienced in the Anglo-Saxon suburbs of Camberwell and Kew. We enjoyed strolling along the streets, hand-in-hand, admiring the dress shops and bookshops. We would eat lunch at one of the continental delis and, for dinner, we would indulge in cold cuts, cheeses, Russian salads, pickles and rye bread in our motel room while watching a film on the small black and white TV. If a good movie was scheduled on one of the three channels, it was indeed a treat. Our honeymoon ended on a real high and we were looking forward to spending the next few months in Sydney.

When I rang the Sydney office, there was an ominous message to call Alan Dick in Melbourne. Ada and I were both deeply disappointed to learn that the Farmers job had been delayed and we had no option but to drive directly back to Melbourne. Our immediate concern was where we would live, so Lida got on the job straight away. Fortunately, by the time we returned to Melbourne, she had rented a lovely two-bedroom apartment in an appealing modern block in Glen Street, Hawthorn, and partially furnished it.[48]

We moved in immediately, started unpacking our wedding presents, and shopped for other basic furniture. Ada resumed her law course, and I made an appointment to see Alan Dick at the Melbourne office.

Our block of flats was modern and airy, and we enjoyed getting to know the neighbours. In the well-furnished flat opposite lived two gay men with whom we became quite friendly. Next to our flat lived an elderly widow who was helpful with domestic advice but, unfortunately, she often cooked lamb and I detested the smell. Periodically, Lida would turn up to help us keep the flat in reasonable shape.

Our days would start with the clinking of bottles from the early morning delivery of milk, deposited by the milkman on a ledge by the back door. This ledge also came in handy for storing Gorgonzola, the smelly cheese I was partial to. Most weekdays, I would drive Ada to university and then continue to the western suburb of Brooklyn, where I was working on a consulting assignment at the Farmers & Graziers Direct Meat Supply Company. After work, I would pick up Ada and we'd stop at the Union House cafeteria for a quick meal. We rarely ate at restaurants; our budget was tight as we were saving for a deposit on a house.

On Saturdays we would fill up our Simca with petrol at the local service station owned by Frank Sedgeman, a retired tennis champion, and go for drives. We also joined a record supply company called The World Record Club, which allowed us to purchase records at reduced prices. To mark an anniversary, we lashed out and bought a Harry Belafonte album set of two records that we played over and over. We led an active social life and enjoyed entertaining friends; I would create cocktail concoctions and impress them with my Balkan Sobranie cigarettes.

---

[48] Unbeknownst to Lida, the rent was too high for my income, so Grandmother often gave me money from her pension.

Unfortunately, my father's deteriorating financial situation marred the pleasant routine and rhythm of our early married years. Although he had arrived in Australia with considerable wealth, he was never able to establish a viable business. He embarked on several ventures that ended up losing him quite a bit of money. At one stage Eva part-owned a shop in Camberwell Junction that sold corsets and ladies' underwear, but that too ended badly. Eventually, the capital had totally eroded and the house in Lansell Crescent had to be sold. My parents moved into a rented flat in Carnarvon Road, Caulfield, that was spacious but dated. Father then secured a job as a salesman in the men's shoes department in the main Myer store in Bourke Street. He had a natural talent for sales, and I thought he was happy there, but he found his descent in status galling and, after a few months, he resigned. In his mind, he needed to succeed in his own business to maintain his self-respect.

With their much-reduced capital, my father and Eva bought a doughnut-making franchise in a busy arcade in Chapel Street, Prahran, where they worked together. Ada's brother Jack, who was then a student at Wesley College, used to drop in after school for a doughnut and milkshake. The American-based franchisor required a detailed weekly report, so every Saturday I would go to the store to prepare the reports for posting on Monday. One Saturday, I was in the doughnut shop when my father collapsed. An ambulance took him to the nearby Alfred Hospital where he was diagnosed with a brain haemorrhage and put in intensive care. Somehow, he slowly improved and, after a few weeks, we received the happy news that he would be transferred to a rehabilitation centre.

A day after the transfer, on 16 November 1963, my father had another stroke, and he did not recover. The medical term for his cause of death was subarachnoid haemorrhage. It was a terrible shock. We found it hard to accept that Father would no longer be with us. Naturally, Eva was distraught, so it fell to me to break the news to Grandmother. When she heard the tragic news, she broke down crying. She had lost her husband and now she had lost her only child.

I made the arrangements with the Chevra Kadisha (Jewish burial service) for a Temple Beth Israel burial ceremony at one of the last remaining plots in the Jewish section of the Melbourne General Cemetery in Carlton. A year later, the family organised a suitable tombstone and we had a religious consecration. For several years after that, Nathan and I would accompany Eva on the *yahrzeit* to mark the anniversary of Father's death. By then, Elijah had left for England. We would wipe the tombstone, leave fresh flowers, and place a stone on the grave, the traditional Jewish way of indicating that the gravesite had been visited. Finally, Nathan and I would recite the *kaddish*, the customary prayer for the deceased.

I think of my father often, and regret that he died such a disappointed man. I am certain that resettling in Australia, where he no longer had an established business or extensive communal support, was a critical factor. It weighed heavily on him that he had lost a substantial amount of the money he inherited, through unsuccessful business ventures. For me, the most upsetting part of him dying at the young age of 59 is that he was robbed of the opportunity to witness the personal and professional success of his three sons— including Nathan's career as a Queen's Counsel and Elijah's phenomenal rise as an internationally acclaimed opera director. It also saddens me that he never got to meet any of his grandchildren. I take solace in knowing that at least he lived long enough to get to know Ada and to celebrate our marriage.

Arthur Andersen Australia

W hen I had returned to the Melbourne office in 1962 after 18 months away, I had naturally been curious to see what had changed since the firm merged with Arthur Andersen. The office was still on the fifth floor of Western House, on the northwest corner of Collins and William Streets, but the gracious old building on the opposite corner had been demolished to make way for a multi-storey building. One of its floors had been leased to the firm for the administrative services (consulting) division, over which Alan Dick presided. William Street was a hive of building activity, with soulless glass towers replacing the solid buildings of a bygone era.

It was apparent that most of the major firms had gone the way of Fuller King and become the Australian outposts of the then 'big eight' international accounting firms.[49] Gone, also, were the milk bars and sandwich shops I had previously frequented. They had made way for more salubrious eating establishments, as the practice of eating a sandwich at one's desk at lunchtime had become passé.

Some things stubbornly resisted the passage of time. As soon as I entered the familiar portals, I was greeted by the same receptionist who said, "Good, now that you are back, could you please take over the changing of the partners' towels. It hasn't been the same since you left!" Mabel Cooper, the office manager, was nearby and fortunately intervened to save me the trouble.

The partners were still ensconced in their separate section and continued to enjoy their time-honoured privileges. I was particularly keen to see Rex Prime, my old manager in the secretarial and accounting section. He had visibly aged and was contemplating imminent retirement, as he sensed that his section didn't fit into the

---

[49] These firms have since been further consolidated into four 'mega' firms.

new direction of the firm and would soon be disbanded. He proved to be right. Following Rex's departure, the work performed by his section was discontinued at the firm, which I thought was a pity as it had provided an excellent training ground for learning basic principles of accounting. In later years, when I supervised newly recruited university graduates, I formed the view that they often failed to grasp basic accounting principles because of this lack of practical experience.

My first day back, I went to see Alan Dick, who now headed an expanding consulting practice. Although a good proportion of his work still came from Ken Little's receivership practice, the consulting work was beginning to evolve in accordance with the Andersen philosophy. But first the audit personnel would have to be trained to recognise when their clients could benefit from system analysis. There was also a way to go in terms of building an atmosphere of trust, and improving communication between audit personnel and colleagues in other departments.

The reports the partners had received about me from Chicago were positive, and Alan told me that I could look forward to a bright future with the firm. He said that I would soon be formally joining the administrative services team, comprising of Americans and Australians. I would be working on a substantial project, which was still being negotiated. However, initially, the partners were keen for me to impart the practical experience I had gained at Marshall Field's. A major review of the audit program of Myer Emporium Limited, the Melbourne office's largest client, was underway and everyone was looking forward to hearing about the specialist merchandising focus of the Chicago office. I would be working directly with Wal Castles, a highly respected audit manager. I was pleased to hear that I was designated an S3 ranking, a senior of the highest level, just below manager. With this came a commensurate increase in salary, which was very welcome.

I was pleased to discover that most of my old colleagues were still at the firm. Betty Cunning was still in charge of the typing pool and welcomed me back warmly, as did Lois Richards who was secretary to several of the senior partners. I caught up with Bill Charlton and had a good meeting with Reg Waddell, during which we reminisced about my initial interview. I thanked him for giving me that first chance and for his advice regarding my studies, and he reminded me that, in addition to my commerce degree, I had to study several more subjects to become a member of the Institute of Chartered Accountants as an associate. In those days, a fellowship at the institute, the highest membership ranking, was reserved for partners of firms of chartered accountants.

Returning to Myer as a senior in charge of the audit was a satisfying improvement on the mundane tasks I had been assigned in my early days. In fact, under the Andersen approach, many of those mind-numbing procedures had become obsolete. Wal Castles was a true gentleman and working with him was a delight. Wal had extensive experience as an auditor but did not resent the changes I suggested to align Fuller King's traditional practices with the Andersen ones. It was a very satisfying working relationship.

We heard that the Myer management was unhappy with the performance of the appliance section, one of the major departments in the Bourke Street store. The problem stemmed from the existence of 'resale price maintenance', whereby the supplier could legally dictate the price at which the retailers were permitted to sell big ticket household appliances (refrigerators, kitchen stoves and ovens) as well as the newly available black and white television sets. This, of course, compromised Myer's competitive edge. The most popular way around this limitation was to invite trade-ins for unwanted items, at prices far exceeding their normal values. The loss to the retailer, on reselling these items, either in store or through the trade, effectively represented the prohibited discount on the new merchandise.

We undertook a detailed analysis of the major cost components, in addition to the outrageous trade-ins offered. Our analysis included a breakdown of the advertising expenditure on individual products and delivery costs. This took many hours of clerical research. Through sheer perseverance, we were able to clearly demonstrate that profits would improve by dropping several product lines. The philosophical issue for the Myer management was how to maintain its image as a 'universal provider' with a wide range of products. Our response was that they should keep the unprofitable items in stock but not spend money on promoting them.

At the conclusion of the Myer project, Alan Dick called me to his office to discuss my future with the firm. He said that after extensive negotiations, he could now reveal the details of a new project. The clients were Felt & Textiles Ltd, Australia's largest manufacturer of carpets, in association with Myer in Melbourne, and Farmers, the prominent department store in Sydney. I would play a leading part in the team, which would be overseen by John Boyle, an American partner from the merchandising industry competence team in Chicago. The objective was to study the profitability of existing distribution arrangements of carpets sold by these stores. Australia was experiencing a period of rapid economic growth, which led to a boom in the construction of carpeted residences. Department stores, with their extensive furniture and homewares divisions, were the natural distributors of carpets but it was necessary to maximise the efficient use of space on the shop floor and carpet sales required large areas.

After detailed discussions with the Felt & Textile people, and surveying the operations of Myer's floor coverings department, as it was called, John Boyle—or Jack, as he preferred to be called—set out a detailed workplan for the analysis of the relevant data. My main task was to access Myer's records and direct the small army of personnel, drawn from both Myer and Arthur Andersen. We were provided with generous space on the seventh floor of the Lonsdale Street building. To Jack's frustration, the record keeping did not suit analysis. For example, detailed data was not pre-sorted, and advertising costs were aggregated and not allocated to product categories.

Jack Boyle was a mid-westerner who had never been outside the United States. Like most of the young American Andersen partners, he possessed a high work and success-oriented ethic. No doubt, he also wanted to get the job done and go home as soon as possible. The problem was that he expected everyone to emulate his work hours, which caused some resentment. Also, there were issues with the Myer security guards, who were not used to people leaving the building at 10pm. Through dogged perseverance, we finally put together an analytical report to present to management at Felt & Textile and Myer.

After the Farmers' project in Sydney was cancelled, Alan Dick formally transferred me to his section, where he had several new projects for me to work on. The most memorable project was for the Direct Farmers & Graziers Co-operative Ltd, an abattoir co-operative that aimed to establish a more equitable payment system for livestock. The new 'abattoir weight and grade' system was considered fairer than relying on estimations from specialist livestock buyers at sale yards. Although the idea was sound, and sufficient money was raised to build a modern abattoir, several problems soon emerged including a slow and bureaucratic payment system. Also, the co-operative ownership structure lacked the driving force of private ownership, resulting in operating losses, which was of great concern to the growers. Our challenging assignment was to analyse the issues and recommend solutions. I was the senior in charge, reporting to Bill Weekes, a manager in the consulting division. I mostly worked with Bill Collis, the co-operative's competent and dedicated cost accountant. However, whenever Bill Weekes turned up to review our progress, I found his behaviour strange and unsettling.

Nevertheless, I remember that time fondly. After work, I would meet Ada for a light dinner at Union House on the university campus. The food was average, but we didn't care as we were happy and life seemed full of purpose. After dinner, we would drive home to our flat in Glen Street, Hawthorn, and settle in for the evening. Sometimes we would informally entertain our friends, but often my evenings were spent rewriting Ada's jumbled lecture notes or reading books we borrowed from a small privately-owned library nearby.

My next assignment at work related to the planned conversion of the currency from the pound to a metrified version. The Australian pound, like the British pound sterling, was divided into 20 shillings and each shilling, in turn, was divided into 12 pence. The complexity of the pound/ shilling/pence system was recognised early, and several attempts had been made to decimalise the system. However, it was not until 1963 that the federal treasurer, Harold Holt, announced that the decimal currency system would be introduced in February 1966, with the base unit to be equal to ten shillings. In other words, the pound would be worth two dollars. Initially, Holt announced that the new currency would be called the 'royal' but this was met with widespread disapproval and three months later it was changed to the dollar. The first paper issues of this new currency were issued early in denominations of $1, $2, $10, and $20.[48] At the same time, new coinage was issued in denominations of 1, 2, 5, 10, 20, and 50 cents. The official switchover date was legislated to be 14 February 1966.

To complement the currency decimalisation, it was also decided to introduce the metrification of other measurements, thus abandoning the imperial system, which the Australian colonies had inherited from the United Kingdom. The process would be staggered over several years as different industries had their own unique conversion issues. Prior to the official regulations taking effect, the government embarked upon a major educational campaign to explain these fundamental changes to businesses and the population. This was partly to address a concern held by many retailers, particularly those selling large ticket items like furniture and appliances, as the price of items might appear to have doubled. The firm felt that this should be complemented with 'hand holding' for any clients who might need special assistance. I was asked to take on this role, which I readily accepted. I enjoyed drafting the necessary explanatory pamphlets, running seminars, and helping individual clients with their conversions.

In 1963, the firm moved to 350 Collins Street, a modern office building with the upmarket menswear store, Henry Bucks, on the ground floor. The culture at Fuller King was markedly adapting to the Andersen's approach. Working papers were totally revamped, rating forms introduced, and regular training sessions were held across various

---

[50] A $5 note was issued in 1973 but the $100 note was not issued till 1984.

disciplines. Training sessions were facilitated by the new partner, Ken Keown, a leading academic at RMIT. Also introduced were the formal Andersen rankings for all staff, from partners to assistants.

In May 1964, Alan Dick informed me that, subject to passing a day-long medical examination, I was to be promoted to the position of M1, the lowest of the manager classifications. There were four more levels to attain before being considered for partnership. The new role came with a significant boost to my salary, and I was also entitled to a small office of my own. I received many letters congratulating me on my new position, including several from my former colleagues in Chicago: Walter Oliphant, the firm-wide managing partner who succeeded the legendary Leonard Spacek; Joseph Glickauf, the partner in charge of administrative services; John H. Jones, the developer of MMA; and Jack Boyle, with whom I had worked on the Myer/Felt & Textiles MMA project.

I continued to be involved with several interesting assignments in the administrative services division, mainly in the development of sophisticated management information systems for large organisations with far-flung activities. I recall my introduction to 'critical path analysis', following the hiring of a mathematician to our division, who trained us in its concepts. I also recall a new client called the Tongala Milk Company, which was named after the town in Victoria's dairy district where the factory was located. The business was the subsidiary of a large Swiss-based organisation. Its aim was to break into the condensed milk market, which was dominated by the corporate giant Nestle. The managing director was Werner Brodbeck, a charismatic Swiss German with an impatient and explosive personality. I worked with the cost accountants to set up the production and sales information systems for the business and, each year, Geoff Cohen, the audit partner, and I would stay in Tongala for a few days to complete the auditing.

A year after being appointed manager, I started to question my future in the organisation. The influence of Bill Weekes continued to be destructive, and several of us who were obliged to work with him decided to take our complaints to Alan Dick, who gave us a respectful hearing. I don't know what transpired, but shortly after, Bill Weekes resigned. Disappointingly, Alan Dick also retired from the firm. Rumour had it that friction had developed between him and Ken Keown, who had become an influential figure in the Melbourne office.

I was very sorry to lose Alan as a personal mentor. I had learned much from him, particularly about writing reports. He had high standards regarding written English and succinct prose. Later, I became respected for the standard of my reports, and I attribute that to him.

I started to informally canvas my options and found that accountants with my qualifications and experience were in high demand, particularly at smaller firms wanting to extend their services to management consulting. I spoke to the partners of Wilson, Bishop & Henderson in Queen Street. It was a prestigious organisation with an excellent audit client list, including Carlton & United Breweries (CUB) and T&G Mutual Assurance. The firm was headed by three partners: John Davis, the senior partner, Barry Hutchins and Darvell Hutchinson. We seemed to hit it off and they were keen for me to join them to start and develop the consulting side of the practice. They offered me an equity partnership within 12 months of starting, if all went to plan.

It was a good opportunity and, after 12 years at Fuller King/Arthur Andersen, it seemed like a sensible move. The new job also came with a significant lift in immediate and potential earnings.

I informed Ken Keown of my decision in July 1966. He took it graciously and did not try to dissuade me, which confirmed that I had made the right decision. On 15 July he sent around a kindly worded memorandum to all the personnel at the firm to inform them of my departure.

I was sorry to leave Arthur Andersen. The firm had been good to me. It had given me every opportunity to better myself as I evolved from an apprehensive young man to a confident and mature person, happily married and ready to tackle greater opportunities.

JayCee News

JOURNAL OF THE MELBOURNE JUNIOR CHAMBER OF COMMERCE

Registered at the G.P.O. Melbourne for transmission through the post as a periodical.   Price

66

April

HAPPY TENTH ANNIVERSARY!

This year, the Chamber's Management Training Course will have been run for the tenth consecutive year. For a project as big and as complex as this one, this continuity is an example of Junior Chamber enterprise. Furthermore the high standard originally laid down a decade ago has been maintained and the syllabus updated to keep pace with management trends.

Each year the convenor and his committee were faced with what seemed to them insurmountable challenges in improving the course. And in each year these challenges were met — syllabus, case studies, presentation, venue, organisation, all came under close scrutiny and evaluation. And what seemed at first impossible turned out to be a new breakthrough in project management and organisation.

The course was first conceived and put into effect in 1956 by a committee under the chairmanship of **Max Sandow**, one of the most outstanding vice-presidents and leaders that the Chamber has ever had. In that year Australia had already begun to shed the universal image of a pastoral country and begun to acquire the look and feel of a sophisticated industrial economy. But although the resources and the desire were there, what impeded the rapid progress of this industrial expansion was the shortage of management qualified to cope with the new demands.

Many organisations responded to the challenge by introducing Management Training Courses. However, most of these were high geared, directed at senior managers, and the Melbourne Junior Chamber recognised the need to direct attention at a more intermediate level — at future managers.

The course consists of a combination of lectures, films, syndicate case study discussions, plant visits and a management game. It normally commences in May and extends over some 17 weeks. Its enrolment has been traditionally limited to 48 participants carefully selected from the many applications received as the result of our circularization of business houses. This selectivity based on qualifications and experience of the candidate is essential for the preservation of the high standard of the course as well as ensuring a student body drawn from a wide cross-section of industries and occupations. This year, after ten years of operation we feel confident, at last, in giving more people the opportunity to attend and participate by increasing the enrolment to 60.

The range of subjects covered is all embracing — from communications and organisation, to marketing, production, finance and personnel. This year the new field of data processing will be included in the syllabus and students will be introduced to the exciting world of the computor which is beginning to play such an important role in management.

Active participation by the students is a key objective of the course. To ensure this, students are divided in syndicates — each containing no more than a dozen, thus permitting a meaningful contribution by all. These syndicates under the direction of an experienced chamber member, discuss a number of case studies dealing with organisation, marketing, production and finance. The case study method which was pioneered by Harvard University has become an accepted method of management training at leading business schools, the world over.

An annual favourite with the students is the management game which will be conducted this year at the end of the course. To test the assimilation of the knowledge gained from the course, students are asked to devote a full day in the fascinating process of decision making under realistically simulated conditions.

To cap the course, students, lecturers and other distinguished guests are invited to a banquet which over the years has become one of the social highlights of the chamber year. This year, in recognition of the acceptance that this course has received from the business community it is proposed to award certificates to those who have successfully completed the course.

Despite the continuing rise in costs, the fee will remain unchanged at **$60 or £30**. If you feel you can benefit from such course, why don't you pick up an application form from the Chamber office. Attending the Management Training Course may be your path to success and higher responsibilities.

Sam Moshinsky,
Convenor, 1966 Management Training Course.

Above: A meeting of the Jaycee economics
section, with a guest speaker from Indonesia

Below: With senior Jaycees

A New Era

After Father's death, Eva felt that she could not run the doughnut shop on her own, so we put it on the market. It was a good business in an excellent location, and we quickly found a buyer. With the proceeds and Father's remaining capital, Eva purchased a small house in Wentworth Avenue, Canterbury, for her to live in with Nathan and Elijah.

While life in our flat was pleasant, Ada and I decided to start looking for a house to accommodate what we hoped would be a growing family. We were attracted to North Balwyn, which was close to our parents and where some of our friends had recently settled. Another advantage was the proximity to the eastern suburbs congregation of Temple Beth Israel, in which I had become involved, including several years volunteering as honorary auditor. After some searching, we settled on a house at 26 Macedon Avenue, North Balwyn, on a sloping street leading from a small group of shops in Doncaster Road called The Village. It was a two-bedroom house with a study at the rear looking over the backyard. The attractive front garden had been lovingly looked after by the owner. Ada had promised she would look after it, which she faithfully did, and in so doing developed a lasting interest in gardening.

It was an affordable purchase for us. To pay the deposit, I sold my investment in the terrace house in Gourlay Street, St Kilda, for a good profit. For the loan balance, Ada's father introduced me to his bank manager, Ron Horne, at the Kew branch of ANZ. The loan was approved, and we moved into our new home over the 1963/1964 summer holidays.

Our first house

Ada completed her law degree in November 1963. Her formal graduation at the University of Melbourne's stately Wilson Hall in March 1964 was a joyous family event. I took great pleasure sharing the details with Grandmother, and I thanked her for her sage advice that Ada should persevere with her studies.

Following her graduation, Ada needed to work for 12 months as an articled clerk at a law firm before being admitted to practice. Finding articles at a reputable law firm was extremely difficult, particularly without personal contacts. Luckily, I remembered that Maurice Cohen had said he owed me a favour for meeting and recommending Henry Shaw at Hillel House in London. Maurice readily arranged for Ada to be interviewed by his partners. When Maurice rang several weeks later, he asked "How are you?", to which Ada replied, "It depends on what you are going to tell me!" He advised that he was formally offering her the position of articled clerk at Maurice Cohen, Jowett & Co.

Earlier, in April of that year, Jack had celebrated his bar mitzvah at the Temple. After our wedding, the Gringlas family had decided to move from the Kew synagogue and become members of Temple Beth Israel, so that on the High Holidays we could all worship together. The bar mitzvah function was held at the popular Southern Cross Hotel. It was a lavish affair and a most joyous occasion.

Our house needed renovating, but our tight budget meant some work had to be deferred. Ada was particularly annoyed by the picture railings on the walls, which were in fashion when the house was built. We decided to tackle their removal ourselves, starting with the second bedroom, which was going to be the nursery. It turned out to be a larger and more complicated task than we had anticipated. When we pulled off the railings, a gap in the wall plaster was revealed. I can still recall the two of us, awash in plaster and water, trying to rectify the situation as we listened on the radio to the rapturous welcome The Beatles received on their first visit to Melbourne. After that, I decided to call in the professionals for all future renovations; but that did not stop Ada from continuing to try to do things herself.

In December, our local general practitioner, Dr Alan Griffiths, confirmed that Ada was pregnant. Our baby was due mid-August 1965 and the doctor arranged for the delivery to take place at the Jessie McPherson Women's Hospital in Lonsdale Street. Ada soon gave up her prenatal classes because she kept falling asleep when one of the exercises required resting on the floor.

As our financial position gradually improved, we started to furnish the house. Because stores were only open till midday on Saturdays and closed on Sundays, it was rare for us to find a whole day to go shopping. However, for some reason, only professional firms observed Easter Tuesday, which meant we had the day off while the shops remained open. That year we bought a television at the Easter sales, but deferred shopping for baby necessities.

In March, Ada completed her year of articles and applied to be formally admitted as a Barrister and Solicitor in the State of Victoria. The admission ceremony was a session of the Supreme Court of Victoria, presided over by the chief justice. When "Mr Moshinsky" was called, Ada stood up, visibly pregnant, and everyone in court laughed. His Honour quickly said, "I could be right!" And it turned out he was.

Our first baby boy was born on 12 August 1965, exactly four years since the day we met. During the birth, I sat on a bench in the hospital corridor smoking my Camel cigarettes while our GP delivered the baby. How different things were back then!

I was told that I could see Ada in her private room and found her well but impatient as to my whereabouts. I was then given a card with 'Baby Moshinsky' written on it and led to the viewing room. After I pressed the card against the window, a nurse brought out a little bundle in swaddling clothes. After admiring the scene for a few minutes, I returned to Ada before calling the family to inform them of the baby's birth and that all was well. Later that day I returned to work, before rushing to the Montefiore Homes to impart the good news to Grandmother. I promised that I would bring the baby for her to hold, which I soon did. The photograph of that occasion is one of my most treasured possessions.

I had hoped that our firstborn would be a boy. It must have been my upbringing in Shanghai, as the Chinese prized male offspring. We named him Mark Stuart Moshinsky and gave him my grandfather's Hebrew name, Shlomo, which pleased my grandmother.[51] Because hospital stays were longer back then, the circumcision took place in hospital. Ada was adamant that Dr Griffiths be present while the *mohel* recommended by Temple performed the religious rites. Fortunately, all went well and, a day later, I picked up Ada and Mark and drove them home.

Ada had started a sole legal practice from home after her admission, and it did not take her long to become quite busy. One of my friends in the accounting profession was Jack Rezak, who ran a very successful practice in the city. He referred work to her, much of it involving taxation law and the setting up of legal structures. Jack particularly appreciated Ada's fast and efficient service and they developed a very good professional relationship. In fact, as she was being wheeled into the maternity ward, Ada called out, "Make sure that there is a telephone in my room." The first large flower arrangement to arrive at the hospital was from Jack, with a note that read: "Hope you're back at work soon."

We soon settled into a new routine. Once or twice a night, I would get up and bring Mark to Ada for feeding. As it was winter and very cold, I would get up early, and stoke up the briquette heater in the lounge. I would then take the tram to work, leaving Ada with the Simca. In those days, unbelievably by current standards, we would just pop Mark in a basket, which we placed on the back seat. We would regularly go out for dinner to a new steak restaurant called Gregory's in Smith Street, Collingwood. I would take the tram from the city and Ada would meet me there. Mark slept in the basket,

---

[51] Following Mark's marriage to Sidra Kranz, they decided to change both of their second given names by deed poll to Kranz, to honour her family name.

placed astride two chairs, while we enjoyed our meal. Occasionally, friends who lived nearby would babysit Mark at their house and we would pick him up on the way home. Fortunately, he was always a good sleeper. Drive-in movies were in vogue, and we often frequented the large outdoor cinema on the corner of Toorak and Tooronga Roads. We would find a spot, hook up the speaker to the car, settle Mark, and enjoy films like the newly released *Zorba the Greek*.

We started to entertain at home more regularly, and we hosted parties to mark special events, including Mietek's 50th birthday and Elijah's 21st. We even hosted an art show at our home for a young painter named Stuart Black.

Unfortunately, our first experience at dog ownership failed. Our dog was so boisterous that we had to give him to Jane Permezel's father for use on his farm in Molong.

Ada's graduation

Grandmother holding Mark

Watershed Moment

O n Sunday 31 July 1966, Grandmother died after several months of deteriorating health, during which I visited her on an almost daily basis. That day, we were visiting our friends, Dario and Annette Zoureff, at their home in Glen Waverley. I received an urgent call on their landline to advise that Grandmother was failing fast. Ada drove me to Montefiore Homes and went home with Mark. I was grateful that I was able to be with Grandmother in her final hours, although I was unsure whether she was conscious of my presence.

Grandmother's death was a watershed moment in my life. Since my parents' divorce in Shanghai when I was four years old, she was always there for me, and I grew up knowing that I was a very special person in her life. Looking back, I felt sorry for the pain my grandmother had endured: the loss of my grandfather, whom she loved and admired, and her many years of widowhood; her descent from a wealthy lifestyle in Vladivostok and Shanghai to a humble life in Melbourne, plagued by financial issues; and the death of her son. I took comfort in the fact that she lived long enough to see me on the road to success as a professional, married to a woman she very much approved of, and that she had held Mark in her arms.

Grandmother's sayings and admonitions, which guided me throughout my life, were many and legendary. To cope with frustrating situations and difficult people, she would tell me, "Let it pass through your soul. Don't let them lodge in you and destroy you." Before I left Shanghai on my own, back in 1951, she drew me aside and said, "You will come across many people. Remember that everybody is like an iceberg. What you see is only the surface 10 percent. The rest is hidden, which could be dangerous. Beware!" The advice I value most is what Grandmother

shared about the three most important decisions in life: who you marry, who your friends are, and who you work with.

Grandmother had never been comfortable at Temple, so I decided to respect her feelings by arranging an Orthodox Jewish funeral. I asked the rabbi at Montefiore Homes to conduct a traditional service and arranged for her to be buried in the relatively new cemetery in Springvale, run by the Chevra Kadisha. It was also a way to honour my grandfather who had been an active supporter of the Chevra Kadisha in Shanghai. Grandmother had not only outlived her son, but all her friends as well, so it was a small funeral. Nathan, Elijah and I recited the *kaddish* at the burial, as I would continue to do every year on the anniversary of her death—her *yahrzeit*—at Temple.

My grandmother's death took a toll on my nerves and Ada felt we should enjoy our first family holiday before I started at the new firm. Fortuitously, I noticed a newspaper advertisement placed by the Italian Lloyd Triestino cruising company regarding availability on the relatively new liner *S.S. Guglielmo Marconi*. The ship's route was from Naples to Australia and back again, and there were cabins available on the Melbourne to Sydney and back to Melbourne leg of the journey. The trip included four days docked in Sydney, sleeping on board. The duration and timing were ideal, and we were excited at the prospect of celebrating Mark's first birthday on the ship.

We were happy with our cabin allocation and the high standard of the cuisine in the tastefully decorated dining room. Ada was particularly appreciative of the Italian waiters' insistence that we try every dessert on offer. The sea voyage to Sydney was smooth and sunny, and everybody doted on Mark. I can still picture the look of surprise on his face as he took his first unaided steps just as the ship started to roll.

On each of the four days that we were moored in Circular Quay, we enjoyed a leisurely breakfast and then put Mark in a stroller and sauntered off the ship. One day, we caught the ferry to Taronga Zoo. We thought Mark would be fascinated by all the animals, but his attention was fixed on the workmen doing road maintenance. Another morning, we went to the top of the newly built AMP office tower to take in the magnificent view of the harbour.

While window shopping in Sydney one day, I noticed the headlines in the morning papers announcing the casualties suffered by the Australian forces in Vietnam, in what became known as the Battle of Long Tan on 18 August 1966. In this confrontation between the 1st Australian Task Force and the Viet Cong, the Australians suffered 18 deaths and 24 wounded.

One evening there was a party on board to celebrate the Sydney premiere of the film *They're a Weird Mob*, based on the popular book of the same name. It's a rollicking comedy about an Italian journalist visiting Australia, in the 1950s, that provides insight into the immigrant experience in Menzies-era Australia. The main character thought he could speak English but was unprepared for the Australian version. The cast party on board was a glamorous occasion, with the stars—Walter Chiari, Claire Dunne and Chips Rafferty—mingling with the prestigious guest list. Selecting an Italian ship for this launch party was inspired, as Lloyd Triestino liners had played an important role in transporting thousands of Italian migrants to Australia.

Having taken on a new complement of passengers, the *Marconi* steamed out of the spectacular Sydney Harbour bound for Melbourne. In my wanders around the ship, I discovered a small museum dedicated to the ship's namesake. I learned that Guglielmo Giovani Marconi was born in Bologna in 1874 and died in Rome in 1937, aged 63. He pioneered a radiotelegraph system and was credited with inventing the radio. Marconi shared the 1909 Nobel Prize in Physics with Karl Ferdinand Braun, in recognition of their contributions to the development of wireless telegraphy.

On our return to Melbourne, we happily settled back into our house and the routine of family life. A few days before I commenced work, Ada paid a visit to Dr Griffiths, who confirmed that she was pregnant again. Our next baby was due early the following year.

The Wilson Bishop & Pannell Kerr Forster Years

In September 1966, I presented myself at the offices of my new employer, Wilson, Bishop & Henderson, at 99 Queen Street. I was welcomed by the three partners and given a tour of the offices before being introduced to several key people including Harry Featherstone, the long serving office manager, a courtly gentleman of the old school. I met Denys Horman, who looked after the medium and small non-audit clients in the secretarial and accounting team, as well as Roy Knight, the manager of one of the largest divisions, which maintained the share registers of listed public companies.

I was introduced around the office as the head of the newly created management consulting division. As I met everyone, I reminded myself of the talk that Joe Glickauf had given us at Andersens in Chicago. He said that our primary marketing targets should always be our professional colleagues and clients. With this in mind, I focused on building constructive relationships with the partners and senior managers at the firm, in the hope they would, over time, refer management consulting work to me.

John Miller, an old friend of Darvell Hutchinson and Barry Hutchins, whom I knew through my involvement with the editorial committee of the Australian Society of Accountants publication, approached me with a novel proposition. He was a partner at Hungerford, Spooner & Kirkhope, the forerunner of the Australian arm of the giant international firm KPMG. John proposed that we create a group of medium-sized firms with management consulting capabilities, and then market this expertise to the clients of smaller firms, with a guarantee that we would not woo their business away from their existing accountants. It was a good idea. The professional accounting scene in the major cities had changed significantly over the years. 'The big eight' had been consolidated down to 'the big four', which serviced more than 90 percent of large public companies and offered an increasing range of ancillary services. The aggression and domination of the big firms was such that smaller firms were reluctant to approach them for special services for fear of losing their client base. John Miller had recognised there was a gap in the market and an opportunity to be seized.

Several meetings later, we had created a group of accountants from smaller firms with management consulting expertise. We laid down the ground rules and we started marketing our services. It did not take long for me to receive an enquiry from an accountant named Bob Johnstone, who had been at Fuller King with me. He was now in partnership with Ian Sinclair, and their client, Diamond Cut Lingerie, needed an efficient sales analysis system involving electronic data processing methods. I agreed to take on the assignment and guaranteed I would not pursue the client at the conclusion of the project.

Diamond Cut Lingerie was based in Smith Street, Collingwood. It was owned by Les Eisenberg who knew of me through my community involvement. He greeted me warmly before introducing me to Les Erdi, his chief sales representative.[52] The assignment involved devising an acceptable coding structure and the supervision of a tendering process to several service bureaus that could process coded data. I suggested that we approach: IBM; ICL, a leading British computer company; and EDP Australia, a smaller, Melbourne-based bureau. My firm had a good working relationship with EDP Australia, which ran a share registry for its publicly listed clients.[53] However, I did not know, nor expect, that several partners at our firm had significant ownership interests in that business. This would become the cause of great embarrassment for me.

The quote from EDP Australia was the lowest, and I saw no reason not to recommend to Mr Eisenberg that it be awarded the data processing contract. I advised IBM and ICL accordingly. The rest of the assignment was going well, and my client seemed pleased.

---

[52] Mr Erdi became a wealthy and generous donor in the Jewish and general community.

[53] Large, specialised companies now operate share registries. At the time, because of the increasing volume of business, the traditional manual handling gave way to computerised methods, but it still wasn't economical to justify the dedicated ownership of mainframe computers.

On 31 January 1967, we were thrilled when Ada gave birth to our second son, Randall, at the newly built St. Andrew's Maternity Hospital in East Melbourne. Our GP, Dr Griffiths, once again performed the delivery. For a middle name we gave him the Hebrew name Aron after Lida's father.[54] I brought Ada her legal files so that she could continue to provide prompt legal service from her hospital bed, and I took leave from work to look after Mark.

A few days later, whilst I was at home with Mark, I received a message from my office to urgently ring Les Eisenberg. When I returned the call, he sounded furious. I asked Eva to babysit while I quickly drove to Collingwood to sort out what had happened. It turned out that the managers at IBM, upset to have missed out on the project, had discovered that the partners at my firm had a financial interest in EDP Australia. They had told Mr Eisenberg, who felt genuinely betrayed that I had failed to disclose the conflict of interest. I expressed my regret and explained that I had been in the dark about the financial relationship. I apologised for not having had a candid conversation with the partners about the arrangement and agreed there was a need for transparency going forward.

I also convinced Mr Eisenberg that there had been no loss or damage to his business, and I assured him that I would personally supervise every aspect of the assignment. In time, the work was completed to his full satisfaction, and Mr Eisenberg harboured no grievances. Whenever I saw him at community events, he was always friendly.

Thankfully, this episode did not prevent me from having a good working relationship with Bernie Taylor, the managing director at EDP, and his senior team. I was also relieved that this incident did not undermine my credibility with our consortium of consulting firms.

Another time I was tasked with unravelling issues involving IBM was for Sam Webb, who owned a successful business importing giftware. Eager to keep accurate track of his sales and inventory, Sam had purchased a large IBM computer system. Initially, IBM sold its computer hardware with its own software as part of a bundled package deal. However,

---

[54] Ada was named after the wife of Lida's beloved brother, Abram Biderman.

American anti-monopoly laws ruled that this practice infringed consumer rights, so the practice was changed to allow consumers to purchase software elsewhere. However, when issues arose, as they did in Sam Webb's case, a blame game would commence about whether the problem was a fault in the hardware or the software. Consulting companies then needed to be engaged to identity the problem, determine which business was responsible for the issue, and devise a solution. I eventually solved Sam Webb's problem regarding who was to blame for the lack of appropriate specifications in his computer system. Sam and I enjoyed a good working relationship for many years after the successful conclusion of that assignment.[55]

The new management consulting initiative was gaining traction and the fees earned were increasing. Every project generated new work and my reputation within the firm was growing. I started to give serious thought to recruiting someone to assist me, as it was getting difficult for me to handle the flow of work.

In April, John Davis advised me that the partners were all very satisfied with the progress of the consulting division and that I had created a favourable impression. Accordingly, he was pleased to confirm that I would be admitted as a partner of the firm from I July 1967. Denys Horman, a long-term senior manager, would also be admitted as a partner on that date. I thanked John for the trust shown in me.

Thus began the next stage of my professional career, which would last 17 years. Over that period, several remarkable transformations took place—mostly due to the vision of Darvell Hutchinson and Barry Hutchins—which beneficially affected the development of the management consulting division, as well as me personally.

In 1967, Wilson Bishop & Henderson was a Melbourne-centric organisation with loose affiliations to several interstate firms. The largest of these was an established and well-respected firm called Bowes & Craig, which was based in Sydney but also had an office in Brisbane. In keeping with the emerging national focus of Australian businesses and the professional organisations that serviced them, the partners of

---

[55] Multi-generational friendships have developed between members of the extended Webb and Moshinsky families. The connection continued when my daughter-in-law, Romy Moshinsky, co-wrote and published Sam's fascinating memoir *Being Bold* in 2015.

the two firms decided to merge under the name Wilson, Bishop, Bowes & Craig.

An affiliation arrangement was made soon after with an Adelaide firm, Whitbread & Company, whose senior partner, Mel Whitbread, was a longstanding friend of Darvell and Barry. Whitbread & Company, which also had an office in Alice Springs, did not have a management consulting division.

Over time, I gained the confidence of the partners, who referred me to some of their other clients, including a notable Indigenous organisation, funded by the federal government, which was tasked with warehousing supplies for several settlements. The organisation had been set up in haste and without adequate training for its Indigenous workforce. In addition, its administrative and accounting systems were inappropriate. My trip to Alice Springs revealed to me the cultural chasm between white Australians and the Indigenous population, which reminded me of colonial Shanghai. This was particularly evident in the conversations I overheard in the white-only clubs where we would congregate after work.

Another memorable aspect of the trip to Alice Springs was that I took Mark, who had recently turned 10, with me. During the days, when I was occupied at the office, the partners organised tours for him to Kata Tjuta and other places of interest. During one of these trips, Mark met a young Jewish couple from Canada, and, to our amazement, he invited them to our home in Melbourne for a Friday night dinner. Ada and I were proud of the way he handled himself when they took him up on the offer and joined us for Shabbat.

Another expansionary development for the firm was the merger, or rather, acquisition, of a small firm of chartered accountants called Davies, Boldeman & Company. Back then, several public companies had joint auditors to certify their accounts. One such company was North Broken Hill Ltd. Our firm shared the audit of this company with Davies, Boldeman. When we heard that several partners were approaching retirement age, we offered a partnership to Ken Flannery[56], the youngest

---

[56] Father of acclaimed environmentalist Tim Flannery.

of the three partners, and a limited consultancy role to the other two. This move locked in our firm as the sole auditors of North Broken Hill. I got on well with Ken and we travelled to Broken Hill together to review the company's procedures. This involved travelling down the shafts with the miners, which was a little different to my usual consulting work.

The next major development was a merger with Cleveland, Scott & Hislop. That firm had six partners, including Albert Shergold and his son, John, who had recently married Shelley Davis, the daughter of our senior partner, John Davis. I presume conversations at family dining tables led to the merger, which could not have come at a more opportune moment.

For some time, our firm had been experiencing cash flow issues, inhibiting further expansion. A major reason was the share registry division, the operations and expansion of which required significant upfront cash resources. Its manager, Roy Knight, was ambitious and was keen to secure new clients. Furthermore, the payment of outstanding fees across the firm was not as energetically pursued as necessary, which was impacting the monthly draws to the partners.

The Cleveland Scott & Hislop firm, though not as large as us, had a very strong cash flow, accompanying its profitability. This was primarily due to its unusual arrangement with one large client, Brick & Pipe Industries, a leading manufacturer and supplier of bricks and clay-based products to the building industry. It was a listed public company that was popular with the investing public. Early in its history, Albert Shergold was instrumental in transforming this struggling client into the large and successful enterprise it had become. He parlayed this success by getting the board to agree to a unique arrangement whereby Cleveland, Scott & Hislop had the contract to manage the company. This arrangement ensured the firm enjoyed a strong cash flow from its services, however there was a question as to whether this could be sustained over the long term. And while the firm's four other partners—David Petley, Brian Vance, Ken Scott and Keith Gouldthorpe—had a respectable client list, a merger would ensure a sensible diversification from its more limited future prospects. The partners were prepared to adopt the Wilson, Bishop, Bowes & Craig name for the combined firm.

I developed a close relationship with one of the new partners, David Petley. He was a keen yachtsman and a senior member of the Royal Brighton Yacht Club. Shortly after the merger, I developed an interest in sailing and, for a while, owned a yacht, which I would sail with my sons and friends from St Kilda. David was keen to nurture this interest and invited me to join his exclusive club, as well as the races he participated in on Saturday afternoons. I recall marvelling at the change in him when he skippered a yacht during races; the mild-mannered gentleman from work turned into a commanding presence when in charge of the yacht's tiller.

Within a relatively short time, the firm of three partners that I had joined, had ballooned to a firm of 12, and become a significant player in the Australian public accounting profession. Moves were also made to strengthen the national framework in parts of Australia where gaps still existed. At its peak, Wilson, Bishop, Bowes & Craig was a national organisation of some 50 partners across all capital cities and major regional centres. A delicate balance was required to project a national brand while retaining the individual ownership of practices.[57] Darvell Hutchinson played a major part in creating this national firm, adding new organisations, preserving financial independence, and ensuring a common philosophy of professional standards. To enhance its corporate identity, he organised several national gatherings of partners in various parts of Australia.

I was a major beneficiary of the significant expansion of the firm as I was the only partner who could provide the appropriate management consulting expertise. In addition, I became active on the speaker circuit of organisations such as the Australian Institute of Management.

After one presentation in Bowral, NSW, the general manager of Metal Manufactures Ltd., one of the country's largest engineering companies, approached me for assistance in improving its management reporting system. This involved travelling to Port Kembla, where I was taken on

---

[57] In contrast, some of the other national players opted for a legal national partnership structure.

a tour of the huge sprawling plant and met the executive team.[58] After reviewing its processes, I detected a conversion issue in the reporting of the copper piping manufacturing system, the mainstay of the business. A conversion issue arises when material is purchased in one medium and the output is sold in another. In the case of Metal Manufactures, raw copper was purchased in tonnes, but the finished copper wire was sold by length. When the standard conversion factor is incorrect, discrepancies arise and, over time, I developed expertise in identifying conversion issues in reporting. It was a prestigious assignment lasting nearly six months and, apart from earning a good fee, it won me much respect among the partners.

I was also approached by Albert Speck, who ran a business school called A. E. Speck & Associates, to lecture at the Chartered Secretaries Institute, which was geared to company secretaries and senior financial executives. This turned out to be a good source of referral work. I also met the institute's longstanding chairman, Vic Gole, a respected author of textbooks. He and I struck up a good rapport and, as he was well connected, he too became a good source of referrals.

Not all projects were strictly in the management consulting field, but they helped grow my developing network. An early, notable client was my friend Keith Beville, with whom I had studied at university (and who later worked with me at the United Israel Appeal). Keith's business, Bevilles, a well-known jewellery and gift store in Bourke Street, was expanding into a chain of stores. After I was admitted as a partner, Keith shifted his audit business to the firm and asked me to be closely involved as a consultant and confidant. It was a great arrangement, and we developed a close professional bond over that period. Ada and I also forged an enduring friendship with Keith and his wife Deirdre. Keith demanded prompt professional attention but always paid the professional fees on time and, when we were experiencing cash flow problems, he even agreed to pay our fees ahead of time to help us out. Bevilles was also a fantastic store for purchasing gifts, and Keith ensured that Ada and I were well assisted with selection and gift-wrapping, especially in the lead up to Christmas.

---

[58] The relevant union was so powerful that, as a consultant, I had to be smuggled onto the premises.

When it became known that I had become a partner in one of the traditionally Anglo-Saxon firms, more work began to flow in from the Jewish community. One day, I was attending a meeting of the executives of the United Israel Appeal when I received an urgent call from Nathan Jacobson, a communal leader who was the senior partner at the law firm Jacobson, Chamberlain & Casen. One of his clients, Morry Majtlis, a successful developer of residential homes, was publicly listing his company Monmia Developments. He was happy with his existing accountants and auditors, a medium-sized Jewish firm with an excellent reputation, however the underwriting brokers were insisting that, upon listing, a well-known city-based firm be named as the auditors and investigating accountants in the prospectus. Securing a newly listed public company was a coup for the firm and for me personally.

It would be hard to conceive of two more different people than Morry Majtlis and me. I vividly recall our first meeting at the offices of Monmia Developments in Elsternwick. Morry was a successful, streetwise entrepreneur, while I was the classic conservative accountant. Born in 1920 in the Polish town of Wolbron, he was the only member of his large family to survive the Holocaust. Morry told me that even in the hopeless postwar displaced persons (DP) camps in Europe, he had the sagacity to establish a thriving business, trading in textiles. After deciding that, "you do not make a future in a graveyard," Morry and his young wife, Mania, moved to Australia, where they had children, and he created another successful business. Despite our differences, we hit it off and maintained contact for many years after Monmia Developments was taken over by L.J. Hooker Ltd, and our professional association came to an end.

I learnt a lot from listening to Morry. He had an innate sense for real estate opportunities and continued to be very successful in the developments he was permitted to undertake after selling Monmia. We would regularly meet for a leisurely lunch at Lazar, a popular city restaurant in a beautiful bluestone building. I appreciated his perceptiveness and ability to quickly find the nub of complex issues, and he valued my straightforward and commonsense approach, particularly regarding family issues.

Another unusual relationship I developed through the firm was with George Schnabl, the managing director of a textile mill called John Foster & Son, a majority-owned subsidiary of a large Yorkshire-based weaving mill. The substantial minority interest was held by the Schutt Trust, one of several large trusts whose trustees were the three original partners of our firm. Today, these professional links could be considered conflicts of interest, but back then they were looked upon as strong captive sources of fees. John Davis, from our firm, was a board member of John Foster and the monthly board meetings were held in the boardroom of our firm. John was contemplating retirement, so he asked me to attend as an observer, with a view to me taking over his board role in the future.

George Schnabl was an incongruous element in this very Anglo-Saxon and patrician board of directors. He was of Czech origin and spoke with a strong accent. He was married to Dorothy, a friendly woman who had a passion for gardening, and they lived in a comfortable home in Park Orchards, a semi-rural outer suburb of Melbourne. I initially suspected that George was Jewish, but this aspect of his heritage did not surface until later. He reminded me of Grisha Sklovsky and his European friends; although they did not deny their Jewish origins, neither did they identify with the organised Jewish community. Judaism had caused them grief in the past and they sought to put some distance between their religion and their lives, yet their ethnic and cultural origins never deserted them. Like Grisha, over time, George became comfortable discussing his Jewish origins with me.

George's expertise in textiles and weaving yarn design was legendary, and the key to the success of the Australian business. He had recently developed a yarn, made from natural wool, which could be woven into a lightweight fabric, ideally suited to the warm Australian climate and popular with those who disliked wearing suits made from synthetic material. Melbourne's largest manufacturers of yarn, Cleckheaton

(Yorkshire) Ltd, a public company (controlled by Fred James, one of the shrewdest businessmen in an industry full of very shrewd people) was contracted to produce this yarn and Fletcher Jones & Staff, then Australia's most successful producer of menswear, was contracted to manufacture the suits.

I soon discovered that John Foster & Son was devoid of even the most rudimentary accounting and costing system. Although his title was managing director, George openly admitted his lack of knowledge in these aspects of business management. My initial role, therefore, was to implement a significant upgrade of the management accounting system. In effect, I assumed the role of finance director, which involved regularly spending time at the company's premises and working closely with George to understand the financial and management needs of the business. Later, I also allocated one of my recruits, Joe Foley, a competent and dogged accountant, to assist me in the implementation of the new systems. Thus began a long, enjoyable and educational association with George Schnabel, who appreciated my interest and dedication. My involvement also generated valuable fees for our consulting division.

After refinements to the financial and costing systems, the business acquired six of the latest Swiss Sulzer weaving looms to replace its old labor-intensive looms. The purchasing exercise was an eye-opener for me, as Sulzer insisted on sending a team of its employees to Australia to ensure the intricate looms were functioning well and to train the operators, before handing them over to the purchaser.

When John Davis retired from the board of John Foster, I was pleased to take his place. By then, through my work with George Schnabl, I was considered the de facto finance director, and I liaised closely with the parent company in the UK and two of its directors, Derek Gallimore and Gordon Hunter, during their regular visits to Melbourne. I also became deeply involved in the dramas associated with John Foster Australia's takeover of a publicly listed textile company, Valley Worsted Mills, which was based in Geelong. John Elder[59], a senior partner at the law firm Madden, Butler, Elder & Graham, and I navigated the minefield

---

[59] John Elder was an erudite gentleman. I admired his legal prowess and learned a lot from working with him.

of financial and legal challenges associated with the merger, including a protracted and expensive action in the Supreme Court brought by a shareholder. Thankfully, we won the case.[60]

Finally, the operational and physical merger of the two mills was completed in December 1973 and the business was relocated to Geelong. The name of the combined entity was changed to John Foster Valley, ending the 50 years of independent existence of Valley Worsted Mills.[61] The board of directors was reconstituted, with Lister Wright the only member of the old Valley Worsted board remaining. He became joint managing director with George Schnabl, while I joined the board as finance director. One of our early issues was the sudden death of Peter Lempriere, the chairman of John Foster, who would have been appointed the chairman of the new entity. I recommended that Darvell Hutchinson be considered for this delicate role and, over the next few years, my judgement was vindicated by his superb performance as chair.

Throughout the merger, as managing director, Lister Wright behaved impeccably and effectively. He understood that the future success of his mill required him to meaningfully cooperate with George Schnabl on operational decisions, and with me regarding accounting and information systems. Over the years we worked well together and developed great respect for each other. I grieved Lister's death in January 1979 and was touched that he bequeathed to me the Valley Worsted corporate seal that I had once admired. It now stands in my study and is a constant reminder of him and our close association.

The John Foster Valley enterprise thrived for a few years after the merger. However, the election of a Labor government under the leadership of Gough Whitlam in 1972, sounded the death knell for much of Australia's manufacturing industries, especially textiles. While many of Whitlam's rapid reforms were enthusiastically received, they came at a high economic price.[62] By mid-1975, inflation had hit over 15%, and wage rises reached nearly 33%. On top of the existing tariff

---

[60] The case was brought by a prominent Geelong bookmaker who briefed an eminent QC. We had to contend with no less than four QCs in succession as each, for varying reasons, dropped out of the case.

[61] Lister Wright's daughter, Judith Rice, has written a comprehensive and fascinating history of Valley Worsted Mills.

[62] Some of the Whitlam government's early reforms included: re-establishment of formal relations with China; repeal of conscription laws and withdrawal from the Vietnam War; introduction of universal health care; abolition of the White Australia policy; introduction of free tertiary education; and significant increase in arts funding.

cuts, which resulted in a 30% increase in imports, several labour-intensive manufacturing industries buckled. This hit John Foster badly. Even after rationalising the various divisions, the economics did not work out, particularly as customers turned to China in the wake of its economic liberalisation.

I resigned from the board of John Foster Valley in 1983 and the business remained a listed company until May 1984 when it was sold to an entrepreneur, Reuben Hall—incidentally, a friend of mine—who later sold it to A-Weave Textiles in Reservoir. It was a great shame that John Foster Valley did not survive the measures devised in Canberra that led to the demise of much of the Australian manufacturing industry. I believe the country remains much the poorer as a result.

I remain proud of the assistance I was able to provide to George Schnabl when he was preparing for his retirement. In discussions with him, I found that his retirement plan was totally inadequate, considering his contribution to the company over many years. I lobbied the directors to redress the issue, and, to their credit, they readily agreed. As a result, George was able to retire with financial security to his Donvale home, where he could indulge his lifelong wish to study piano, and Dorothy could continue her passion for gardening in their spacious grounds. I would visit quite often and was pleased to see George so content in his twilight years.

Despite the demands of the John Foster business, I continued to work hard to expand the reach of Wilson, Bishop, Bowes & Craig's consulting division, including into our interstate offices. One of the Sydney-based partners, Peter Gosling, indicated his interest in consulting work, and I shared with him my approach and experience in this emerging specialty. He readily took to it and, over the years, we developed a fruitful working relationship. This grew to include consulting for the tourism and hospitality industries because of our association with the international firm of Pannell Kerr Forster.

As my division grew in size and credibility, other partners in our national firm asked me to advise their major clients. For example, Mel

Whitbread, the senior partner in Adelaide, introduced me to the office's largest and most prestigious client, the Royal Automobile Association (RAA) of South Australia. The RAA was seeking to mechanise its manual members' records, thereby increasing the level of service it would be able to provide to its members. I would regularly fly to Adelaide to work on this assignment.

The flow of work was exhilarating, but it reinforced the need to hire new staff. Over the years, I built a talented team. Looking back, I am proud of the people I engaged; we formed excellent professional and personal relationships.

One of the first consultants I hired was Bruce Leslie. Initially, Bruce approached me because he was interested in the emerging field of farm management analysis, and he had heard that our firm had a substantial number of clients with large rural properties. I did not know anything about this area but was prepared to give it a go. We identified several potential clients, who were initially skeptical about modernising their systems, so we had to win them over with discounted fees. Regrettably, after several unprofitable years, we decided to suspend our consulting services in this area.

At that time, discussions were also underway with the London firm of Pannell Fitzpatrick & Co for our firm to join an international network of accountancy firms. The international team would include a substantial Canadian national firm, Campbell, Sharp, Nash & Field, as well as Harris, Kerr, Forster & Co, a medium-sized New York-based national firm.

Of particular interest to me was that Harris, Kerr, Forster & Co had developed a specialty in the hospitality industry and were already involved in discussions with the new Australian Tourism Commission to investigate the tourism potential of the Great Barrier Reef marine park. Chuck Kaiser, the partner in charge of the US firm's consulting division, considered that it would be advantageous for political purposes, to include an Australian firm on the study team.

As this arrangement did not involve Wilson, Bishop, Bowes & Craig relinquishing any control over its operations, or any international profit sharing, it did not take long for us to join the association. Initially the various component firms practiced under their national names, but a few years later, in line with other such firms, we decided to adopt the Pannell Kerr Forster (PKF) name internationally.

The general client composition of the component firms was such that there was hardly any referral work in the audit and taxation areas. Nevertheless, the senior partners of the national firms did find it of value to schedule regular international get togethers. These conferences gave us an opportunity to get to know each other, to share information about our firms, and to learn about the special aptitudes of the individual practices.

In the consulting area, however, there was an immediate benefit to our Melbourne and Sydney offices and to our fee-earning potential. With an Australian firm on board, Chuck Kaiser was able to formalise two major tourism studies with the Australian Tourism Commission: the Great Barrier Reef and the Central Australia studies. I decided to give Bruce Leslie the opportunity to be the resident consultant on these assignments, working with Chuck Kaiser and George Lipp, the partner in charge of the Honolulu office. Bruce took to the work like a duck to water and carved out a great career for himself in the hospitality industry.[63]

The American firm developed, and introduced us to, an invaluable statistical exercise to determine hotel and motel occupancy. This data became a key source of information to bankers when deciding whether to finance the purchase or construction of new hotels. It soon became impossible to enter financing discussions without such a report, which was produced by the firm under a strict code of independence and ethics. This became a lucrative source of income, usually paid by intending developers or hotel operators. Once the viability of a project was established, our consulting services were extended to creating spreadsheets to calculate the effect on profitability of planned ancillary services.

I tasked Bruce Leslie with the job of establishing this type of service in Australia, which he eventually did, successfully overcoming the initial reluctance of some very conservative people. The Australian version, although expensive to establish, became a vital feature of our country's

---

[63] I saw Bruce years later and was pleased to learn that over the course of his career he held several senior managerial positions running hotels and was able to retire to run a farm, his original love.

hospitality consulting. The investment paid off as we became involved in the preliminary planning of major hotel and resort developments. A significant number of these resort and hotel studies were based in Queensland and, at the request of the Queensland Tourism Authority, we established a tourism-dedicated office in Brisbane. We were the only major accounting firm to take this unique step. This office was established amid much fanfare, and repaid its initial establishment costs, thanks, in part, to the authority's strong support.

At one of the Pacific Area Travel Association (PATA) conferences, Chuck introduced me to Susan Calwell, who was earning a name for herself as the dynamic new manager of the Melbourne Convention and Tourism Authority. She revealed that The Oberoi Group had expressed interest in establishing a presence in Melbourne as part of its expansionary plans. I was later introduced to several Oberoi executives who advised, confidentially, that they had the venerable Hotel Windsor in their sights.

The Oberoi Group, founded in 1934 by Rai Bahadur Mohan Singh Oberoi, was an award-winning luxury hotel and resort group, headquartered in New Delhi. Realising the group would be an excellent source of work for our fledgling Australian tourism consulting practice, upon returning to Melbourne, Bruce Leslie and I shared our hotel financing data with some of the Oberoi executives. That was the start of an ongoing advisory relationship with the group.

The Windsor Hotel was an interesting choice. The original hotel had been commissioned by shipping magnate George Nipper and designed by the leading architect Charles Webb in 1884. The name was changed from The Grand to The Windsor in 1923 in honour of a luncheon the hotel hosted for the Prince of Wales. Over the years, adjoining properties were acquired for the extension of the hotel. However, the property gradually became rundown. The only remaining vestige of its proud past was its traditional Sunday afternoon, British-style high tea.

In 1976, the Victorian state government purchased the hotel and then leased, and later sold, it to The Oberoi Group. Serious money was spent restoring the property to its former glory. Particular attention was paid to the grand dining room, where the huge brass chandeliers were faithfully reproduced. It was in this magnificent room that Ada and I were seated alongside the official guests to mark the Windsor's reopening. Seated close to us was a Saudi Arabian sheik, who was one of the financiers of the project, and Graeme Samuel, another financial advisor to the group (who would later become the head of the ACCC). I found it ironic that Saudi money had funded the many Jewish advisors on the project.

A few years later, Ada and I spent a long weekend at the Windsor Hotel to celebrate our anniversary. We were delighted to be upgraded to a spacious suite overlooking Spring Street. Our three sons were suitably awed by the top-hatted doorman and the grandeur of the dining room when they joined us for a special dinner on the night of our anniversary.

Electronic data processing was the next consulting growth area. As computers became cheaper and smaller, they no longer required expensive space and add-ons, such as false flooring for the cables and dedicated air conditioning, and companies began to invest in their own equipment and tailored software. This required our firm to engage specialists, such as Maurie Munsie and Brian Wilby. Together, we worked on many assignments in this rapidly developing field. One major assignment, for our largest audit client, Carlton & United Breweries, was to redesign its active share registry, which it operated in-house.

Amid the flurry of new projects, there were the demands of managing the firm, which were incumbent on all partners. Our firm still valued goodwill as an asset of the individual partners. In time, tension developed over salaries between the younger incoming partners and the older equity partners. Partners' meetings were delicate affairs and extreme tact was necessary to steer them.

Nonetheless, ours was a reasonably harmonious partnership. I particularly enjoyed the conviviality of the partners' Friday night drinks in the boardroom, which provided an opportunity to keep abreast of the latest developments in the firm.

The pace of progress in the consulting division earned me considerable kudos within our national firm and I was elected as the international chair of the management consulting committee at PKF. This was more a coordinating role, as each national firm controlled its own operations. Inter-firm referrals were a constant, and important, item of business. On several occasions, I had to disentangle potentially embarrassing conflicts. For example, on one occasion, I learned that representatives from both the American and British firms were in Cairo to pitch a hotel feasibility study to the same international company!

The hectic pace of driving the expansion of the consulting division was mirrored by an equally busy time in our home life. In 1967, we bought a block of land at 6 Tara Court in an undeveloped estate in Doncaster, next to the Eastern Golf Club, and eventually Sybil Builders delivered the desired rustic, yet modern, house built of clinker bricks. Ada would regularly go to the building site and, one day, she was horrified to notice that the bricklayer had diligently separated the blue toned bricks from the red ones and built the front of the house accordingly. Ada insisted that the wall be pulled down and re-erected with the various hued bricks used randomly.

Our rugged split-level house did not resonate with everyone. When we were showing the house to Eva and her sister, Nusia, who was visiting from Sydney, Nusia pulled me aside and, pointing to the exposed heavy timber beams, said if we couldn't afford to finish the ceiling, she would be happy to advance me the money.

On 20 October 1969, two days before Ada's 29th birthday, our third son, Richard, was born at St. Andrew's Hospital, East Melbourne. He brought a sense of completeness to our family.

A few months later, we received a visit from Leon and Lauretta Silver[64], with their baby son, Jamie (who would soon become Richard's closest friend). They were living a cosmopolitan life in South Yarra but were also considering settling down in the suburbs and were keen to see our house. They liked it enough to purchase one of the remaining blocks of land in the court and to commission the same builders. More than 50 years later, we remain very close to Leon and Lauretta, and we were devastated when Jamie passed away in 2022.

---

[64] Lauretta's parents, Mr and Mrs Klings, were friends of Ada's parents.

Above: With Richard, Randall & Mark
Below: Mietek & Lida with the boys

In my position as international chair, I would attend the large gatherings of PATA in major tourism-oriented centres, including Hawaii, Malaysia, Indonesia and Japan. In January 1971, Ada was able to come with me to Malaysia.[65] It was our first trip since our honeymoon and the first time we had been away from our three sons. By then, Mark had started at Doncaster Park State School, which was directly behind our property, Randall was due to start kindergarten and Richard had started walking, so it was a logistical challenge to arrange for them to be looked after while we were abroad.

While in Kuala Lumpur, I reconnected with one of the Colombo Plan students, Mohamed bin Anas, who had worked for me at Arthur Andersen. Since returning home, he had become a successful accountant and he was eager to show off his achievements. He picked me up in his chauffeur-driven limousine and took me to his hairdresser for a haircut, manicure and pedicure. It reminded me of my life in Shanghai, when I would sometimes accompany my father for a similar experience in Avenue Joffre. Later, Mohamed took me to the Selangor Country Club, an exclusive establishment dating back to the British colonial days. There I had a massage and drinks before partaking in a lengthy and sumptuous lunch. It was not till mid-afternoon that I was taken back to the hotel. Ada was waiting for me and was eager to share the details of her day of shopping and touring, which included a visit to the zoo, where she was photographed cuddling a lion cub. The photograph appeared the following day in the local English language newspaper.

<hr />

In the winter months of 1972, Lida began to feel unwell. When she failed to regain her health, she sought medical advice and, tragically, was diagnosed with pancreatic cancer. The family was plunged into despair when it became clear that she would not recover. Lida died on 17 December 1972 at just 52 years of age.

---

[65] In 1972, Ada also accompanied me on a business trip to Japan.

Lida's premature death seemed particularly unjust after surviving the war and overcoming the difficulties of adapting to life in a new country. While she had lived to see Ada happily married, to see three grandsons born, and to see Jack finish his secondary education as dux of his school, Lida missed out on many precious decades of life. She never got to meet Dianne Rutman, who Jack married in 1977, or their four fantastic children. And she was denied the chance to grow old in the company of her beloved husband.

Mietek was bereft after the loss of Lida, but did his best to maintain a positive outlook. After some years, he married again but, sadly, his second wife Stella also died of cancer.

⬤ ◆ ⬤

Over the years, the merger with Cleveland, Scott & Hislop (CSH) had brought about several profitable opportunities for some of the partners. The first was the development of Nubrick House, on the northwest corner of William and Little Lonsdale Streets. CSH was originally located on that corner in an old low-rise building, whose freehold they owned, while we were still in Queen Street in premises that were becoming progressively inadequate due to our expansion. Albert Shergold came up with a proposal for the development of a multi-storied modern office building on that corner site, which would house our merged firm over several floors, and Brick & Pipe and some other clients on other floors, including a branch of the National Australia Bank on the ground floor. The financial arrangements between the equity and general partners of our merged firm had to be diplomatically handled. Eventually, Nubrick House was sold, with the partners of our firm reaping a good profit, and the firm moved to rented premises in the newly built National Bank House in Bourke Street in 1981. The traditional parts of the firm occupied the 14th floor, with the management consulting division ensconced in a separate part of the building on the 21st floor. Coincidentally, the barristers' chambers where Ada had her practice were located on a lower floor in the same building, so we could easily visit each other. We always drove in separately, however, and parked in the same area of the building's carpark.

Another of Albert Shergold's entrepreneurial initiatives was the purchase of a huge agricultural property in New South Wales called Coketgedong. The partners each had the option of buying an interest in the 50,000-acre property. I used to joke that it was bigger than Israel! Some partners who invested enjoyed the chance to spend time on the land, like country squires. Ada and I took a financial interest, but never managed to go there. Eventually, the property sold for a good profit. I shall always be grateful to Albert Shergold for his foresight and generosity.

———— ◆ ————

Wilson Bishop Bowes & Craig conference. Darvell Hutchinson is seated second from the left

Lister Wright's wife planting a tree outside the John Foster Valley offices in Geelong, 1973

PATA conference, c.1973

Smoking a pipe while sitting on my Jaguar with the boys

Randall, Mark and Richard on the first day of the school year, 1975

The United Israel Appeal (UIA)

Even now, after so many decades, most older people in the Australian Jewish community know me through my long association with the United Israel Appeal (UIA), the fundraising body for Israel, established by the Zionist Federation of Australia (ZFA).

The fact that my community profile remains connected to the organisation says less about the importance of my roles—I was state treasurer, then federal treasurer, and then federal chairman—and more about the powerful reach of the UIA under the dynamic and visionary leadership of Isador Magid.[66] The UIA is the Jewish community's principal vehicle of financial support to Israel and, from 1967 to 1992, just about everybody in the community received a receipt with my signature, thanking them for their financial support.

Looking back, I am surprised that it took as long as 15 years of active participation in Melbourne's Jewish community before I became involved with the UIA. It wasn't as though I had no affinity with Zionism or pride in the creation of the Jewish State. Even as a boy in Shanghai, I had been involved in the Zionistic Betar movement, and later, in 1960, I had been exhilarated by my first visit to Israel.

In June 1967, it was impossible to ignore the events unfolding in the Middle East that culminated in six days of armed conflict between Israel and a coalition of Arab states. Israel was victorious and Jewish people around the world were euphoric. I too felt buoyed by Israel's swift and convincing retaliation. But I was a passive observer until, shortly after the Six-Day War, I assumed a role at the UIA that galvanised my interaction with Israel.

One weekend, Ada and I were invited to afternoon tea at the Balwyn home of Isador and Ira Magid. Like all their friends, we looked forward

---

[66] The Magit family changed their name to Magid in 1957.

to these visits which featured Ira's delicious Russian-style pastries and the opportunity to enjoy the modern and classical sculptures throughout their stylish house and gracious garden.

The Magids were one of the few other Shanghai Russian Jewish families that had settled in Melbourne—most of the others lived in Sydney. In Shanghai our families had socialised together at the Russian Jewish Club, but Isador and Ira were younger than my parents and the two couples were not close. However, in Australia, our families forged strong connections: Elijah was friendly with Ralph Magid, the youngest of Isador and Ira's children; and Ada was close friends with their daughter Nora. Ada and I both attended Nora's wedding to Danny Goodridge—a senior academic from Sydney whose Russian Jewish family also hailed from China, specifically Tientsin—which featured the Russian tradition of drinking vodka and then smashing the glasses against the fireplace.

⬤◆⬤

Both Isador and Ira were born into the thriving Russian community in Harbin, Manchuria. When the Japanese seized control of Harbin, they, like many other Jews, resettled in Shanghai where life was safer and where there were better business opportunities. In Shanghai, Isador's leadership qualities came to the fore and, before long, he was appointed secretary of the Ashkenazi Jewish Communal Organisation. When it became clear that the Communists would seize control of Shanghai, Isador was instrumental in getting Moshe Yuval, then an assistant consul of the newly established State of Israel, to come to the city to issue permits to the stateless Jews of Shanghai who wished to migrate to Israel. After Moshe Yuval's departure, the Israeli government gave Isador the role of honorary consul and he undertook the urgent and complicated process of attempting to transfer all the properties owned by the Russian Jewish community, including the New Synagogue and the Shanghai Jewish Club, to the State of Israel. Unfortunately, these efforts were in vain and, ultimately, the properties were 'acquired' by the communist municipal authorities.

The Magids left Shanghai at the end of 1950. They lived in Sydney for several months before settling in Melbourne. Initially, Isador started a business importing goat hair, which achieved moderate sales to automotive carpet manufacturers. He then purchased a popcorn business and, to bolster its offering, he imported a machine from the US that produced a type of snack food. After changing the settings, Isador manufactured a curled, yellow, cheese-flavoured chip that he named 'Twisties', now an iconic Australian food item. He eventually sold the business to Monty Lea of the confectionary company Darrell Lea.

Like many Jewish entrepreneurs, Isador gravitated to real estate development. His company, Overland, purchased swathes of land in outer Melbourne that he developed into large suburbs that later featured extensive shopping malls, including Brandon Park and Fountain Gate.

A passionate Zionist, Isador also dedicated himself to numerous organisations supporting the fledgling State of Israel, and, in June 1967, he was appointed co-president of the Victorian Chapter of the United Israel Appeal (UIA).

⬤ ◆ ⬤

Our afternoon tea at the home of the Magids passed pleasantly. As the guests started to make their farewells, Isador asked us to stay behind. He invited me into his cosy study, dominated by photographs of him with notable public figures, including Israeli prime ministers and presidents. Isador explained that an avalanche of support from the Melbourne Jewish community following Israel's remarkable victory in the Six-Day War had overwhelmed the administrative capabilities of the UIA office. He asked me to investigate and recommend a viable solution to speed up the dispatch of receipts for donations. Of course, I readily agreed to assist and Isador asked that I contact Sigmund Stock, treasurer of the ZFA, and Nettie Warda, the UIA office manager. I had no idea at the time that Isador's request would lead to such a lengthy and defining involvement with the UIA.

Neither Nettie Warda nor Sigmund Stock were overly enthusiastic about the need for an investigation into administrative procedures, but they both acknowledged that if such widespread community support for Israel continued, the financial systems at the UIA office would have to be modernised to cope with the volume of donations. It was clear that the struggle to issue receipts was due to antiquated manual procedures and a policy to minimise expenses.

Within a few weeks I presented a detailed report containing my findings and recommendations to Isador and the UIA co-president Henry Krongold. I was thanked for my work and secretly hoped that this pro bono job would eventually yield some consulting assignments. Instead, to my great surprise, I was offered the position of deputy honorary treasurer of the UIA (Victoria), with full power to implement my recommendations and to ready the office for future expansion.

All this was a prelude to the UIA assuming a more significant presence in the Australian Jewish community. Isador had correctly assessed that the Six-Day War had changed attitudes and increased the generosity of Jewry throughout the world towards Israel. The unification of Jerusalem and the capture of the West Bank certainly played a part in this shift, particularly among the religious Orthodox communities in America. Concerns expressed about the fate of the large number of Palestinians living in the West Bank were drowned out by exultation over the trove of biblically significant sites under Jewish rule after so many years. Qualms regarding the governance of these territories were not seen as relevant by many Jews until much later. In any event, the Arab states who lost the war responded with their infamous 'Three No's' resolution[67], which put paid to any serious bargaining of land for peace.

Isador actively recruited dynamic, young volunteers, as well as older, well-connected people to aggressively encourage giving throughout the community. My friend, Keith Beville, became an outstanding chairman of the Victorian appeal. In addition to Keith's strong commitment to

---

[67] The 1967 Arab League summit in Khartoum resulted in the Khartoum Resolution which includes 'The Three No's'—No peace with Israel, no recognition of Israel, no negotiations with Israel.

Israel, he was organised and had the extensive business skills sorely needed at the expanding UIA. Isador also recruited Saul Same, an older man with extensive connections in the business and political realm. Saul's networking capabilities proved invaluable, as Isador believed in personal approaches to targeted people, rather than impersonal communication by phone or mail.

This energetic nucleus of committed volunteers would regularly meet around the kitchen table at the Magids' home. We called ourselves 'The Kitchen Cabinet' and our conversation was sustained by hearty consumption of Ira's delicious pastries. We pooled our collective knowledge of various individuals' capacity to donate and decided on a strategy of personal approach.

In those days, much of the UIA giving population was organised around common interest groups whose fundraising efforts would culminate in private 'drawing room meetings' where donations would be read out to applause. Prominent among these were 'The Landsmanshaften', the social groups of Eastern European—mostly Polish—Holocaust survivors who had found refuge in Melbourne. Such groups were often named after the cities and towns where the members had lived before the Nazis uprooted their lives. They were, in the main, staunch Zionists who strongly believed that their increasing personal financial success should be reflected in their generosity to Israel. Sometimes, when the chair of a group felt that the pledges tallied at the meeting were not enough, they would initiate an on-the-spot supplementary appeal to boost the final donation.

I decided that the starting point for my reforms would involve recording the details of these 'drawing room meetings'. Although the atmosphere at these meetings was joyous, from an administrative point of view they were challenging as the details were often vague. I determined that a UIA representative should be present at every meeting to record the pledges so that donations were duly paid and processed the following day. I tried to personally attend as often as possible, often flitting from one meeting to another during the peak of an appeal and not returning home till after midnight. In this way, I gradually earned the respect of the donors and everyone at UIA, which paved the way for me to propose further administrative reforms.

Next on my agenda was upskilling the staff at the office, situated at Beth Weizmann, the Jewish community centre in St Kilda Road. I had been concerned that the office accountant, Jacob Labiner, an older Polish Holocaust survivor, would be unable to cope with the transition to a mechanised system. In any event, Jacob pre-empted my concerns and decided to retire, mainly due to his wife's failing health. I was pleased to host a luncheon to thank Jacob for his many years of devoted service. Fortunately, Sylvia New, an experienced accountant and a dedicated Zionist, was available to fill the role successfully for many years to come.

The expansion and success of UIA was, in part, due to rigorous adherence to several fundamental fundraising principles. We spent considerable time researching what a potential donor would consider to be a fair donation to Israel. Nathan Jacobson, a successful and witty lawyer, enunciated the principle: If you LIVE like a king, you ought to GIVE like a king! Isador also insisted on personal meetings and allied to this principle, the moral imperative that the person approaching a donor should have made an appropriate personal donation him or herself.

The UIA executive was aware of the changing demographics of the Melbourne Jewish community and the need to accommodate these changes. It became obvious that the influence of the Landsmanshaften, hitherto the mainstay of its campaigns, was waning with the increasing age of its members, and the generosity of this group was not mirrored by the next generation, so new groupings had to be established. Among the most successful was the establishment of the women's division, which benefitted from a series of energetic leaders. Others, like the professional groupings and a division catering to younger members, were moderately successful. New accounting systems were implemented for each new group, which was only possible because of the excellent UIA staff and successive upgrades of the computer system.

As the reach of the UIA continued to expand into every nook and cranny of the Melbourne Jewish community, it was decided to appoint George Zbar as chief executive/business manager. George had recently sold his textile manufacturing business and personally knew many successful businesspeople. He also had chutzpah, which was exactly what we needed to support our volunteer canvassers and to translate pledges into actual payments.

The ever-increasing activities of the UIA meant that I had to devote more and more attention to this voluntary work, at a time when I was dealing with extensive responsibilities as head of the firm's expanding and demanding management consulting division. I decided that, in order to manage my time most effectively, I should devote Wednesday mornings exclusively to UIA matters. For many years, everyone knew that was when they could find me at the UIA office.

The UIA office was put to the test with the sudden outbreak of the Yom Kippur War in 1973. News of the totally unexpected invasion of Israel by Egypt and Syria hit Jewish communities throughout the world like a thunderclap. The attack, which occurred on the holiest day of the Jewish calendar, was aggravated by the early military gains of these two powerful foes of Israel. We held genuine fears for Israel's future existence. An urgent executive meeting in Melbourne decreed an Australia-wide emergency UIA appeal. This appeal was to be George Zbar's first major assignment. He quickly displayed his shrewdness by suggesting that we first capitalise on our donors' anxieties for Israel by collecting the unpaid amounts from their pledges made at the regular appeal in April, before announcing the new appeal. His intuition proved to be correct. We were able to collect virtually all unpaid pledges and, contrary to the fears of some, the emergency appeal was unaffected. To the contrary, as news from the conflict continued to be bad, the community rallied as never before. The foyer of Beth Weizmann became a pledge and cash collection centre. Long lines of people waited, sometimes impatiently, to do their bit for Israel. At the end of several hectic days, we had raised *three times* the amount donated in our annual appeal. At Keith's suggestion, we incorporated the pledges into our donor database, as a guide for future requests.

My partners and staff at PKF, none of whom were Jewish, supported my involvement with the UIA and showed interest in Israel's position in the Middle East conflict. I was particularly pleased when, in July 1976, my partners decided to celebrate the successful counter-terrorism rescue by Israeli commandos of 103 hostages being held at Entebbe Airport in Uganda. To mark the occasion, they opened a prized bottle of cognac in the boardroom.

In Israel, the absorption of immigrants has been a particularly challenging economic and social issue. After Menachem Begin was elected prime minister in 1977, he suggested that Keren Hayesod, the parent body of the UIA, allocate donated funds to specific projects that support targeted groups of struggling migrants, including elderly Eastern European Jews and, later, Jews from Ethiopia. Fundraising for specific purpose-built facilities, such as aged care homes and specialised schools, opened the possibility of offering naming rights to major donors. This was particularly appealing to donors who wanted to commemorate the memory of loved ones who perished in the Holocaust through plaques and enduring signage on the buildings being created under a scheme called Project Renewal.

George Zbar and I developed a close working relationship. I came to value his sagacity and his readiness to carry out difficult tasks, particularly those that required his particular brand of humour and his keen insight into the personalities of those in our orbit.[68]

The growth of the UIA cemented its reputation as the community's principal fundraising organisation for Israel and hastened the formal separation of the UIA from the Zionist Federation. Fortunately, the logic of the separation was accepted by Mark Leibler, who later became the head of the ZFA. Ironically, the immediate effect was more greatly felt in Israel than in Australia. We soon received a message from the Keren Hayesod head office in Jerusalem that its

---

[68] Unfortunately, due to ill health, George had to retire earlier than we all would have liked. I was honoured to be asked by his wife, Tusia, to say a few words about George at the Elwood Synagogue service held in his honour, following his funeral. I still think about George often and continue to miss his company.

director of finance, Motka Meron, would be travelling to Australia and New Zealand to review our financial operations.

Motka Meron and his wife arrived in Melbourne and spent time with Isador, Saul and Keith. Motka also spent many hours with Sylvia New, poring over the accounting systems for pledges and their conversion into cash receipts. In the evenings I would meet him to discuss his findings. After discovering that Motka was interested in wine, I arranged a tour of the wineries in the Yarra Valley. Ada and I also hosted a Sunday lunch in Motka's honour. As several of the guests were kosher, we converted our kitchen, underestimating the effort (an acetylene blowtorch was involved) and attendant costs. Fortunately, the luncheon was a great success. Motka was duly satisfied with the financial management of the UIA and, as a result of his visit, we developed a close working relationship.

<hr />

Shortly after Motka's departure from Australia, Sigmund Stock announced his intention to retire as federal treasurer of the UIA. Saul Same, as federal chairman, asked me to take on the position vacated by Sigmund, which I readily accepted, knowing that it would not impinge on my work as Victorian UIA state treasurer. Saul began to regularly invite me to his office in Collingwood for a sandwich lunch and a chat. He was the head of a substantial shirt manufacturing business called Gloweave. Saul showed genuine interest in my professional work and soon he engaged me to review the costing structure of his Gloweave operation. We developed a very good professional relationship over the following months, and he gave me free reign to investigate all sections of the manufacturing operations. I found that Saul was a benevolent employer who knew the names and personal circumstances of every one of the workers at Gloweave. As a result, he could not bring himself to implement some of the harsher measures that I recommended. Many similar businesses in the textile industry were improving their bottom lines by shifting operations to one of the low-cost countries in Asia. Knowing the negative impact this measure would have on his cherished employees, Saul recoiled whenever he was confronted with this difficult decision. In the end, reality asserted itself and Gloweave moved its manufacturing to Indonesia, and its extensive site in Collingwood gave way to new apartment buildings, as part of the gentrification of the area.

Saul Same was one of the most well-connected people I had ever met. He was a strong Labor party man, on first-name terms with all its leaders. Sitting in his office and listening to him taking one call after another from politicians and business leaders was an awe-inspiring experience. He and Isador worked very effectively together in guiding the UIA to the heights it attained.

In 1983, I was thrilled to visit Israel for the second time. That trip, like all my many subsequent trips to Israel, was paid for personally in accordance with the UIA rule that all honorary officers of the UIA must fund their own local and international travel. That gave me the freedom to apportion some of my trip to personal travel and the opportunity to spend time with Ada, who arrived in Israel soon after me, and with Mark, who was living on a kibbutz as part of Netzer's gap year program.

When my plane landed in Israel, I was met by Motka at Ben Gurion Airport and, for the first time, received VIP treatment, which included waiting in a comfortable room while my passport and luggage were swiftly processed. Motka then drove me to the historic King David Hotel, where I had always dreamed of staying.

It was wonderful to observe how much had been achieved in the 23-year period since my first visit to Israel. The country's agricultural developments, military strength, rising wealth and significant social progress, including the establishment of well-functioning health and education systems, were simply amazing. To me, there seemed to be an atmosphere of peaceful coexistence with the Arab population, particularly in the now united Jerusalem, where it was possible to wander freely throughout the fascinating Old City with its myriad of food stalls, markets and holy sites.

Motka took great pains to ensure the trip was a success. He spent time showing me how the remittances from Australia were merged with monies from other Keren Hayesod offices around the world to fund projects through the Jewish Agency. I found the scope of the fundraising operation impressive. Motka also drove Ada, Mark and me to Masada, where we enjoyed an excellent tour of the ancient site. On the way, Motka shared, with great pride, the news that his son had recently been selected into an elite paratrooper unit of the Israel Defense Forces.

On that trip, we also met, for the first time, Mietek's distant relative, Aaron Zucker, his wife Rikki and their daughters, Anat and Michal. Aaron was in his mid-30s and had formerly worked for the minister of defense in a senior capacity. We listened with interest as he described travelling on official business to Germany. Upon arrival in Berlin, the Israeli delegation had been escorted with much fanfare in a motorised procession to their hotel. We were all struck by how much had changed in the decades since Aaron's parents fled the Nazis to escape to Palestine. Aaron was working in a merchant bank at the time of our visit, and I couldn't have imagined that we would one day work together.

After our time in Israel, Ada and I were excited to join the European cruise we had booked. However, when we boarded the ship in Athens, we were disappointed to find that the standard was well below our expectations. In the dining room, the cruise managers seated us at a table with the only other people on board who spoke English. Saud and Huda Bukhar were from Saudi Arabia, and the irony of a Jewish couple sitting with a young Arab couple, from a country zealous in its hatred of Israel, was not lost on us. As the cruise progressed, we discovered a little about Saud's life as an executive at Aramco, the official Saudi oil company, and noticed that Huda seemed taken aback by the non-deferential way that Ada spoke to me. We also realised that we had several things in common with our table partners, including the fact that we all rejected the pork dishes on offer.

Above: Farewell lunch for Jacob Labiner
Centre: Speaking at the UIA national conference, c.1975
Below: At the UIA Operation Commitment Plus meeting, c.1975

Temple Beth Israel (TBI)

Our family was initially drawn to Liberal Judaism (or Progressive Judaism as it is sometimes known) by Rabbi Dr Herman Sanger's charismatic personality and the fact that we lived near Temple Beth Israel's (TBI) affiliated congregation in Melbourne's eastern suburbs. But, after attending several services in spacious old homes in Lorne Grove and Royal Crescent in Camberwell, Grandmother decided that this more modern denomination of Judaism was not for her.

My brothers, Nathan and Elijah, each celebrated their bar mitzvah at the Temple under the direct supervision of Rabbi Sanger, who visited our home and admired our carved Chinese furniture. We also attended the High Holiday services at Box Hill Town Hall before they were moved to Melbourne Town Hall to accommodate the growing Liberal Jewish community.

By the early 1960s, we were an entrenched Liberal Jewish family and the Temple in Alma Road, St Kilda, was an obvious choice for our wedding ceremony. At the time, many young Jewish families were, like us, migrating to the northeastern suburbs of North Balwyn and Doncaster. This augmented the membership of the Liberal congregation and prompted discussion about the viability of a new American-style Jewish centre with sports facilities, social amenities and a synagogue. Ada and I supported the vision for a communal centre and gave, what was for us, a considerable donation.

The North Eastern Jewish Centre was finally built but, to our dismay, we discovered that the Orthodox orientation of the synagogue would dictate the tone of the social and sporting activities. The young, newly appointed Orthodox rabbi, with support from the administrators, decreed that no sport would be played on Shabbat or religious holidays. We were particularly distressed that one of the hard-working founding members was not allowed to host his son's bar mitzvah party on the premises because the rabbi refused to recognise his wife's conversion. We were so scandalised by this and other incidents that we cancelled our membership.

In mid-1975, while I was in Hawaii attending a PATA Conference, I received a call from Ada advising that Mark had been moved up a grade at school. This meant that our plans to move closer to Wesley College when he commenced there in year 7 would have to be accelerated. As soon as I returned home, we started to look for a house in earnest.

Although the house Ada found in Bellaire Court, Toorak was in a poor state, its layout made sense. As I was feeling optimistic about my prospects with the firm, and with the adage of 'position, position, position' in mind, in July 1976 we decided to buy it.

In January 1977, we moved into our new house. Randall and Richard were enrolled in the local state school, a short walk from home. For the first week of school, Ada drove behind Mark's tram to ensure he arrived at Wesley safely. To our amusement, our friend Natalie Miller was coincidentally driving behind the same tram to ensure her son, Ashley, got off at the right stop.

For the boys, leaving our life in Doncaster to move into this sub-standard abode was a great disappointment. However, after several renovations, 9 Bellaire Court proved to be one of our most rewarding purchases and is still our home more than five decades years later.

We decided to leave the eastern suburbs congregation and become members of TBI in Alma Road, St Kilda. By 1977, TBI and its two affiliated suburban congregations had become an integral part of the Melbourne Jewish community, despite the Orthodox rabbinate continuing to deny the legitimacy of Liberal Judaism. TBI's standing in the community was, in large part, due to the indefatigable efforts of Rabbi Sanger, who retired from the role of senior rabbi in 1974. The board of TBI immediately invited Rabbi John Levi to succeed him.

To honour Rabbi Sanger for his immense achievements, TBI president, Dr Jack Morris, conferred on him the title of 'Rabbi Emeritus,' and renamed the TBI building, 'The Herman Sanger Centre'. Unfortunately, Rabbi Sanger was not destined to enjoy a long retirement. He passed away on 24 January 1980, only a few weeks before TBI celebrated its golden anniversary. Rabbi Levi spoke movingly at the funeral and his words were echoed in Canberra by the rabbi's good friend of many years, the governor-general of Australia, Sir Zelman Cowen. I mourned Rabbi Sanger's untimely passing and still believe that his inspirational sermons guided the direction of my spiritual life. For me, both literally and metaphorically, Judaism was about 'the singer', rather than 'the song'.

When Mark turned 12, I went to Temple to enrol him in Rabbi Levi's Sunday school bar mitzvah class. I was pleased to become reacquainted with Rabbi Levi; we had lost touch since my initial memorable encounter with him at the MJYC leadership training course. By the time he was teaching Mark, Rabbi Levi was already distinguishing himself as Rabbi Sanger's successor.

While I was there that day, board member Philip Appelboom attempted, unsuccessfully due to my UIA commitments, to interest me in getting involved in the organisation. At the time, I had no inkling of just how involved I would later become. Despite my protestations, in 1978, Theo Tropp, the senior vice-president of TBI, approached me to join the board. He expected to take over as president when Sol Segal retired at the forthcoming AGM and he had heard about my work at the UIA through Isador Magid. Theo said that TBI's communal standing belied its true problems and he felt that young and driven board members were essential to its future survival.

A short time later, I received a call from Isador urging me to accept the offer. He also hinted that he was planning to give generous financial support to the organisation. This was real pressure! Over the next few months, other members made similar approaches. In my heart, I knew that the die had been cast. But my first focus was to plan for Mark's approaching bar mitzvah, with Ada.

As expected, on 12 August 1978, Mark performed his bar mitzvah faultlessly and made us very proud. Luckily, the black eye he had been given during a cricket match at Sunday school the week earlier cleared up just in time. Following the Temple service, at which Rabbi Levi officiated, we hosted a celebratory luncheon in one of the smaller reception rooms at Leonda By The Yarra.

After the bar mitzvah, I could no longer avoid the question of my future involvement on the board of TBI. I decided to accept on a one-year trial basis. So, at the AGM of 1978, I was elected to the board under the leadership of Theo Tropp as president and Gunter Lesh as senior vice-president. Meetings were held monthly, with Rabbi Levi playing an important role in all the discussions. Our cantor, Avraham Jacobi, a Sephardi Jew born in Israel (to parents from Greece's ill-fated Jewish community of Salonika) also attended some of the meetings.

My first years on the board were mostly devoted to listening and learning about the manifold activities of TBI. It was clearly a period of expansion. Attendances at weekly services were good and the High Holiday services drew increasingly large crowds. Our main concern was maintenance and upkeep of the Temple building and, more importantly, the lack of facilities needed to deliver TBI's ambitious programs. Nothing highlighted this situation more than the fact that at our winter board meetings we would keep our coats on and sit huddled around a small electric heater.

Theo Tropp was the initial driving force behind the reconstruction program that would physically transform the Alma Road site over the next decade. Under his leadership, Frank Steen (who later served as president of the King David School council) of the architecture firm Steen & Tan was engaged to design and supervise the project. Unfortunately, Theo did not live to see the work commence, as he died whilst still in office in July 1981. He was succeeded by Gunther Lesh, who served as president for the following three years. During that time, my position on the board continued to consolidate and, in 1983, I was appointed senior vice-president.

One of the positions I held along the way was honorary treasurer. I found the accounts in good order but determined that the systems needed to be digitised. Temple member Jenny Gorog provided advice regarding the purchase of a computer system. However, before we could input all the membership data, we needed to check that the names, addresses, and dates of *yahrzeits*, birthdays and special anniversaries were correctly recorded and up to date. I was unprepared for the resistance that came from several members, scarred by the Holocaust, who were concerned that comprehensive communal record-keeping could expose them to the risk of being rounded up or arrested, as had occurred in Europe during World War II.

Board membership also involved interstate meetings for the Australian Union for Liberal Judaism and the opportunity to connect with other board members. In particular, I had the opportunity to hear the interesting life story of fellow board member Peter Kolliner. Peter was born in Hungary, where his parents converted from Judaism to Catholicism. Peter married a Catholic woman but, as he told me, he had always felt the pull of Judaism. After his divorce, Peter married Barbara, a warm and delightful Jewish woman, and he returned fully to Judaism via TBI and the Liberal movement. Peter was also a successful businessman in the metallurgical field and a lover of classical music. The more I got to know him, the more I liked him, and I felt that he would enjoy a great future in the leadership of TBI.

I also successfully recruited two close friends to the board, both of whom made significant contributions through their advice and generosity: Geoff Opat, a professor of physics; and Adam Ryan, a successful developer and businessman. Ada and I were also close to their wives, Diana and Yoko.

At the time, our primary focus was to rebuild the Temple. Rabbi Levi worked closely with the architects and my time was mostly spent devising fundraising strategies. We knew that raising the funds would require a herculean effort from our membership base which, fortunately, had grown substantially.

At an initial planning meeting held at the home of Philip and Doreen Appelboom, we invited several engaged and connected members of the congregation to contribute their ideas. Frank Mahlab advocated for a $3000 per family donation target, payable over three years, and, after some discussion, that was adopted as the best approach. Paul Littmann, a professional marketer, and Lionel Carrick, who owned a photography studio, offered to produce, on a pro bono basis, the presentation materials required to show to potential donors.

Our next challenge was to establish an appropriate structure for this ambitious project. The catchy name finally selected was 'Fund for The Future' and a tax deductible trust was established by TBI's solicitor, David Payes, of Phillips Fox & Masel. I was nominated director of the trust and we were honoured that Victorian Supreme Court Justice William Kaye agreed to act as the inaugural chairman of the appeal.

In August 1981, the Fund for The Future was finally launched and the personal canvassing work began. We undertook a detailed analysis of TBI's membership and allocated members to volunteers. The potential donors with the highest giving capacity were put into a separate category for Rabbi Levi and me to approach personally.

For the next few years, regularly approaching members became my substantive role. I would call a prospective donor and request the opportunity "to discuss the Temple". It was difficult for members to refuse a visit from Rabbi Levi, so high in regard was he held among the general membership. Generally, three meetings were scheduled per week: two on weeknights and one each Sunday morning. The pattern was always the same: the members were invited to discuss their likes and dislikes and, after they had unloaded their feelings about TBI, Rabbi Levi would deftly address their issues. I would then begin the sales pitch and show the architectural sketches in the promotional materials. We were regularly surprised by the members' generosity. Initially we expected to raise $750,000, but ultimately, we raised pledges in excess of $2.4 million.

Several very large pledges enabled us to arrive at this gratifying total. Isador Magid had promised to be generous if there was evidence of successful fundraising from the general membership. When we felt ready to discuss our progress, Rabbi Levi and I met with Isador. We showed him the plans and drew his attention to the resources centre, which would incorporate a library, meeting rooms and offices. He was impressed and readily pledged $100,000, a huge sum in those days that dwarfed, by far, any other donation. It then seemed logical to name the centre the Isador and Ira Magid Resource Centre. I returned home feeling quite triumphant. That was a particularly happy day because it coincided with Mark receiving news of his outstanding HSC results.[69]

The next major fundraising coup came from a totally unexpected source. Lorraine Topol had recently immigrated to Melbourne from Johannesburg and had quickly become an involved member of the congregation. She called me one day and invited me to her apartment in Toorak where she lived with her two daughters, Caren and Sheryl. She revealed that she wished to donate $100,000 in honour of her late father, Bennie Slome, a successful businessman who had once been the chairman of the United Liberal Congregations in South Africa. We decided to name the large room behind the *bimah*— planned to be the venue for *kiddushim* after services, as well as major social events— Slome Hall. Lorraine later joined the board and, in 1990, was elected president, serving a distinguished two-year term.

My next approach was to Mark and Joyce Southwick, who were part of an established and generous Jewish family. Mark was happy to hear about the plans and the progress of the appeal. He pledged a donation of $50,000 and was pleased to be offered the naming rights for The King David School preschool located behind the Temple. Mark would go on to serve as president of The King David School

---

[69] Following in the footsteps of his uncle, Jack Gringlas, Mark was the dux of Wesley College. In 2021, Richard's daughter Mia Moshinsky was also dux of Wesley.

council from 1980 to 1987. I was also very pleased to receive a sizable donation from Raymond and Mary Lou Orloff for the new library.

Once we had raised sufficient funds, we commenced the rebuilding program whilst continuing to operate from the site. That year, when members had to walk over builders' planks to attend services, was one of our most successful fundraising periods. The signs of activity gave donor members confidence in the project.

In April 1983, a fantastic launch ceremony at the rebuilt Temple marked the culmination of our efforts. The newly elected prime minister of Australia, Bob Hawke, a close friend of Isador Magid, performed the dedication, and the major event was followed by a sumptuous lunch at the Magid home.

Mark's bar mitzvah, 1978

The extended Moshinsky family, c.1980

Launching the Isador & Ira Magid Resource Centre at Temple Beth Israel in the presence of prime minister Bob Hawke, Rabbi John Levi, Isador Magid & Mark Southwick, 1984

A Crossroad

At the beginning of 1982, I started to give thought to my future with the firm. I did not believe I had the stamina to continue for another 17 years until the mandatory retirement age. I was getting tired from the frantic pace of building the consulting division, and Ada noticed my diminished sparkle and zest. She suggested that it was possibly time for change. I thought about transferring to another division, but I had been out of the tax and audit departments for too long and I was not across all the developments in those areas.

To preserve my goodwill in the practice, I gave 12 months' notice of my resignation, and my national partners expressed their regret that I was leaving. Shortly after, at a meeting in Houston, Texas, I shared the news with my international partners, who also expressed their sadness at the news. At a post-meeting cocktail party at Chuck Kaiser's home (he had moved from LA to Houston), Chuck stunned me by saying that my intended retirement was due to "male menopause" and that the cure was to take charge of the American practice.

I was, naturally, taken aback. The American consulting practice was based in Denver, Colorado, with 20 offices around the country. In Chuck's opinion, it was not achieving its potential under the leadership of Don Jacob, who had also signified his intention to retire. Chuck intimated that the remuneration would be substantially above my Australian earnings. Other aspects of this position were also couched in the most attractive terms. I left his house with my head reeling from this sudden turn of events.

I returned home via San Francisco, where I discussed the offer with my close friend from Shanghai, Reuben Wekselman, and his wife Edna. They cautioned me against rushing into it. Their feeling was that I possessed a romantic, but unrealistic view of life in the United States. As a visiting partner, I had become accustomed to being picked up at the airport by limousine, staying at good hotels, and being offered free tickets to shows and ball games. Even my experiences in Chicago, back in the 1960s as a young bachelor, were no preparation for relocating a family to America. The job would also involve constant travel, so Ada would regularly be left to deal with the boys on her own in a new city.

I ruminated upon this on the long flight home, feeling the initial exhilaration waning. I gave thought to the sacrifice I would be asking of Ada, who was experiencing a promising start to her career as a barrister.

At home, there was a letter from Chuck Kaiser outlining further details of the position and requesting a swift response. I now faced a real dilemma! Ada suggested that I speak to Morry Majtlis, as she knew I had developed great respect for his judgement. Morry regularly provided me with invaluable, down-to-earth advice.[70]

Morry's opinion was clear and his reasoning simple: America was a huge country that worshipped wealth, without which, it was difficult to make an impact. He believed that a good reputation was the most important attribute a person could have, and, as far as he was concerned, I already possessed that in Melbourne. He could not see the value of "wasting time" re-establishing it in the United States. His clarity on this issue was convincing.

The following evening, I ran into an old friend, the businessman Richard Pratt, at a cocktail party to celebrate the launch of Rockman Regency Hotel, for which I had done some feasibility studies. While chatting, I shared with Richard that I was at a crossroads in my career. To my surprise, he responded that there was a senior finance position open in his business and that he would love me to join the team at Visy Board (now Visy). He invited me to his home on Sunday morning to discuss the position before I made a final decision about the American offer. I had much to talk to Ada about that evening.

---

[70] Ada and I used to visit Morry and Mania when they lived in a grand house in Dandenong Road. I grieved with Morry and his three children when they lost his beloved Mania, who died prematurely. Luckily for him, he met Sonya soon after and they moved to South Yarra after the children all married. I was honoured when Morry asked me to speak at his 97th birthday party, and I researched the tragedies and triumphs of his life with great enthusiasm. Unfortunately, at the last moment, the gathering had to be cancelled due to his ill health and he died on 13 January 2018. I will always treasure the memory of our friendship.

That Sunday, we enjoyed an informal breakfast before Richard got to the point of the meeting. He had recently hired Michael Naphtali as his finance director, but with the substantial expansion of the business and his vision for the enterprise, he was looking to hire somebody who would bring financial discipline to the company, and he felt that I was the right person for the job. I was naturally pleased with the offer and agreed that I would be open to the opportunity.

Richard said he believed in paying people generously and not haggling over remuneration. He then offered me a $100,000 salary plus a car, which was more than I had been earning. His only proviso was that I make my mind up on the spot, so we could shake hands on it. So I did! He found a used envelope and, with a stubby pencil, wrote the terms, signed it, and asked me to show it to Michael Naphtali who would work out the details. Richard offered to walk me to my car, and I had the distinct impression that he was interested to know what I was driving. I was pleased that I had come in the Jaguar I had bought from one of my partners.

When I got home and told Ada what had transpired, she was elated and relieved that we would not be leaving Melbourne. I called Morry Majtlis to thank him for his advice, and he also seemed very pleased. I then wrote to Chuck Kaiser, politely declining his tempting offer. The decision was the right one; the American practice of Pannell Kerr Forster later collapsed under the weight of severe financial pressures.

The following morning, I imparted the news to my partners, who seemed genuinely happy for me. My next important task was to finalise who would take over as head of the consulting division in the Melbourne office. It had not been clear who would take over the role, but recently a senior accountant named Andrew Lamb had joined the division and was performing very well. He was a diligent worker who quickly absorbed the consulting ethos. He took charge of some of our major assignments, including the feasibility study for the new Intercontinental Hotel in Sydney, as well as the prestigious work for the National Capital Development Commission. The partners agreed that Andrew should be my successor, and I spent several months doing a handover. I was pleased to leave the firm, confident that what I had created over the years would continue in the right hands.

I ended up spending 17 years at Wilson, Bishop & Henderson and its subsequent incarnations—the longest I spent in any organisation during my long professional career. It proved to be a happy period of my life, though not without its challenges.

The partners held a lavish farewell party in my honour at the Hilton Hotel. Denys Horman spoke on behalf of the partnership, lauding my achievements over the years, and he was followed by Keith Beville, my close friend and valued client. I was touched to receive an excellent antique map as a parting gift, and I will always remember, with warmth and appreciation, the generous way in which my partners marked my departure.

HEMISPHERE   MERIDIONAL

pour voir   plus diftinctement

LES TERRES   AUSTRALES

Par Guillaume De l'Isle   de l'Academie Rle des Sciences

A AMSTERDAM chez JEAN COVENS et CORNEILLE MORTIER Libraires

Left: Denys Horman presenting me with an antique map from my partners
Above: Richard, Randall and Mark on the first day of the school year, 1982

PART THREE

1983 - 2022

The Visy Years

I was first introduced to Richard Pratt by Nathan Fink in the mid-1950s. At the time, Richard, or Dick as he was known, was a fellow commerce student at the University of Melbourne and lived at the home of his parents, Leon and Paula, in White Avenue, Kew. A small enclave of Jews—including members of the Fink, Sweet, Mahemoff and Smorgon families—had settled in that leafy suburb, away from Carlton and St Kilda where most of Melbourne's Jewish population resided. They were the founders and principal supporters of the Kew Hebrew Congregation.

Richard was born in the Free City of Danzig (now known as Gdansk, Northern Poland) and migrated with his parents to Australia in 1938 at the age of four. The family settled in the regional Victorian town of Shepparton where there was a small community of Jews working mostly as orchardists. It was there that Leon Pratt first came up with the idea of manufacturing corrugated containers, a much better system for the transport of fruit than the standard cardboard box. By the time I met Richard, his family had moved to Melbourne and their nascent corrugated packaging manufacturing business was operating from a factory in Reservoir, an industrial suburb in northern Melbourne.

Richard already had a reputation quite unlike that of most other Jewish youngsters. Apart from being tall, slim, handsome, and popular with the girls, he was an Australian Rules football player at the Carlton Football Club in the under-19s team. In addition to his prowess as a ruckman (he was awarded the Morrish Medal for 'best and fairest' player in 1953), Richard had an interest in acting. He scored the major role of Johnnie Dowd in the 1955 Union Theatre of Melbourne University production of *Summer of the Seventeenth Doll*, which also toured in London and New York.

While I was able to leave work in time for the start of evening lectures, Richard struggled to get to the university by 5.15pm, so I would reserve him a seat next to mine and I'd bring him up to speed upon his arrival. I also tutored him in accounting as the exams approached. This arrangement worked well for several years, and we became good friends, even though my lifestyle was far less exciting than his.

After university, Richard married Jeanne Lasker, a journalist from Sydney. They eventually settled in Melbourne and had three children: Anthony, Heloise, and Fiona. To his parents' relief, Richard decided to work in the growing family business rather than pursue a career in acting. When his father died in 1969, Richard took over the reins at Visy and spearheaded the company's phenomenal expansion.

In the mid-1960s, Richard had approached me to become Visy's first full-time accountant and invited me to the Reservoir plant to view its recently acquired corrugated machinery. I had already decided to leave Arthur Andersen, but the prospect of one day becoming a partner at another prestige accounting firm was more appealing, so I told Richard that, unfortunately, I would have to decline his offer.

Over the following few years, Richard and I were in contact on an intermittent basis and we continued to get along well. Occasionally we would run into each other at Melbourne airport (then still in Essendon) and sometimes found ourselves seated next to each other on an interstate flight. As treasurer of the UIA, I noticed that over time Richard's donations were steadily increasing—a sign of his growing financial success—and he was soon classified as a major donor. I was also aware that he continued to take an interest in my professional trajectory.

In 1983, when I accepted Richard's generous offer to join Visy, the company was a far cry from the promising, but much smaller, business he had inherited. Indeed, those who, like me, knew Richard in his university days, could not have envisaged that he would possess the determination and vision to create one of Australia's largest manufacturing companies. Some of this success was due to Visy's delivery of outstanding service to its customers. In one legendary example, Richard responded to an after-hours urgent request for corrugated boxes by commandeering a truck, packing the order himself, and driving the truck to the customer.

Great service was not the only mantra of the organisation. Costs were tightly controlled and there was a disciplined reporting structure of key performance indicators. Each plant manager was expected to submit detailed sales and cost reports within 24 hours of the end of each month. It was felt that managers should know monthly results in order to properly, and profitably, manage their operations.

Considerable efforts were also made to foster customer loyalty. Christmas dinners were lavish affairs at leading hotels, featuring top performers. Richard would also entertain the crowd by singing and telling jokes. At the end of the evening, guests would be presented with professional photos in souvenir frames as a memento of the event. These parties were held in every city where there was a Visy plant, and Richard and Jeanne always made a point of attending. Other end-of-year events included well-catered factory tours for senior customer representatives, during which they would be shown recently acquired manufacturing equipment and innovative new products.

Another popular marketing and staff-relationship initiative was the annual AFL grand final lunch and tickets to the iconic match. Each year, Visy purchased hundreds of grand final tickets for select customers and key members of the workforce. The event would start with a sumptuous barbecue lunch at a park by the Yarra in Hawthorn, and then buses would materialise to take the guests to the MCG. Ada and I attended our first such event shortly after I joined Visy. At the park, Richard asked to see our tickets and was unhappy about the position of our seats, so he arranged for the tickets to be exchanged. We were amazed that he would attend to such a minor matter whilst hosting hundreds of people.

Richard was mindful that the success of the organisation depended on employing the right people, fostering a positive culture, and implementing efficient systems. He had been actively recruiting excellent people for several years and, when I started at Visy, the rudiments of a management structure were already in place to complement the small group of experienced people who had been with the business since the early days.

Leon Lunski had been at Visy for decades and he had one of the shrewdest minds I had ever encountered. Richard appointed him to the position of chief purchasing manager. His job was complex; he was responsible for the purchase of items ranging from large machinery to mundane stationery. Michael Naphtali was a finance graduate from the University of Chicago and an alumnus from Hill Samuel, the predecessor firm of the fabled Macquarie Bank. Michael served for many years as Richard's 'right-hand man' on matters of finance and the funding of Visy's phenomenal growth. More recently installed was human resources director Rick Jones, a young man recommended to Richard by Harold Bridger, an Englishman connected to the prestigious Tavistock Institute of Human Relations. Richard had a penchant for using advisers to identify promising people and develop business strategies.

Shortly before I joined Visy, Richard had announced his decision to sponsor an Australian entry in the upcoming America's Cup, the prestigious yacht race. The event was usually won by the Americans, but in 1983 there were two strong Australian contenders. The other challenger, backed by entrepreneur Alan Bond, became the first yacht to beat the Americans in 132 years, ending the longest winning streak in sporting history and sparking celebrations across Australia. Richard's surprising move to sponsor a sailing endeavour had not been popular within Visy and the Pratt family were worried about the publicity. Richard had seen beyond those narrow concerns and felt that it was time to promote his profile. Ultimately, it was a successful strategy that paid off in attracting good staff and business opportunities.

The Pratt name and reputation had already been enhanced some years previously, in 1981, when the family purchased Raheen, a heritage-listed Italianate mansion located at 94 Studley Park Road, Kew. Since 1917, Raheen had belonged to the Roman Catholic Archdiocese of Melbourne and had been the official residence of Archbishop Daniel Mannix, as well as several of his successors.

Jeanne engaged the promising young architect, Glenn Murcutt[71], to restore the house to its original state. This was a complex undertaking that required significant historical research. Jeanne's vision was that the grand ballroom at Raheen would be used for fundraising functions for a range of worthwhile causes. One of my early duties at Visy was to monitor the financial arrangements for the building project. Later, Glenn Murcutt was also engaged to design a spectacular modern extension for the family's private use.

In addition to dealing with the building project and raising funds for the America's Cup sponsorship, during those initial years I was the 'trouble shooter' for several of Richard's financial ventures, including Pratt & Co Financial Services, a newly established merchant banking operation. The chairman was Sir John Knott, who had an illustrious career in the senior branches of the Commonwealth public service.[72] I developed a good rapport with John; we were like-minded in our approach to project analysis and adherence to proper practice. The managing director was Bob Reece, who often clashed with Richard; they had vastly different personalities and attitudes regarding which projects were worthy of investment. Several other bright people were involved in running the company, including a young financier called Ashok Jacob. The death knell for the merchant banking operation came with the 1967 stock market crash, after which the decision was made to wind up the venture.

The disappointing flirtation with the financial services sector did not hinder the expansion of Visy's core business. New manufacturing plants continued to open throughout the country, including in key provincial areas, which entailed a large capital expenditure program managed by Michael Naphtali. This rapid expansion created some administrative and accounting issues, which I was asked to investigate. At that stage, most of the paper needed for the manufacture of corrugated boxes was purchased from Australian Paper Manufacturers Ltd (APM). The APM contract was reputed to be the largest commercial purchase agreement in Australia at the time and I spent many long nights dealing with the inevitable complexities.

---

[71] Glenn Murcutt was later recognised as a leading Australian architect who won several awards including, in 2002, the prestigious Pritzker Architecture Prize.

[72] Sir John Knott was also director general of the Postmaster General's Department and chair of Epworth Private Hospital.

The Visy Years

Eventually I was asked to take over the accounting for the entire Visy manufacturing division and to modernise its administrative systems. The role was challenging as the fast-paced growth subjected the existing systems and personnel structure to considerable pressure. Updating the computer systems was an early priority, and we initiated several evaluations before settling on a viable system. I quickly learnt that all computers were ultimately dependent on the people operating the system and that training was paramount. I also had to engage tech-savvy staff. My most outstanding recruit was Vin O'Halloran, whose role grew with the demands of the organisation. By the time I left Visy, he had attained the most senior financial position in the hierarchy.

I got on well with the plant and manufacturing managers, a competent and tough group of people who coped well with Richard's performance-demanding and 'no nonsense' attitude. My closest association was with John Wheeler, who was recruited as human resources manager. Over time, John's innate management skills were recognised by Richard and he quickly rose through the ranks to head the corrugated manufacturing complex.

Richard's decision, in the late 1970s, to expand into paper recycling signalled the beginning of a turbulent period in the company's history. Visy's commercial dependence on APM, combined with the fact that a new machine had become available that could recycle wastepaper into usable paper for the manufacture of corrugated cardboard, led to this prudent diversification.

Although the cost/benefit analysis of this new source of primary materials was financially compelling, the problem was that, initially, the quality of the corrugated end product was inferior. Naturally, the plant managers were unhappy about using recycled paper as they had to deal with the repercussions of producing inferior corrugated cardboard. Richard held fast, however, and through sheer dint of his strong personality, was able to prevail. Over time, the quality of the recycled raw materials substantially improved, and this resource, coupled with the expansion of sales, proved to be immensely profitable.

President of TBI

In addition to the frenetic tempo of fundraising and attending meetings, when I became president of TBI in 1984, I had the privilege of sitting on the *bimah* during the Friday night and Saturday morning Shabbat services. Each week, I would also congratulate the young person who had completed their bar or bat mitzvah and present them with gifts to mark the occasion.

I took the trouble to remember the names of most of the congregants and I tried to converse with as many members as possible at every occasion. I took to heart the advice of a wise, long-standing Temple member. He said, "Sam, the Temple office can make mistakes (he was referring to errors such as the dates of *yahrzeits* or anniversary announcements), but if you remember the member's name and the substance of a previous conversation, they will always forgive you!"

As president, I would attend meetings of the newly formed Australian Union for Liberal Judaism, which were often held in Sydney. There, I would meet with the likes of Hans Jensen, Ted Waxman and Dr Philip Bliss. On one occasion, Ada and I hosted a long and entertaining lunch for a senior delegate from the World Union for Liberal Judaism, Rabbi Alexander Schindler, and his wife, Rhea. Alex was a true raconteur with a great fund of stories and jokes from his days as a paratrooper with the United States Army.

I was regularly invited to attend the annual World Union conference in Jerusalem, which coincided with my trips to Israel on UIA/Keren Hayesod business. At one conference, Rabbi Levi introduced me to the head of the Liberal movement, Rabbi Richard Hirsch, and his Russian-born wife, Bella. Over time, I got to know them both quite well and I was frequently invited to the eclectic gatherings held at their Jerusalem apartment. Rabbi Hirsch also visited Australia on several occasions and was a strong supporter of the initiative to establish The King David School. Philip Bliss and I also worked with him to establish the UIA Progressive Fund, an entity created specifically to raise funds from Liberal Jews in Australia.

During my presidency, I became committed to making TBI's poorly attended annual general meetings (AGMs) more popular and engaging. In that vein, I suggested we combine the 1985 AGM with a celebration to mark the 25th anniversary of Rabbi John Levi's ordination. The idea came to me after John shared the story of how he had serendipitously discovered the whereabouts of the mysterious 18th century illustration that adorned the cover of the book *Australian Genesis: Jewish Convicts and Settlers 1788-1850* that he had co-written with Dr George Berman in 1974. John had accidentally stumbled upon the original artwork when exploring the bookshops and galleries of Soho in London. He finally discovered that the work was by Robert Dighton (1782-1814), an acclaimed artist and social commentator. When John recounted that he had wanted to purchase the illustration, but the price of the work was unfortunately beyond his means, I realised that it would be the perfect gift to express the gratitude of the congregation for his 25 years of service to our community. I contacted John's close friend from his schooldays, the celebrated entertainer Barry Humphries, who was living in London at the time, and I was thrilled that he was able to successfully acquire the work on behalf of TBI.

We advertised that there would be a surprise presentation at the AGM that year. As anticipated, we had a record attendance, and the atmosphere was particularly festive. After we quickly dispensed with the formalities of the AGM, I had the great pleasure of presenting the original artwork to Rabbi Levi.

My second, and final, year as president was largely devoted to continuing our fundraising efforts. Rabbi Levi and I were pleasantly surprised by the readiness of our members to financially support TBI. I also enjoyed the opportunity to get to know many members of the congregation well and to address any issues they raised.

As I had done at the UIA, I attended the TBI offices every Wednesday morning for a briefing with Rabbi Levi, to sign cheques and to make a myriad of minor decisions. The administration at TBI was ably managed by Margot Joseph (who, together with her husband Peter, were friends of ours). We got along well, and I believe Margot appreciated the regularity of our interaction.

No account of my years on the board and as president of Temple Beth Israel would be complete without mention of Irene Benjamin, the indefatigable, long-standing president of the TBI Women's Guild and a regular attendee at Friday night and Saturday morning services.[73] Nothing was too much trouble for Irene, who assisted at every function. We worked well together, and I continued to visit her until she died at the impressive age of 100.

By the middle of 1986, it had become abundantly clear that Peter Kolliner would be my deserving successor, and I took pains to keep him informed of all developments to ensure a smooth changeover. Just before the AGM that year, Peter asked me to continue chairing the board meetings, as he felt, with justification, that the roles of chairman and president should be split. I agreed to his request and for the next two years I was the ex-officio past president as well as chairman of the board. (This arrangement was later dropped by presidents who felt comfortable executing both roles.) The AGM did not have the fanfare of the previous year but, pleasingly, it was well attended by members interested to hear about the progress of our fundraising efforts and the second stage of the reconstruction plans.

I finally stood down from the board in 1988, many years after I took Mark to his first bar mitzvah lesson. In that time, I also experienced, with immense pride, the bar mitzvahs of Randall and Richard at Temple Beth Israel. I will always treasure that intense period, which included some of the most satisfying years of my life.

The only vestige of my role as TBI president is that I continue to be invited each year, along with all the other past presidents, to sit on the *bimah* for the concluding *neilah* service on Yom Kippur. It is truly an honour.

---

[73] As mentioned in the book about Temple Beth Israel, *A Time to Keep*, Irene was born in England, and raised within the orbit of Rabbi Danglow's St Kilda Hebrew Congregation. She became involved with TBI through her late husband, who liked the idea of sitting together as a family during services.

With Barry Fradkin, Isador Magid & Lorraine Topol at TBI, c.1990

Media Businesses

Richard Pratt was an avid gatherer of information, but he didn't have the patience to read lengthy documents. He preferred to have complex information relayed to him verbally—and succinctly. To this end, he would invite certain people to walk with him in the Royal Botanic Gardens on Sunday mornings. A favoured walking companion was the celebrated journalist, Sam Lipski. On one walk in 1987, Sam imparted to Richard that the Rubinstein family, descendants of the founder of the Melbourne edition of the *Jewish News*, were interested in selling the newspaper.

Richard decided to buy the newspaper and install Sam Lipski as its editor-in-chief. Richard then approached me to join him and Sam as a director on the board. Sam's reputation was such that, immediately upon his announcement as editor-in-chief, the number of subscribers increased significantly. I took my position as director seriously and enjoyed the break from the accounting and administrative demands at the Visy head office. Working with Sam was a delight and I always looked forward to our conversations.

There was much to do on the financial and administrative side of the media business and, when Richard was unable to attend, I would chair the monthly board meetings. At one meeting, Sam proposed that the masthead merge with the Sydney *Jewish News* to form a national newspaper that would service the whole Australian Jewish community, including Canberra where a fledgling Jewish community was establishing itself in the nation's capital. The Sydney *Jewish News* was owned by the Klein family. Peter Klein managed the business while his sister, Susan Bures, served as editor. Personnel integration issues needed to be addressed but, in due course, a workable arrangement was achieved.

While this foray into community journalism was interesting and diverting, an ominous situation was developing within Visy's flagship manufacturing operations. After a significant drop in paper sales to Visy, APM decided to expand its business operations to include the manufacture of corrugated paper. Before long, a savage competitive environment emerged that resulted in neither company making any profit and customers taking full advantage of the buying bonanza. The diabolical financial situation generated much tension at Visy. Looking back, I admire the way that Richard held his nerve and coped with the strain. In the end the situation was resolved, but not without a financial toll.

Towards the end of a driving holiday in New Zealand, I received a call from Michael Naphtali, informing me that I was needed to travel to Israel as soon as possible to carry out due diligence on *The Jerusalem Post*, the iconic newspaper that served as the main English source of news in Israel. I was told that Robert Maxwell, the infamous English Jewish businessman and publisher, had bought *Davar*, the leading Hebrew evening newspaper in Israel, and now had *The Jerusalem Post* in his sights. The word was that Maxwell's predilection for cost-cutting took no account of journalistic ethos and the team at the *Post* were fearful. They were looking for a white knight, and felt that Richard Pratt fit the bill, based on his success with the *The Australian Jewish News* and his reputation as one of Australia's most successful businessmen.

On arrival in Jerusalem, I met Ari Rath, the publication's long-term editor-in-chief. No doubt he hoped that with the newspaper under Richard Pratt's ownership, he would enjoy the same editorial independence as Sam Lipski. After a quick tour of the production facilities, I spent time with Shalom Weiss, the newspaper's treasurer. Unfortunately, the *Post*, which was owned by the Histadrut (the General Organisation of Workers in Israel), was not making money. The only profitable part was an investment in the Israeli equivalent of the Yellow Pages. The newspaper's plant was outdated and so was the culture of the organisation. I then met with some of the senior people from the Histadrut and formed the impression that they had lost interest in *The Jerusalem Post*. Through my own sources, I learned that some American interests, associated with the right-wing Herut movement, were also seeking to buy the newspaper, to change its editorial position from left-wing to right-wing.

On my return home, I felt compelled to write a negative report. I could not see how the Pratt Group could invest the effort and funds needed to resuscitate the neglected newspaper. However, since *The Jerusalem Post* was a prestigious newspaper with a valuable masthead, after much internal debate and consideration, we made a low offer. Unsurprisingly, we were quickly outbid by the right-wing group.

I thought that the negativity of my report and the trumping of our offer would be the end of the matter. However, much to my surprise, Richard wasn't prepared to let go of the opportunity to own an Israeli newspaper. He had gleaned that there was probably room for a second, more balanced, lively and informative publication, so he asked Sam Lipski whether he knew someone who could head such a venture. Sam Lipski suggested Hirsh Goodman, a South African-born Jew who had made *aliyah* to Israel and developed an excellent reputation as a journalist. Hirsh Goodman was invited to Melbourne and, after several discussions, the concept for *The Jerusalem Report* was born.

On my next trip to Israel, I worked closely with Hirsh to establish the magazine. We offered the position of financial controller to Aaron Zucker, who welcomed the challenge of setting up the administrative and financial structure. Sam Lipski and Hirsh recruited several excellent journalists, including Ehud Yaari, the award-winning commentator and author. The magazine got off to a great start and, from the beginning, filled the void, sensed by Richard Pratt, of serious analysis of pertinent issues. In due course, Charles Bronfman, from the preeminent Canadian family of wealthy philanthropists, was brought in as a shareholder to relieve some of the budgetary pressures generated by the magazine's rapid expansion. I knew Charles Bronfman in his capacity as a board member of Keren Hayesod, and I enjoyed and valued my association with him.

Meanwhile, back in Australia, the newspapers were becoming a distraction from the pressing needs of running the ever-expanding Visy business. Eventually, in the mid-1990s, Richard sold his interest in *The Australian Jewish News* to Peter Klein and, later, he also sold his remaining interest in *The Jerusalem Report*.

Soon afterwards, I decided it was time to consider my retirement. I advised Michael Naphtali and Richard Pratt that, after eight years at Visy, I wished to retire from full-time work. Richard accepted my resignation with some reservation. Naturally, I agreed to his request that I find a replacement and stay on during the transition period. After a thorough search, Steven Crawford was appointed to the position, which he held for several years.

Around the same time, John Wheeler retired as general manager of the corrugated manufacturing division, which was a great loss to Visy as he was an extremely capable executive. Before he left, John arranged to take an interest in Glama Pak, a Visy subsidiary specialty packing company, with a right to sell it back to Visy at a point in the future. Richard asked me to serve on the board of Glama Pak to look after his interests, which I was happy to do.

I left Visy feeling that I had learned as much as I contributed. It was an organisation unlike any other I had previously worked for. Visy was entrepreneurial in the extreme, with an emphatic passion for success, founded on sound judgement and instinct. In particular, my experience confirmed that expecting high performance from individuals need not be at the expense of fair, or even generous, treatment.

I could not end this narrative of my years at Visy without acknowledging Richard and Jeanne Pratt for their kindness and generosity. Ada and I were regularly welcomed to their home for dinners and lunches and were always included in family events such as bar mitzvahs, weddings, and birthday receptions. They were incredible hosts. We also greatly appreciated their invitations for us to holiday on their marvelous yacht in Sydney Harbour, as well as at their superb holiday homes in Honolulu, London and New York.

———◆———

On 28 April 2009, I was devastated to hear an ABC news broadcast announcement that Richard had died from prostate cancer. He left an enormous legacy and his funeral service at Kew Hebrew Congregation was appropriately full of mourners from all walks of life.

I remain particularly sorry that Richard did not live long enough to fully witness the success of his son, Anthony, who took over the reins of his business empire, and to experience the joy of watching his growing number of grandchildren find their place in society.

Above: With Charles Bronfman
Centre: At a meeting to finalise the purchase of AJN
Below: Reviewing documents with Sam Lipski

The first cover of *The Jerusalem Report*, October 1990, signed by Hirsh Goodman

Opposite, above: With Aaron Zucker
Below: Sam Lipski & Richard Pratt, 1995

Federal Chair of UIA

In 1989, I was surprised to learn through the grapevine that Saul Same intended to relinquish the position of UIA federal chairman, and I wondered who would be asked to fill this prestigious position. One wintry Sunday evening, I was working in the front garden when Keith Beville dropped by. He asked me if I'd heard that Saul Same was retiring, and then floored me by saying that my name was being bandied about as Saul's possible successor. I was caught off guard and impulsively blurted out that I could be interested. Within minutes, Saul and Isador both rang to congratulate me on my new role.

After confessing to Ada that I had inadvertently accepted the position without discussing it with her, I spent the rest of the night wondering what I had gotten myself into. After further reflection about how I would balance it with the demands of my work at Visy, I felt confident that I could navigate both roles successfully. I was also excited by the prospect of frequent visits to Israel.

My first task as federal chairman was recruiting my replacement as treasurer. Fortunately, Joseph Frank, a respected partner at the accounting firm Lowe Lippmann, accepted the role.

I then decided to strengthen the UIA's connection with the smaller Jewish communities outside of Melbourne and Sydney. I started taking regular trips to visit local fundraisers in Australia's smaller cities, which widened the reach of the annual appeal, and yielded worthwhile increases in the number and size of individual pledges.

In South Australia I found a willing ally in Hilda Hines, the matriarch of the Adelaide Jewish community. Her husband and son were leading local businessmen and they all generously facilitated introductions to potential donors. Mark Leibler kindly agreed to speak at one very successful Adelaide campaign launch.

Another Adelaide visit was particularly notable. Ada had agreed to join me and, on the morning of our scheduled trip, she received word that there was a sealed letter at her barristers' chambers at National Bank House from the Chief Justice of Victoria. We stopped off on the way to the airport to collect the letter. To her delight, she discovered that her application to 'take silk' had been successful. She was to become a Queen's Counsel (QC), the third woman in Victoria's history to be bestowed such an honour. We were both overjoyed.

My decision to include Tasmanian Jewry in the federal UIA campaign was accepted despite considerable skepticism regarding the cost-benefit of visits to Hobart and Launceston. Even though it was one of the oldest Jewish communities in Australia, extending back to the convict days, the Jewish population in Tasmania had substantially diminished with the growth of the Melbourne and Sydney communities. I organised an event in Hobart and invited Sam Lipski to speak, and his wife, Aura, a talented musician, to perform. It was Hobart's largest Jewish gathering for many years, and Sam's rousing words and Aura's soulful Jewish music created a moving atmosphere. That night, scud missiles from Iraq fell on Tel Aviv and I told the crowd that the people of Israel would be heartened to learn that this most distant Jewish community had gathered to show their solidarity at a critical time. The amount collected in cash and pledges at the end of the meeting was a state record.

Over several years, I also successfully opened appeals in Perth and Brisbane. As these initiatives gathered pace, the federal executive decided to recruit a professional federal director, Yitzhak Lev. He was an energetic and hard-working Israeli who successfully organised federal conferences for honorary participants from around Australia, as well as key professional staff. These annual gatherings alternated between Melbourne and Sydney and provided valuable opportunities to share information and fundraising techniques and, above all, to cement significant relationships.

Another important initiative was the resolution of the long-standing and vexed issue of tax deductibility for UIA donations. The UIA was considered an overseas charity and therefore donations were not tax deductible under Australian tax law. The issue was also politically challenging because UIA funds were sometimes directed to communities of new migrants (many of whom had escaped antisemitic persecution in the USSR) who resided beyond the 'green line', the areas controlled by Israel since the Six-Day War.

Several people at the law firm Arnold Bloch Leibler (ABL), most notably Mark Leibler and Helene Teichmann, tirelessly lobbied the government in Canberra to introduce the deductibility arrangements by highlighting the humanitarian issues and the extraordinary projects supported by the UIA. Their campaign was bolstered by the fact that Helene had travelled extensively and was able to provide first-hand accounts of the plight of the prospective migrants. Once government approval was finally secured, it was necessary to create the legal framework for the UIA to meet its obligations under the arrangement. This work was undertaken by several people, including ABL lawyers Joey Borensztajn and Michael Dodge who worked with me. I have endless admiration and gratitude for the work done to effect this change, which had an enormous enduring impact for the UIA.

One year, Ada and I were pleased to be invited to the national ZFA conference in Canberra organised by Helene. There we met interesting people, listened to informative talks and attended the closing dinner at Government House. Ada was lucky to be seated next to the governor-general, Bill Hayden, and they discussed their shared passion for art. After the formalities, he gave Ada a private tour of the extensive art collection at Government House which she greatly enjoyed.

There were several pockets of the Jewish community that chose not to donate to the UIA for ideological reasons, including he Bundists—members of the secular Jewish movement that promotes Yiddish culture and eschews Zionism. However, other groups didn't donate to the UIA seemingly because they were unaware of its significant work. Embarrassingly for me, many members of my own Liberal congregation at Temple Beth Israel (TBI) and its affiliates fell into this category. Possibly it was because Central European Jews, who founded TBI, were never as ardently Zionistic as Eastern European Jews. Whatever the reason, the demographics of the Liberal Jews of Melbourne were changing, and I felt the time had come to test their attitudes towards Israel, particularly because Rabbi John Levi, our highly respected senior rabbi, was openly pro-Israel, and Isador Magid, an extremely generous member of TBI, was widely known as the leader of the UIA. With the tax deductibility issue favourably resolved, the three of us felt confident about directly approaching members of the Liberal Jewish community of Melbourne to fundraise specifically for projects initiated and controlled by the Movement for Progressive Judaism in Israel, and did so with great success. I remain pleased that the UIA continues to engage successfully with the Progressive/Liberal communities in Australia.

Each year, I would travel to Israel three times to attend the meetings of the world board of the Keren Hayesod and the general meetings of the Jewish Agency. These meetings gave me great insight into the Israel fundraising scene, particularly the different challenges experienced in appeals across the globe. These trips also facilitated introductions to key Jewish leaders from across the Diaspora, as well as some legendary personalities in the Israeli political scene. I was fortunate to meet the global campaign leaders—many of whom were towering figures, both in their personal achievements and in their contributions to the UIA—including politician Shlomo Hillel, who masterminded the transfer of 120,000 Iraqi Jews to Israel. He was world chairman of Keren Hayesod, and a hero in Israel. I felt honoured to serve with him. Another memorable figure was Mendel Kaplan, head of the South African appeal. He was a steel tycoon and a dynamic and visionary Zionist, the epitome of Herzl's famous saying: If you wish it strongly enough, it is no longer a dream! I was also inspired by Julia Koschitzky, who raised prodigious sums while heading the Canadian appeal. Julia's energy, effectiveness and true love for Israel and the Jewish people was infectious.

On several occasions, I travelled to Israel with Keith Beville, and I enjoyed serving the UIA with such a close friend. When visiting Israel with Ada, we always stayed at the famous King David Hotel. I would request a room on level five, facing east so we could watch the sun rise over the Old City—a magical experience—before indulging in the legendary buffet breakfast. The King David Hotel was the hotel of choice for important people attending international conferences and one morning I found a top-secret message had been slipped under the door, addressed to a diplomat with a similar name to Moshinsky!

<hr />

There was much excitement, particularly amongst the local South African Jewish community, when it was announced that Nelson Mandela would be visiting Australia in October 1990, just a few months after being released from prison after 27 years of incarceration.

Jews from South Africa first started arriving in Australia in the late 1950s after the strict introduction of Apartheid. That inflow gained momentum in the wake of the Sharpeville massacre in 1960, when police killed 69 Black South Africans during a race riot. Culturally, the South African Jews were similar to many of their Australian brethren as they were mostly descendants of Lithuanian Jews who left Europe to escape antisemitism. They were also like Australian Jewry in their fervent and generous support of Israel. As a result, they integrated relatively smoothly and, before long, started to occupy senior positions in Jewish communal organisations, including the UIA.

Nelson Mandela appreciated the ongoing support he had received from the Jews of South Africa and understood their deep connection to Israel. However, he also voiced support for Yasser Arafat and the Palestinian cause, which the Jewish community struggled with.

There is no doubt that Mandela was a great leader and merited the adulation he received worldwide. Despite his long imprisonment, he did not preach any hatred towards his oppressors. His advocacy for a truth and reconciliation policy, rather than a campaign of revenge against his tormentors, won him considerable respect.

I was very pleased to be invited to a much-anticipated meeting attended by Nelson Mandela and Jewish community leaders at the Hyatt Hotel in Melbourne. Mandela had a mesmerising persona and the guests hung on to his every word. I remember one electrifying story of suffering endured under the Apartheid regime's secret police. Mandela described how two policemen threatened to immerse a newborn baby headfirst into a pot of boiling water unless the nursing mother revealed the whereabouts of her husband, who was suspected of being a member of the Black resistance.

At question time, Mandela was asked about his supposedly close relationship with Arafat, to which he blithely replied, "Your enemy is not necessarily my enemy!"

That meeting will long remain a vivid highlight of my communal involvement.

⟫◆⟪

I was particularly fortunate that my years as federal chair coincided with the waves of migration of Ethiopian Jews and Jews from the former Soviet Union. To me, the rescue operations that resulted in these vulnerable Jews settling in Israel with dignity were the epitome of Zionist ideology in action.

Operation Moses was a co-operative effort between the Israel Defense Forces, the CIA and Sudanese security forces to rescue thousands of Ethiopian Jews languishing in refugee camps in Sudan and suffering from famine and antisemitic persecution. Over a seven-week period, from November 1984 to January 1985, the world watched on in awe as 30 flights transported at least 8000 Ethiopian Jews to Israel, including 1000 orphaned children. In 1991, under the covert Operation Solomon, a further 24 flights brought thousands more Ethiopian Jews to Israel.

At the time, Isador Magid was also the chair of the Jewish Agency's Immigration and Absorption Committee, which had the mammoth task of overseeing the integration of these new immigrants, many of whom were suffering from starvation and dealing with significant trauma. For us, raising funds through the UIA to support this project felt exhilarating.

For several years there had been a growing campaign in the Jewish world to liberate the Jews in the Soviet Union. Australia played a leading role, spearheaded by Isi Leibler, an important Jewish community leader.[74] The Jews in the Soviet Union were forbidden from expressing their religious and cultural traditions, and were also subject to growing state-endorsed antisemitism. The cruel persecution of Jews in that part of the world was, of course, nothing new; it was the reason my own ancestors had escaped Russia in the 1920s and eventually moved to Shanghai. Unfortunately, the unexpected death of Stalin in 1953 had not improved the situation for Russian Jews. Merely expressing the desire to leave the Soviet Union could earn extreme opprobrium. Even Jewish children were subject to persecution in the playgrounds.

The campaign to liberate Russian Jews assumed worldwide dimensions. Then, finally, in the late 1980s, Mikhail Gorbachev, the courageous new general secretary of the Soviet Union, lifted restrictions on emigration. I still vividly recall the special meeting of the Keren Hayesod world board when Mendel Kaplan told us that we should prepare for an annual influx of 100,000 Jews from the Soviet Union. He then revealed the magnitude of the additional funds—tens of millions of dollars—needed for the Jewish Agency to integrate these new *olim* into Israel. While the brunt of this cost would fall on the government of Israel, Diaspora Jewry would also be

---

[74] The efforts of Isi Leibler, and that of many other communal leaders, is meticulously documented in the award-winning book by Sam Lipski and Suzanne Rutland, *Let My People Go.*

expected to contribute. We left the meeting sobered by the immensity of the task ahead.

The influx of Russian Jews, welcome as it was, presented unique problems for the Jewish Agency and the Israeli government. Identifying who, in fact, was Jewish, was an inevitable issue, particularly as intermarriage was common in Soviet society and circumcision was rarely practised. While previously some Russian Jews had tried to pass themselves off as non-Jewish, now (possibly for the first time in history) there were non-Jews who were trying to pass themselves off as Jews so they could migrate to Israel.

Despite these challenges, there was much enthusiasm for welcoming back Jews, many of whom were in danger of losing their Jewish identity. Moreover, family reunions were finally possible for Russian Jews after decades of limited contact with relatives in the Western world. During the communist era, such reunions were discouraged and often dangerous. In the case of our family, Eva was finally able to re-establish contact with a long-lost family member when he moved to Israel.

Over time, the Russian *olim* contributed significant talent to Israeli society across many disciplines, particularly in the fields of music, science and medicine. There were, however, inevitable complications regarding the recognition of professional qualifications, and unfortunately not all of them were able to work in their professional fields. I recall visiting an Israeli printing press that employed several recently arrived Russian immigrants. As a Russian speaker, I asked a foreman what his job had been in Russia, and he sheepishly replied that he had been a senior director of the Soviet scud missile program.

Without doubt, some of our most memorable moments involved witnessing the arrival of travellers on flights from Moscow, Leningrad and other major Soviet cities. Ada and I vividly recall a spectacular dinner hosted by Israel's president, Chaim Herzog, in a hangar in Lod airport. As the customary speeches ended, we were asked to rise and congregate near the hangar's entrance. A small band materialised and, a few minutes later, an airplane taxied towards us. The plane doors opened and out stepped Israel's newest immigrants, direct from Moscow. Whole families, including those with young children, started to descend to the sound of traditional Israeli music. The atmosphere was electric. We rushed over to greet them, and everyone began dancing the hora. Several passengers, who had been carrying violin cases, played along to the joyful music. Ada and I were moved to join in the spirit of the occasion and enthusiastically danced with the children. Then several buses arrived to take the passengers to their accommodation for their first night in the Jewish State of Israel. We all agreed that the conference could not have ended on a better note.

On that trip I had one last important job in Jerusalem before returning to Australia—to secure the future leadership of the UIA. For some weeks I had been in discussions with Frank Lowy (now Sir Frank Lowy), who succeeded me as the federal chairman under the updated constitution, which mandated that the federal chairmanship should oscillate between Sydney and Melbourne. He had called me from Sydney to let me know that he would be unable to join the conference because he was under too much pressure from his giant business. I let him know that I did not wish to take up the role again, and I suggested that we persuade Mark Leibler to take it on. Frank authorised me to make the approach.

Coincidentally, Mark Leibler was in Jerusalem on World Zionist Organization business and was staying at the King David, so we set up a meeting in the coffee shop at the hotel. Mark agreed to consider the idea and, once the federal executive approved the offer, he formally accepted the position. Mark was a very successful choice, and his leadership of the UIA over several years did much to enhance its profile and credibility.

Fortunately, Jewish Australians were also buoyed by news of the influx of Russian Jews to Israel, and the Victorian UIA Appeal was able to capitalise on this enthusiasm. Over the next few years, record levels of pledges were received.

The 1992 campaign opening was slated to be the most ambitious ever. The gala event was held in the prestigious Great Hall of the National Gallery of Victoria, with its magnificent Leonard French stained-glass ceiling. Every seat in that large hall was taken by supporters and prospective donors eager to hear Julia Koschitzky, the inspirational keynote speaker. I was also honoured to receive the Askan Award to mark my 25 years of involvement in the UIA, including three years as federal chairman from 1988 to 1991. I was thrilled that Ada, our three boys and other members of our extended family were able to attend that night. When Isador presented me with the award, he rightfully claimed credit for recruiting me to the UIA way back in 1967. He also lavished praise on Ada, as was customary. At that point, one of our sons turned to their uncle Jack to ask what Ada had done to merit the praise. In his usual fast-thinking fashion, he loudly retorted, "She didn't divorce him!"

For several more years I sat on the world board of Keren Hayesod and I was appointed chair of the Financial Oversight Committee. During the October 1994 meeting of the board in Israel, we were informed that a peace treaty, brokered by US president Bill Clinton, had been secretly negotiated between Israel and the Kingdom of Jordan. This was an historic moment as the only other peace deal between Israel and an Arab state was the 1979 treaty with Egypt. It was announced that the official signing ceremony would take place at the southern border crossing of the Aravah on 26 October 1994, and that everyone at the meeting was invited, subject to security clearance by the US Secret Service. I was thrilled that Moshe Gur was able to wrangle a last-minute invitation for Mark and his wife Sidra, who were living in Jerusalem at the time. The venue was festooned with national flags, and our allocated seats were close enough for us to get a good view of Bill Clinton, Yitzhak Rabin and King Hussein as they addressed the huge crowd and ceremoniously signed the treaty document. It was an unforgettable experience. I left Israel feeling eternally grateful to Isador Magid for introducing me to UIA all those years ago and nominating me to the world board.

Bracing for a Soviet influx

With the gates of the Soviet Union now opening up, Israel could face an influx of immigrants unprecedented since the mass migration from the Arab countries in the early years of the State. Recently back from Israel, SAM MOSHINSKY, executive chairman of the United Israel Appeal of Australia, presented this report on the huge challenge facing Israel to the UIA of Victoria's annual general meeting earlier this month.

Sam Moshinsky: 'A new Esther, in the form of glasnost, has made it possible, for Jews to leave in numbers we dared not hope for...'

"In expectation of mass aliyah from the Soviet Union, the Government of Israel has declared that it will absorb every Jew who wishes to come on aliyah to Israel, and together with world Jewry, will allocate the necessary resources so that klitah will be efficient and successful.

The Government of Israel and the Jews of the Diaspora are aware that this is an historic moment, in which access has been regained to the Jews of the Soviet Union, who for many years were cut off from the rest of the Jewish world, and that everything possible must be done to absorb them successfully in Israel."

We live in troubling government Israel underlines. The official expectation is that 100,000 Jews from the Soviet Union alone will make aliyah. The cost of this program will be $US2 billion. 1.5 billion will be absorbed by the people of Israel, burdened as they already are by a sluggish economy, high taxes and the grinding demands of their military obligations.

World Jewry, including the affluent United States and other western Jewish communities, will be asked to shoulder only one quarter of the total sum, $US500 million.

The money will be spent on the following:
• Construction of 25,000 new housing units.

• Renovation of 5,000 existing public housing units.

other bodies to ensure that the primary fund-raising efforts are not splintered.

Not since those exhilarating days of 1948 and the massive aliyah which followed, has the Jewish world and Israel so confronted the basic purpose of the founding of the State.

For this greatest of movements of Jews from their established homes is not only

Ironically enough, glasnost is also the cause of this modern exodus, as well as facilitating it. The increasing assertiveness of the many nationalities making up the Soviet Union, whether they be Moslem, Latvian or Ukrainian, spells trouble for the commonly held undercurrents of anti-semitism. Local nationalism is not good news for us. Mr Sharansky believes that

Soviet olim, of all ages, arrive in Israel to star

18 — THE AUSTRALIAN JEWISH NEWS — FR

The Australian Jewish News, 1989

EXODUS II
U P D A T E

EXODUS II CONTINUES INTO THE NEW YEAR

Some of the most significant events in the recent history of Israel and Russian Jewry would not have been possible over the past 12 months without the strong support of Jewish communities around the world according to the Federal Chairman of the United Israel Appeal, Sam Moshinsky, who has prepared this special message.

As we approach the end of another Jewish year we can truly look back upon a very remarkable 12 months.

For the past year has witnessed an ingathering of the Jewish people, unprecedented since those heady days in 1948 following the birth of the State of Israel.

As I write these words in the first week of September, Israel expects to receive this month alone, nearly 20,000 new Olim from the Soviet Union.

This is a figure greater than the total number of all arrivals from Russia for the past nine years!

By the end of 1990 some 150,000 arrivals will have made their home in Israel.

My friends, the financial burden of sustaining this modern Exodus is placing intolerable strains on Israel and her people. The resources of her fragile economy simply cannot cope with absorption and at the same time provide basic services to the existing population, many of them young people just out of the Defence Forces.

The Australian Jewish Community has responded generously to this joint responsibility of the Jewish world and Israel in ensuring that the lifeline of Exodus II can continue uninterrupted.

BUT PLEDGES DON'T HELP - ONLY MONEY DOES!

PLEASE TRANSLATE YOUR PLEDGES INTO CASH, AS SOON AS POSSIBLE.

Sam Moshinsky

Together with my Federal colleagues, Isador Magid, Saul Same, Joseph Brender, Michael Faktor and Keith Beville, I thank you for your full support to date.

On behalf of the United Israel Appeal of Australia, we wish you and your families a Shana Tova, Well over the Fast and, another milestone Jewish Year, full of achievement and pride.

Prime Minister Shamir's Letter - Page 3

With Keith Beville (above), Frank Lowy (centre) and Moshe Dayan (below)

Above: Addressing the UIA federal conference, 1991
Below: With Hilda Hines, chair of the Adelaide UIA

Opposite, above: With Saul Same
Below: With Meron (Ronnie) Medzini

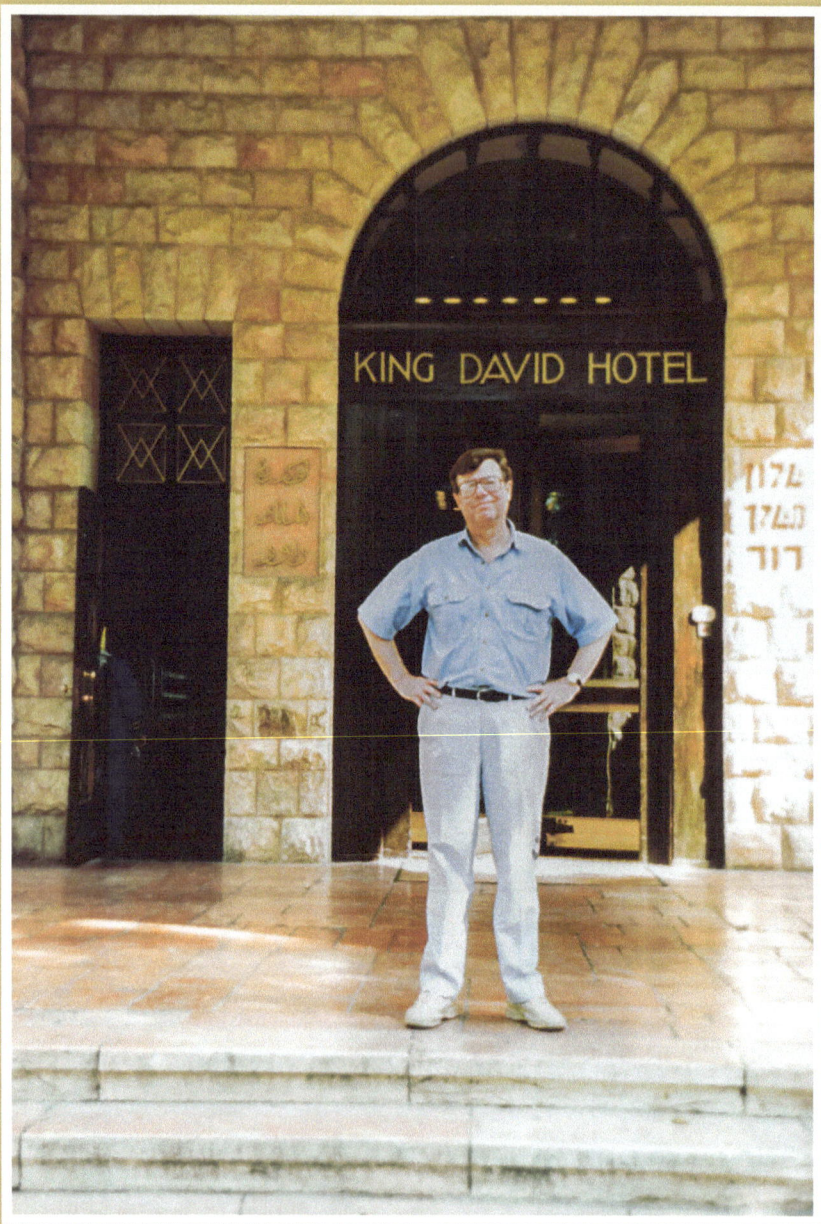

Outside the King David Hotel, my favourite place to stay in Jerusalem

Above: Dancing on the tarmac with Ada and the Russian *olim*
Below: President Bill Clinton addressing the audience at the Jordan-Israel peace
treaty ceremony, the Aravah, 26 October 1994

Semi-Retirement

I decided to parachute gently into the final stage of my working life. I liked the idea of working on my own as a financial consultant in a congenial part of Melbourne. Luckily, I already had three fee-paying roles, all connected to Visy. One was the directorship of Glama Pak, representing Visy's interests. I was also a member of the newly established Visy audit committee and of the Visy superannuation committee. All of these involved regular meetings that I found interesting, and which gave structure to my working life.

I was pleased to find a well-appointed serviced office in Osborne Street, South Yarra, which had a dedicated car spot and a boardroom available for hire. When I discovered that the office had a 'modern' switchboard, with a receptionist who would answer my calls as if she were my personal assistant, I immediately signed the lease.

Fortunately, it did not take long for new clients to materialise. I soon received invitations to join the new audit committees for the state government's Department of Treasury and Finance, and the City of Melbourne. I was steadily developing expertise in this new area of corporate surveillance in the private and public sectors.

Before long, other opportunities arose, including an offer from Ada's brother Jack to become chairman of CMG, the growing electric motors business that he had taken over from Mietek. This was a particularly enjoyable assignment. I chaired regular board meetings and introduced the discipline of analysing the cost benefits of proposed courses of action. The arrangement worked well because, even though Jack owned the business, he adhered to the spirit of good corporate governance under my chairmanship. It was particularly satisfying to witness the strong growth of CMG Electric Motors, which became a leading player in the industry.

I was also pleased that Peter Klein invited me to stay on the board of the *Australian Jewish News* and to act as chairman of the organisation. This was a prestigious and paid role that involved management of the financial affairs of the newspaper. The position also entailed regular trips to Sydney to report to Rodney Adler, son of the deceased Sydney financier Larry Adler, who had invested in the paper.

Rodney was always gracious and friendly. At one of our meetings, he joked about being disappointed to discover, after due diligence, that he could find no 'fat' to trim to increase the AJN's profitability. I was pleased to hear this, as it reflected well on my financial stewardship over the years. Rodney would later cede control of the Adler family's holding to his two sisters, Kathy and Roxanne.

I enjoyed my years as chairman at the AJN. I would devote every Friday morning to the affairs of the paper, arriving early for a meeting with Sam Lipski, the editor-in-chief, to discuss communal matters and operational issues. We would then meet with the senior staff to resolve any problems and to discuss special editions and other initiatives to increase subscriptions. I would then review expenses and sign cheques. After that, time permitting, Sam and I ('the two Sams') would go out for a light lunch to review the morning's events and indulge in community gossip. Each month, Sam and I would also travel together to spend time in the AJN's Sydney office.

Another valued client was Lorraine Topol, who sat on the board of TBI and managed a considerable portion of her family's wealth. She engaged me to be her personal financial consultant. Meetings with Lorraine and her investment advisor usually took place at her home in Toorak. Lorraine was keen for her daughter, Sheryl, to learn about managing wealth so, whenever possible, she would also attend the meetings. Tragically, Lorraine's other daughter, Caren, had died many years earlier while piloting a light aircraft.

Lorraine was both astute and willing to learn, and we developed an excellent working relationship. I also greatly respected her generosity as a philanthropist. When Lorraine, her sister Renee Super, and their

New York-based brother, Ian Slome, decided to form a family board to manage their joint fund, Lorraine asked me to represent her interests on the board. I was also asked to chair the regular family meetings, which were held either in the US or in Melbourne. A 'junior' board was also established for the benefit of the next generation, under the guidance of Renee's financial advisor, Grahame Leonard, and me.

Towards the end of 1994, I met the prominent businessman, Michael Buxton, at a social function. He asked for my business card and, a few days later, he rang to request that I undertake a special assignment. Michael was in the process of amicably dissolving his partnership with Max Beck. The two men had started their successful property development business, Becton, in 1976, and he needed an experienced accountant to monitor adherence to all the steps of the dissolution. The value of the varied assets was considerable, ranging from multimillion dollar properties down to prestige cars. I agreed to take on the job as it sounded challenging and interesting.

Upon completion of the assignment, Michael asked if I would accept the honorary position of chair on the board of his newest initiative. The Michael Buxton Contemporary Australian Art Collection, a family trust, already had a board comprised of art advisors, prominent lawyer John Fast, and family members. My role would involve managing financial and administrative matters relating to the trust and chairing the meetings.

Ada was an astute art collector, and, through her, I understood enough about the Australian art world to know that this role could be interesting for both of us. Michael Buxton did not just spend serious money on acquiring notable artworks based on the recommendations of his panel of experts. In his enthusiasm for collecting art, permeated with a distinct sense of individualism, he would host regular events with renowned artists such as Howard Arkley, Peter Booth, Mike Parr and Tony Clark. The collection grew to include significant works by Juan Davila, Rosalie Gascoigne, Bill Henson, Tracey Moffatt, Callum Morton, and many others of that illustrious calibre. Somehow, in addition to establishing another successful property development enterprise, the MAB

Corporation, with his brother Andrew, Michael also found time to enrol in the same modern art course at the University of Melbourne that Ada was attending. After their lectures, Michael and Ada would go for coffee and discuss art. This association resulted in Ada being invited to join the board several years after I retired as chair.

———— ◆ ————

I have a deep voice that, over the years, many have compared to that of the actor James Earl Jones. Having often been asked whether I had my own radio show, I was elated when, in 1995, Jewish community icon, Dulcie Kanatopsky, invited me to present a monthly program on the Jewish radio network, broadcast on stations 3EA and 3ZZZ. The Sunday morning timeslot was a prized one, and I was told that I could speak on any topic of interest to Jewish listeners. The program would allow me to indulge in my lifelong fascination with current affairs and, finally, I would be putting my resonant voice to good use.

Every Thursday, before the scheduled Sunday broadcast, I would go into the radio station and record my show. I read widely and seemed to have an instinct for the unusual, so I spoke on a variety of topics pertaining to local communal issues, the Jewish world, and Israeli politics.

According to Dulcie, with whom I enjoyed a robust and enjoyable dialogue, the series was a success, with increasing numbers of listeners, so my initial term was extended. However, after approximately 25 shows, I decided that it was time to move on from radio, and Dulcie reluctantly agreed to release me from our arrangement.

Following the radio show, it was a logical progression for me to start giving public talks about world events. In later years, I gave monthly talks on a wide variety of topics to the residents at Emmy Monash Aged Care. These were very popular, judging by the growing attendances. As an expression of their gratitude, Maureen Shulsinger and Shirley Jacobs, who scheduled my talks, threw a wonderful birthday party for me.

In 1995, I was approached to become the chair of the Jewish Museum of Australia: Gandel Centre of Judaica.[75] The Jewish Museum, the brainchild of the late Rabbi Ronald Lubovsky, was a relatively new institution that had quickly become the pride of the Melbourne Jewish community under the guidance of its inspiring executive director, Helen Light, and with generous support from Pauline and John Gandel.

I was impressed by the dominant influence of so many successful women at the museum, both on the board of management and amongst the large cohort of volunteers. Leah Mann, Zelda Rosenbaum, Sandy Benjamin, Emma Kranz, Lee Liberman and other like-minded women at the museum were resourceful and energetic. They seemed to enjoy excellent working relationships and held great respect for Helen Light and each other.

The museum had already developed a reputation for mounting educational and meaningful exhibitions. However, I quickly realised that the institution's constitution required an overhaul. Despite being a busy senior partner at ABL, John Fast spent many hours working on a pro bono basis to produce an excellent revised constitution, which had an enduring positive impact on the institution.

I was comfortable chairing the board meetings and overseeing the museum's financial and administrative processes. I also identified several areas that required improvement, including the museum's shop, which carried a range of books and Judaica. The shop was run by a capable committee but lacked the necessary funds to expand its product range. I approached my friend and former client, Morris Majtlis, who readily agreed to provide an interest free loan of $50,000, which he later commuted to a donation.

Another boost to the museum's annual budget came via Helene Teichmann who, in her capacity as a consultant to the National Australia Bank (NAB), suggested a liaison arrangement through the bank's outreach initiative. We successfully negotiated that NAB would contribute $50,000 each year to become the curatorial sponsor

---

[75] My friend Barry Fradkin became co-president of Montefiore homes the same year, and our appointments were featured together in the AJN.

of high-profile exhibitions. This mutually beneficial arrangement lasted for several years.

In roughly 1996, at his request, the museum hosted a visit by the Catholic Archbishop of Melbourne George Pell (who was later elevated to cardinal, and whose reputation was tarnished by child sex abuse allegations before his death in 2023) and a retinue of senior men from the diocese of Melbourne. Archbishop Pell had heard about the museum's reputation for excellence and was keen to emulate aspects of it in a museum for the Catholic community. Helen Light and Zelda Rosenbaum, a long-standing board member, gave the group an extensive tour. Following the formalities, I showed Archbishop Pell photographs of me from my St Francis Xavier days in Shanghai, standing in the playground with fellow students and our Marist Brothers teachers in front of a prominent statue of Jesus Christ. I remember saying, "I'm guessing you didn't expect the chair of this museum to have had a Catholic education in Shanghai!"

———◆———

In the mid-1980s, I was pleased to receive a call from Grisha Sklovsky, whom I hadn't caught up with for some time. We went out for lunch, and I learnt that since retiring from his role as the chief information officer at ICI, Grisha had become the foundation chair of SBS, the public service broadcaster dedicated to informing Australia's increasing multicultural population. SBS had been established in the mid-1970s as two 'ethnic' radio stations and was later also expanded to include a television station broadcasting in numerous languages. I remember being surprised by how much Grisha's views had changed since the 1950s, when he had strongly advocated that immigrants should assimilate into the dominant Anglo-Saxon culture.

Grisha had done such a fine job at SBS that he had recently been awarded an Order of Australia. After hearing more about my extensive community involvement, he suggested that I might also be eligible for such an honour. At the time I thought little of it but, after Grisha's death in 1995, the idea was rekindled.

A few years later, Ada asked our son Mark to spearhead the nomination process, and, on 14 April 2000, I received an official letter from Government House in Canberra confirming that I was being considered for an award of the Medal of the Order of Australia and requesting my consent to accept the honour. Of course, I immediately replied in the affirmative. On 12 June 2000, my name was listed in The Queen's Birthday 2000 Honours List in the daily newspapers. As was the practice, the *Australian Jewish News* published my photograph in its next edition alongside a detailed narrative of the achievements of all the Australian Jews who received an award.

We celebrated with a cocktail party at home, at which our friends, Margot Costanzo and Chris Arnold, entertained the guests with a witty skit in my honour. A few months later, on a beautiful autumn day, at a formal ceremony at Victoria's Government House, my medal was presented to me by our friend, the governor of Victoria, Sir James Gobbo. It was a humbling and exhilarating occasion for an immigrant from Shanghai. I owe my deepest gratitude for this honour to Ada, Mark and everyone else who supported my nomination.

———◆———

In 2004, as my 70th birthday approached, I decided to fully retire from professional life and community work. I was humbled that all my clients expressed regret at my departure and touched that many expressed their gratitude with special gifts, including Lorraine Topol who gave me a carefully curated selection of choice wines. At a Jewish Museum meeting, Zelda Rosenbaum thanked me profusely on behalf of the museum and presented me with a book on the life and sayings of Isaiah Berlin, knowing that he was one of my favourite philosophers.

John Wheeler arranged a sumptuous Glama Pak retirement lunch at Cosi, a terrific restaurant. John owned a vineyard and was a lover of fine wines, so Ada and I gifted him a book on Bordeaux wines as a token of our appreciation. After several speeches, John produced an envelope with a card inscribed by him and his wife Coralie, as well as the Glama Pak board and executives. Inside was a voucher for two business class around-the-world airline tickets! Ada and I were absolutely stunned by the generosity and thoughtfulness of this incredible gift. I could not have hoped for a more exciting and gratifying end to my working life.

———◆———

I enjoyed those years in my Osborne Street office. I would often go out for lunch in South Yarra with friends and clients, and, after retiring from the law, Ada would regularly work at the second desk in my spacious office. During that time, we began discussing the possibility of me writing a memoir to document my early life in Shanghai. I suspect she hoped that such a book would put an end to me endlessly repeating stories about Shanghai whenever anyone asked where my accent was from. The more we talked about the idea, the more I warmed to it.

Barry Fradkin

Sam Moshinsky

Montefiore Homes, Jewish Museum get new presidents

THE Montefiore Homes for the Aged and the Jewish Museum have new presidents following recent annual meetings.

At Montefiore Homes Barry Fradkin succeeds Graham Slade as president with Sue Blashki as vice-president and chairperson.

Dr David Fonda is the other vice-president, with Max New as secretary and Keith Nathan as treasurer.

At the Jewish Museum Sam Moshinsky takes over the presidency from foundation president Rabbi Ronald Lubofsky who has stepped down after 17 years in office.

Rabbi Lubofsky was named foundation life president and the meeting payed glowing tribute to his work for the museum since its inception.

With Mr Moshinsky on the executive are June Helmer (vice president), Zelda Rosenbaum (chairperson), Sandy Benjamin (hon. secretary) and Maurice Weiskop (hon. treasurer).

The *Australian Jewish News*

At a Jewish Museum of Australia function with Sir Zelman Cowen (in the centre)

Governor-General of the Commonwealth
of Australia and
Chancellor of the Order of Australia

To

SAMSON ABRAHAM MOSHINSKY

Greeting

NOW KNOW YOU that, with the approval of Her Majesty Queen Elizabeth The Second,
Queen of Australia and Sovereign of the Order of Australia, I have been pleased to award you
the Medal of the Order of Australia in the General Division.

I DO by these Presents authorise you to hold and enjoy the dignity of such an award
together with membership in the said Order and all privileges thereunto appertaining.

GIVEN at Government House, Canberra, under the seal of the Order of Australia
this twelfth day of June 2000.

By His Excellency's Command

Secretary of the Order of Australia

Receiving a medal of the Order of Australia from Sir James Gobbo

At Government House with fellow Order of Australia medal recipients,
Barry Hutchins and Darvell Hutchinson, 2000

Loss

On 21 June 2005, whilst holidaying in Port Douglas, Ada and I received the devastating news that Ian Permezel had died. His death came as a terrible shock, as I had seen him the previous week and he had seemed to be recovering well from hip surgery. I was, of course, absolutely devastated to lose such a close friend. I had already experienced the grief of losing a best friend and confidant when Alex (Sasha) Vinogradov died prematurely in 1986.

Ian's funeral service at the Boyd Chapel at Springvale Botanical Cemetery was crowded with hundreds of mourners—diverse friends and colleagues from throughout Ian's life—who had come to pay their respects. I was honoured to be asked to speak, along with Aubrey Schrader who had known Ian since boyhood.

Aubrey shared wonderful anecdotes about Ian and their Scotch College days. I chose to concentrate on Ian's extensive and impactful involvement with not-for-profit organisations and I expressed my enduring gratitude to Ian for helping me to integrate into Australian society by encouraging participation in communal organisations.[76] I also shared a story about a fateful lunch at the iconic Ceylon Tea Centre, during which Ian had revealed his desire to leave the world of merchant banking to work for an organisation with a worthwhile social purpose. By coincidence, immediately after that lunch, Barry Hutchins had advised me that the James McGrath Foundation, responsible for the Odyssey House drug rehabilitation program, was looking for a chief executive officer. I put Ian's name forward and, within days, he was offered the job.[77]

Ian was cremated and his ashes were strewn at the base of his favourite tree in Fawkner Park, where he and his wife Susana used to enjoy sitting on Sunday mornings.[78]

I think of Ian often and miss him very much. It would have been so wonderful to experience this stage of life with Ian and Sasha, and to reminisce about the fascinating times we shared. But it is not to be, and I am much the lonelier for that.

---

[76] Ian introduced me to the Jaycees, the RMIT Capital Funds Appeal Committee, and the Lord Mayor's Children's Camp Appeal. [77] I served as a director of the James McGrath Foundation from 1982-1985.
[78] Ian married Susana after his marriage to Jane ended in divorce.

With Aubrey Schrader, Ada, Ian & Susana Permezel

Work-Life Balance

A narrative of my 'four score' years, would not be complete without painting a picture of my diverse and active life outside of work and community involvement.

I am grateful for the hobbies and interests that have provided balance and great pleasure throughout my life. I first discovered the joy of reading in the well-stocked library of the Jewish Club in Shanghai, where I stumbled upon *The Razor's Edge* by Somerset Maugham. I then devoured all his other books. Many years later, Ada and I stayed at the Oriental, an historic hotel in Bangkok, and I was thrilled to learn that it had been frequented by Maugham. I also came across the writings of Upton Sinclair at an early age, and proceeded to read everything he had written, including the celebrated Lanny Budd series of historical novels.[79]

Around the same time I discovered books, I was also being inculcated with a love of history by the Marist Brothers at St Joan of Arc's College and St. Francis Xavier's College, the last two schools I attended in Shanghai. World War II history became my dominant interest, followed closely by books on Israel and China. I am very proud of my personal library, which heavily features books on these subjects.

After the defeat of Japan in 1945 and the entry of American troops into Shanghai, the city was flooded with all manner of exciting consumer goods, including kits to make wartime planes, ships and tanks out of balsa wood using a penknife or razor blade. The enjoyment I derived from constructing model fighters and bombers complemented my interest in reading about the war, and this soon became a staple hobby. In Melbourne, I discovered the shop Hearns

---

[79] I was so taken by the series that many years later I decided to collect all 12 books by hunting through Melbourne's secondhand bookstores. Later I discovered that there was a 13th book in the series that I finally tracked down whilst holidaying in New York. I discovered the elusive tome in the antiquarian section of the Strand Bookstore. I finally had the satisfaction of owning the complete series which, happily, I still possess in my library today.

Hobbies, which stocked a wide range of kits, and I became a regular customer. More recently, when my brother-in-law, Jack, built a sophisticated model railway, I was pleased to construct the numerous stations and other railway facilities.

My enduring interest in photography was first kindled in Shanghai with the discovery of old Lumiere plates. This led to a failed attempt to set up a serious photography enterprise called Ascot Photo Studios. In Melbourne, as soon as I was able to afford it, I purchased a Minolta 35mm camera, which I used to comprehensively record the early lives of Mark, Randall and Richard. In the 1990s, I upgraded to video photography, which had become increasingly available to amateurs like myself.

Wonderful holidays have been a special feature of our family life. Carefree trips to Phillip Island when our children were young were soon upgraded to holidays in Surfers Paradise, usually accompanied by Ada's parents and brother Jack. As the boys grew older and our financial position improved, we enjoyed a number of holidays overseas. In the early 1980s, our family travelled to North America. The trip featured skiing in Aspen, and visits to Disneyland and Universal Studios, as well as to Mexico City and Acapulco. The highlight of the trip, for me, was the unexpected and joyous reunion with Reuben Wekselman, my close boyhood friend from Shanghai, and his Israeli wife, Edna, in San Francisco. Reuben had become a successful orthopaedic surgeon and we remained in contact until his passing.

Another much-anticipated trip was to Asia, in May 1986, in the immediate post-Mao era. Returning to Shanghai with my wife and three sons was an emotional and enlightening experience, with a mandatory personal guide to ensure that we did not stray too far from the approved itinerary. Many Chinese people were still wearing the drab Mao uniform, but I was relieved that Shanghai had retained much of its original charm and character despite so many decades of communist rule. Japan also proved to be a real eye-opener as it was, at that time, at the forefront of modern electronics, and Tokyo was brightly lit with neon signs. This manifestation of prosperity made it hard to believe that Japan had been so abjectly defeated in World War II.

Shanghai continued to hold a special place in the hearts of the European residents who left after the defeat of the Japanese in 1945 and the eventual capture of the city by Mao Tse Tung's Red Army in 1949. As a result, reunions of Jewish Shanghailanders, dispersed across the globe, became commonplace. The shared refrain at each reunion was that we had lived in a unique place, during a particularly significant period of history.

The first of these Shanghai reunions were held in the United States and Israel, where most of the German and Austrian Jews, who had sought refuge in Shanghai during World War II, had migrated. They wished to commemorate their deliverance from the Nazis, despite the hardships encountered in the Hongkew district where they were incarcerated by the Japanese authorities. In documentaries produced in the aftermath of the reunions, many of these Jews acknowledged the lack of antisemitism they had experienced from their Chinese neighbours in Shanghai—a stark contrast to the virulent hatred they had encountered from local populations in Europe.

Russian Jews tended not to participate in those initial reunions, as our experiences in Shanghai had been vastly different. However, in September 1991, I was invited to a special Shanghai reunion in Philadelphia that was open to all former Shanghai Jewish residents. I was assured that the program would include wider facets of the Shanghai experience, so I accepted with alacrity; I was keen to reunite with the many close childhood friends I had not seen for decades.

Much water had flowed under the bridge, but it was an absolute pleasure to reconnect and share the stories of our new lives. The reunion reignited several significant friendships with the Wekselmans, the Toochins and the Tomkins.

Following the Philadelphia reunion, I flew to New York to stay with my close friends, Ehud and Naomi Houminer, at their home in Scarsdale, New York.[80] I went to his impressive office at Phillip Morris,[81] which featured a framed photograph of Ehud in the White House, standing next to the president, George H. W. Bush.

⸺◆⸺

Once the boys had grown up, Ada and I enjoyed the opportunity to plan our own trips. Europe, particularly Paris, was a great favourite and we regularly enjoyed cruises (although Ada never enjoyed them as much as I did). Memorable holidays include: a trip with Jack and Dianne on the Regent Line to Vietnam in 2007; a cruise to the Galapagos Islands with Erica and Harry Frydenberg; and another fascinating cruise through the Panama Canal, with a glorious morning entry into San Francisco Bay.

In November 2010, Ada and I joined Leah and Leon Mann, on a trip to Broken Hill, the frontier mining town in the far west of New South Wales. The purpose of the journey was to participate in the commemorative events organised by the Broken Hill Historical Society and the Australian Jewish Historical Society to mark the centenary of the Broken Hill Synagogue.

I had been in Broken Hill on business decades earlier but had not seen any vestiges of Jewish life. However, Leon, who was born in the town, is an expert on the brief, but remarkable, Jewish history of the region. The Jewish community in Broken Hill (mostly Lithuanian and Russian Jews) thrived for several decades following the 1880s, but by 1960 the number of Jewish residents had dwindled to only 15.

---

[80] I had previously stayed with the Houminers at their home in Geneva.
[81] Ehud was the CEO of Philip Morris USA (1988 - 1990).

The Broken Hill Synagogue, a simple 20th century stone building located in Wolfram Street, was closed in 1962 and eventually taken over by the Broken Hill Historical Society, which restored the derelict property. The property is now the Synagogue of the Outback Museum and the headquarters of the Historical Society. Leon, together with Professor Suzanne Rutland and Margaret Price, marked the occasion by co-writing a book called *Jews of the Outback: The Centenary of the Broken Hill Synagogue 1910–2010*.

We were surprised to discover that approximately 200 Jewish people, mostly from Melbourne and Sydney, had also made the long trek to Broken Hill. The packed schedule of celebratory events included the book launch and a visit to the Jewish section of the Broken Hill Cemetery. The highlight of the weekend was the re-enactment of the laying of the foundation stone of the original synagogue on 28 November 1910. At Leon's request, I was pleased to play the role of Abraham Rosenberg who had chaired the original ceremony.

All the events were reported in the local newspaper, *Barrier Truth*. It was a wonderful and unforgettable experience.

———◆———

Indulging my interest in video photography

Above: With Mark, Randall & Richard outside the Doumer Apartments, Shanghai, 1986

Opposite above: Alumni of St Francis Xavier's College in Shanghai, celebrating the school's 130-year anniversary in 2004

Opposite below: At the Philadelphia reunion with Reuben Wekselman, Joe Toochin & George Tomkin

Extended Family Life

The past 30 years have been a period of incredible growth in our family. Our three sons have all enjoyed great success in their careers. Mark is a justice of the Federal Court, Randall is a cardio-thoracic surgeon and inventor of medical devices, and Richard is a solicitor, specialising in corporate and commercial law. Pleasingly, they remain very close to each other. This is partly due to the good fortune of their marriages. Our three wonderful daughters-in-law, Sidra, Natalie and Romy, are all intelligent women, supportive wives and great mothers. Ada and I also feel fortunate to enjoy close relationships with the Kranz, Fookes and Sormann families. Our extended family gatherings are a delight.

Our eight grandchildren—Danita, Jamie, Amira, Joey, Tommy, Hannah, Sonny and Mia—arrived in rapid succession between 1995 and 2003. We have so many happy memories of their early years, featuring parties, sleepovers, Shabbat dinners and holidays at our beach house in Lorne.

Their childhoods were meticulously preserved by me on video! Over many years, I improved my filming and editing skills by joining specialist clubs. I am particularly proud of the eight films I produced that chart each grandchild's journey from birth to bar or bat mitzvah.

Our grandchildren continue to fill us with pride. We are extremely impressed by their values, as well as their intellectual and scholastic prowess.

Celebrating Joey's bar mitzvah, 2011
[Back] Amira, Hannah, Danita & Joey [Front] Tommy, Mia, Jamie & Sonny

After Nathan's marriage to Anne Heggie, and Elijah's departure to England, Eva sold her modest house in Canterbury, and moved to Sydney to live with her widowed sister, Nusia, with whom she was very close. Nusia owned a comfortable flat near Bondi Beach, and the sisters enjoyed a happy and very social life.

When Nusia developed dementia, she moved to a specialised nursing home and Eva visited her every day. Subsequently, when Eva's own health began to deteriorate, she reluctantly returned to Melbourne and moved into a flat at the Montefiore Homes for the Aged. Nathan and I went to see her regularly, and she occasionally came to our home on Friday nights for Shabbat dinner with the family.

Eva was eventually diagnosed with stomach cancer and suffered great pain. One sad day, I passed on the news that her sister, Nusia, had died in Sydney. She replied simply, "Now I can go." A few days later, on 16 October 1999, Eva died, aged 87 years. She is buried in the Rose Garden in the Bet-Olam section at Springvale Cemetery.

Mietek was a wonderful father-in-law to me and to Dianne, and he had a particularly close and loving relationship with Ada and Jack. He also greatly enjoyed his role as grandfather and great-grandfather. The family loved visiting the home he built in Orrong Road, Toorak, which was filled with fascinating contraptions and gadgets, and appreciated his warmth, great sense of humour and generosity.

After his third marriage to Dita Gould resulted in divorce, Mietek struck up a connection with a good-natured and caring woman named Barbara Marker, who was his companion throughout his later years. He remained active and social throughout this time, often meeting with close friends at a favoured café in High Street, Armadale.

Mietek had continued to work at CMG for many years, as Jack built it into the leading electric motor manufacturing and distribution business in Australia. Fortunately, Mietek lived long enough to see the business sold for a significant sum to a large American corporation in 2010.

Mietek never lost his zest for life. He took the extended family on two wonderful holidays to Club Med Lindeman Island, and we are still amazed that, at the age of 90, Mietek singled-handedly organised his own birthday party at Leonda.

Mietek passed away on 28 December 2010 and was buried next to Lida. He left a remarkable legacy, and we think of him often.

With Eva, 1993

Jack, Ada & Mietek, 2010

Goodbye Shanghai

My first memoir, *Goodbye Shanghai*, was launched in 2009 on my 75th birthday. Around 450 people attended the festive event at the Astor Theatre, an Art Deco building reminiscent of the buildings in the French Concession of Shanghai where I grew up, and watched a short film about my early life. That night, I could not have anticipated the wonderful reception the book would receive, nor the fascinating journey that it would take me on.

The book received positive publicity locally and, over the next few years, I was also invited to speak at several literary events in Shanghai. I was thrilled when, in 2011, the Shanghai Publishing Company published an edition of the book in Mandarin, which was housed in the libraries at several Chinese universities that offered courses in the Jewish history of Shanghai. In 2012, my memoir was released as an eBook and, at Ada's urging, an audio edition, narrated by me, was also made available for sale.

I unwittingly became the go-to expert on the Jewish history of Shanghai, and, in the ensuing years, I was consulted on numerous books, plays and films. I have also been interviewed on many radio and television programs. *Goodbye Shanghai* has engendered my retirement years with interest and purpose. It has also allowed me to indulge in my love of history and sharing family stories.

By far, my most enjoyable travel experience was an extended family trip in 2012 to celebrate our forthcoming 50th wedding anniversary.

Goodbye Shanghai

Ada and I decided that, rather than celebrating our anniversary with a lavish party for our friends at a fashionable venue, we would enjoy a special celebration with our children and grandchildren, as we felt especially happy and proud of the family we had produced. Ada came up with the brilliant idea of a family holiday with a difference; China was an immediate and obvious choice.

Mark and Sidra recommended their travel agent, Cher Roscoe, who had a good relationship with a specialist China tour group, Eastern Journeys. We departed in April 2012, when all the grandchildren were on school holidays, and, for a special treat, we all flew business class on China Airlines.

For the next two weeks, our group of 16 toured Xi'an, Shanghai and Beijing, mainly in our own private bus and accompanied by informative and interesting guides. We were particularly impressed with Eastern Journeys and its influential connections when we visited Emperor Quinshihuang's Mausoleum Site Museum, and were able to gain exclusive access to the lowest of the three levels, so that we could get a better view of the Terracotta Warriors.

We spent a week in Shanghai, staying at the Donghu Hotel, in the middle of Route Doumer (the old name of Dong Hu Lu). By 2012, Shanghai had regained its famed preeminence. We could sense the vibrancy as soon as we entered the inner city and the former French Concession appeared to have maintained all its pre-war elegance.

Our first stop in Shanghai was a short walk from our hotel to visit the Doumer Apartments, the flats our family once owned and occupied. Although the building was off limits to the public, I showed the guards some of the old photographs I had wisely brought with me, which convinced them to grant us admittance. All 16 of us then walked the short distance to the former Jewish Club, now a conservatory of music, as well as to our synagogue around the corner, now a pizza restaurant. We could still see the markings on the side wall where the Stars of David had once been attached.

The highlight of our time in Shanghai was the visit to my school, St. Francis Xavier College. The new heads of this school, now called the Bei Hong Senior School, respect its history, and have preserved much of its heritage, including the main building. They had even nominated a senior teacher to act as liaison with its alumni. As our family alighted from our tour bus, I was thrilled to be greeted by a large sign, welcoming me back to my alma mater. I showed our entourage my old classroom and addressed another class of students about my time at the school more than half a century earlier. It was, however, seeing my grandchildren interacting with the students in the very playground where I had played in my youth, that affected me most deeply.

On our final night in China, at the Peninsula Hotel in Beijing, our grandchildren showed their appreciation to Ada and me with an outstanding performance they had somehow found the time to rehearse. Ada and I deeply appreciated their effort and sentiment.

However, the true finale to the China trip did not take place until a few months later, after we had all arrived home and resumed the normal tempo of our lives. Closer to the actual date of our wedding anniversary in June, Ada arranged for us all to enjoy drinks at home, and to watch the footage I had taken of the trip, followed by a celebratory Chinese banquet at a restaurant in Toorak Village. Just as we finished watching the video, a bus, like the vehicle that had driven us around China, entered Bellaire Court. Ada had secretly devised this surprising touch and had gone to some trouble to organise it. She had also arranged for dinner to be served on two round tables of eight, to reflect our typical Shanghai dining experience. After the banquet, the bus again materialised to take us back to Bellaire Court. It was a most fitting way to commemorate our wedding anniversary trip and a wonderful reminder of Ada's capacity for originality and fun.

Goodbye Shanghai

Of course, *Goodbye Shanghai* has been shared widely amongst many Jewish people who, like me, lived in Shanghai before being dispersed across the globe after the communists came to power. Since its publication, I have regularly received emails from people from my past, and from others for whom the book has rekindled strong memories.

On 3 February 2013, I received an email from Liza Zaslavsky, a resident of Ottawa, Canada. I immediately knew that Liza must be a relative, as my biological mother's name was Bronia Zaslavsky. As recounted in *Goodbye Shanghai*, I only saw my mother intermittently after my parents divorced in 1939. I believe she left Shanghai in 1945 after the war ended. She did not call me to say goodbye, and I never heard from her again. On my part, I never sought information about Bronia, out of respect for Eva, who was a caring stepmother to me and a wonderful grandmother to our sons (who only discovered later in life that she was not, in fact, their biological grandmother).

My book had been recommended to Liza by Lily Indyk (née Prosterman), whose family were old friends of hers—and mine—from Shanghai. They had briefly been our tenants at the Doumer Apartments. Lily and her family had settled in Sydney after the war. When Liza opened the book, she immediately recognised the photograph of me as a young boy on a tricycle as the same framed image that had sat near the entrance of her aunt's home in San Francisco.

Liza explained that she was the daughter of Bronia's brother, Abrasha Zaslavsky. She advised that Bronia had settled in the US and married a man named Norman Samuels, but that they had never had any children. Liza recalled asking about the photograph and Bronia simply replying, "That is my son in Australia" and nothing further!

I will never know what attempts Bronia made, if any, to find out about my life or to contact me. I did not hear from her at the time of my bar mitzvah, nor when I got married. Liza knew only that her father had advised Bronia not to complicate my life through any kind of intervention.

Hello Australia

In her email, Liza mentioned that she would soon be holidaying in Australia. So, a few months later, I travelled to the airport to meet a blood relative from my mother's family for the first time. That weekend, Liza came to our home to meet the rest of the family. It was lovely getting to know her and hearing about her life in Ottawa, where she taught English to French-speaking Canadians wishing to join the Canadian civil service.

Liza shared that Bronia had led a modest life and enjoyed visiting her large family of six sisters, one brother and numerous nephews and nieces who lived in cities across the United States. Bronia died from pneumonia on 8 February 1993 at the age of 84.

When we were in San Francisco in 2014, Ada and I met Liza's sister, Mira Engel. She showed us the apartment building where Bronia last lived and took us to the Jewish cemetery where she is buried. To bring closure to this poignant chapter in my life, I left a stone on my mother's grave and recited the *Kaddish*. Afterwards, Mira gave me some photographs she had discovered in her aunt's apartment, including a photo of Bronia with my father on their wedding day in 1933. I had never seen the photo—which features numerous Zaslavsky relatives I cannot identify—and I was struck by the evident opulence of the wedding party.

Above, left: Speaking at the Shanghai launch of *Goodbye Shanghai* at The Glamour Bar on The Bund
Above, right: With my friend Professor Pan Guang, who was instrumental in securing a publishing deal for *Goodbye Shanghai* with the Shanghai Joint Publishing Company
Below: The English language and Mandarin editions of *Goodbye Shanghai*

Above: With my grandchildren outside the Doumer Apartments, Shanghai, 2012
Below: With Randall, Richard and Mark

Above: The whole family, outside the Dong Hu Hotel, Shanghai, 2012

In Xi'An, 2012

From Law to Art

Ada enjoyed a distinguished legal career as a Queen's Counsel in Victoria. She co-wrote a seminal book on trusts and was considered an expert in tax law. After several years of intensive court appearances, including in the High Court of Australia, Ada retired from the Victorian Bar in 2000 to spend more time with family and to pursue her many other interests.

From 2010 to 2020, Ada embarked on an incredible art journey in partnership with our sister-in-law Dianne Gringlas. Applying her many years of experience as an avid collector, Ada took on the role of curator at Ten Cubed, a collection of Australian contemporary art owned by Jack and Dianne. Their mission was to collect at least 10 works by each of 10 artists over a 10-year period, and to share them with the public at the modern gallery they opened in Malvern Road, Glen Iris.

The patronage project was an overwhelming philanthropic success. Hundreds of works were collected and enjoyed by the viewing public and by the many groups of school children who attended the gallery each year.

As planned, the gallery closed in 2020, but the impact of Ten Cubed has been recorded for posterity in a beautiful book entitled *Ten Cubed: Concept Collection Gallery 2010–2020.*

The Ten Cubed experience fortified Ada's already strong bonds with Jack and Dianne. We are also extremely close with their four children: Mikki, Robert, Adam and Stevie; their partners, Gidon, Belinda and Gemma; and all the children in the next generation: Raphy, Elijah, Lotte, Oliver, Willow, Ava, Teddy and Alfie.

Above: Jack, Dianne & Ada at Ten Cubed, 2018
Below: Gidon, Mikki, Belinda, Robert, Adam, Gemma & Stevie

My Brothers

The large age gap between me and my younger brothers, Nathan and Elijah, prevented us from having a true brotherly relationship when we were young. Fortunately, as we grew older, the age differences mattered less and a closer relationship emerged, just as our parents had hoped.

Nathan enjoyed a distinguished career as a barrister and later a Queen's Counsel. He served as a crown prosecutor in Hong Kong and solicitor general of the Solomon Islands. Nathan and Anne had two children, Joshua and Natasha, both of whom attended Wesley College with Richard. Tragically, Joshua died in 1991 and is greatly missed.

Since retiring, Nathan has taken up painting. He has had several exhibitions and won notable prizes. Nathan and I speak regularly and take each other out for lunch for our respective birthdays.

During his university years, Elijah attracted acclaim through his stage productions, and won a scholarship to study at Oxford University. He married Ruth Dyttman before leaving Melbourne.[82]

In London he achieved early success and became an internationally renowned director of theatre, television and opera.

Elijah's productions have been staged at the leading opera houses in the world, including the Royal Opera House and the Royal National Theatre in London, and the Metropolitan Opera in New York. Over the decades, we proudly attended many of his productions at Covent Gardens in London, at the Arts Centre in Melbourne, at the Adelaide Festival, and at the Sydney Opera House.

Very sadly, Elijah contracted COVID and died on 14 January 2021, a few days after his 75th birthday. His death is a great loss, particularly for his two fine sons, Benjamin and Jonathan.

---

[82] The marriage later ended in divorce.

Unfortunately, Elijah did not live long enough to meet his first grandchild, Zachary, who was born in 2022 to Jonathan and Martha.

The opera world mourned his passing and his obituary appeared in newspapers around the globe. According to Opera Australia, Elijah was "not only one of the greatest opera directors to ever emerge from Australia, but one of the world's true greats. He created productions that captured all of the beauty, drama and whimsy of the finest operas ever written."

Despite living on different continents, Elijah and I had enjoyed a strong connection and regularly spoke on Sunday nights. I dearly miss his witty conversation.

A Work in Progress

In the past few years, my mobility has become increasingly limited. I am no longer able to walk unaided, and now use an electric wheelchair. For this reason, it became necessary, in 2021, for me to move into Emmy Monash Aged Care. Difficult as it is, I am grateful that I can still visit family and friends, dine out at my favourite restaurants, and enjoy the sunshine in our beautiful garden at Bellaire Court. I have also been able to continue my role as 'guest speaker' at Emmy, providing lectures on current affairs to the other residents.

Adjusting to living apart from Ada has been the most challenging part of this new phase of our lives, however she continues to be an incredible source of strength. Ada's resourcefulness knows no bounds and I am incredibly grateful for her dedicated love, care and attention. I am also thankful for the support of our three sons, our daughters-in-law, our eight grandchildren, and our many close and caring friends. I am so proud of our grandchildren, who are all studying at university or embarking on their own careers. Spending time with them is an absolute joy, and it is a pleasure to observe how much they enjoy each other's company.

My life is a work-in-progress, so it has been difficult to know where to end this memoir. Ada suggested that the death of Queen Elizabeth II on 8 September 2022 would be an apt and poignant moment to conclude this book, particularly as, soon after my arrival in Australia, I happened to be in Parliament House when it was announced that King George VI had died and the words "Long live the Queen" rang out.

Much has been said about how the world changed during Her Majesty's historic 70-year reign and about how Australia has matured as a nation. I hope this book appropriately underscores how fortunate I feel to have lived, worked, and raised a family in this wonderful country.

[Standing, back] Mark, Sonny, Tommy, Jamie, Joey & Randall
[Standing, front] Sidra, Natalie, Romy & Mia
[Seated, back] Richard, Sam, Ada & Hannah
[Seated, front] Amira & Danita

Acknowledgements

The credit for this book is overwhelmingly due to Ada. She encouraged me to start writing *Goodbye Shanghai*, and then again to write *Hello Australia*. I am eternally grateful for her support of my many communal activities and for the positive and defining influence she has exerted throughout our marriage.

I'd also like to acknowledge and thank the many close friends and colleagues who have made my life in Australia so meaningful and enjoyable. It has not been possible to name you all in this book, but I hope you all know how much I appreciate your friendship and support.

My heartfelt thanks go to Romy Moshinsky, my talented editor and publisher, for her dedication and professionalism. Thanks also to her partner at Real Publishing, Georgie Raik-Allen, for her invaluable editing assistance. I am also grateful to Natalie Moshinsky for proofreading the final draft, to Stevie Gringlas of Picos Media for readily assisting with the images, and to Jacki Starr for the book's elegant design.

Together, we have produced another book of which we can all be especially proud.